THE WALL STREET JOURNAL.

COMPLETE
RETIREMENT
GUIDEBOOK

THE WALL STREET JOURNAL.

COMPLETE RETIREMENT GUIDEBOOK

How to Plan It, Live It and Enjoy It

GLENN RUFFENACH AND KELLY GREENE

THREE RIVERS PRESS

NEW YORK

For Karen

For Rick

Library of Congress Cataloging-in-Publication Data

Ruffenach, Glenn.
  The Wall Street Journal complete retirement guidebook : how to plan it, live it, and enjoy it / Glenn Ruffenach and Kelly Greene.—1st ed.
    p. cm.
Includes index.
  1. Retirement—United States—Planning. 2. Retirement income—United States. I. Greene, Kelly. II. Wall Street journal. III. Title.
IV. Title: Complete retirement guidebook.
  HQ1063.2.U6R84 2007
  646.7'9—dc22   2006101399

ISBN 978-0-307-35099-2

Printed in the United States of America

Design by Mauna Eichner and Lee Fukui

10 9 8 7 6 5

First Edition

CONTENTS

INTRODUCTION

Few events in our lives can produce as much satisfaction—and as much anxiety—as retirement.

We fantasize about the day when we finally can walk away from the duties and demands of our jobs—and wonder if we'll miss our friends at the office. We make lists of things to do in retirement—and worry whether our nest egg will be big enough to allow us to chase those dreams. We see ourselves aging gracefully in our home and the neighborhood that we love—and ask if poor health in later life will rob us of our independence.

If you find yourself with some or all of these thoughts, congratulations. You are perfectly normal. Survey after survey shows that most Americans are looking forward to retirement, but we aren't sure if we're ready or able to take the first step. In which case, it helps to have a plan.

The Wall Street Journal Complete Retirement Guidebook is just that: a blueprint for building a successful retirement. Like any good set of instructions, these pages will identify the tools you need to start: an understanding of how personal time, finances and relationships can change in later life. After that, we'll show you how the various pieces—savings, Social Security, relocation, new careers, volunteer work, estate planning, health care, leisure and more—come together as you create your plan for a personally fulfilling retirement. Needless to say, this isn't the first book that has been written about retirement planning, and it won't be the last. With 78 million baby boomers now sporting more than a hint of gray in their hair, we can expect as many roadmaps to later life as there were guides to raising children in the 1950s. So far, most of these retirement books have focused either solely on the financial side of retirement or solely on lifestyles. We're going to take a different tack. First, we address both money and time: how to organize your finances *and* your days in your fifties and beyond. After all, it's almost impossible to answer the most frequently heard question among would-be retirees—Have I saved enough money?—unless you have some idea of how you plan to spend your time in retirement. Depending on your vision (A modest retirement close to home? Days filled with travel?), your nest egg might be more than sufficient or in need of major repairs.

Second, if many of us fail to consider how finances and lifestyles go hand-in-hand, it's because we tend to regard retirement as an event, something that happens on a weekday afternoon. Actually, the best retirements are a *process,* one in which many decisions and refinements are made along the way. That's the approach we'll take in this guide: looking at later life as a series of steps involving your lifestyle and finances. In doing so, we think you will end up with a more rewarding and productive retirement.

Only a few years ago, a guide like this would have been a tough sell—and a thin piece of work. From the 1950s through the early 1990s, retirement in the United States had much the same look and feel. A husband (and it was almost always the husband) collected a gold watch between the ages of sixty-two and sixty-five. He and his wife would spend about ten years at play and then ease toward their respective sunsets. Decisions and guesswork, for the most part, were kept to a minimum. Your former employer calculated what your pension would be and sent you a check every month. Uncle Sam did the same with Social Security. Some friends might move to Florida or Arizona, but nine out of ten older Americans stayed right where they were. The finish line for most was clearly marked: On Friday, you were working; come Monday, you were retired.

Today, in the space of a single generation, retirement for many has become a puzzle—with dozens of decisions and far too much guesswork. Four changes, in particular, have made the process more complicated: extended life spans, the demise of traditional pensions, women's entrance into the labor force, and the rising cost of medicine and long-term care.

Consider that the average sixty-five-year-old today can expect to live to age eighty-three—and spend almost two decades in retirement. Only about one in three Americans is covered by a defined-benefit pension plan; in other words, retirees—and not their former employers—are now shouldering the risks and responsibilities for creating a paycheck in later life. Almost 60 percent of women are working outside the home; thus, couples increasingly find themselves trying to plan and coordinate two retirements instead of just one. Meanwhile, health-care bills—even for those covered by Medicare—already eat up one of every six dollars in Social Security benefits. The average cost of a one-year stay in an assisted-living center is about $35,600, according to MetLife; the average tab for a private room in a nursing home runs $75,200.

These changes mean that questions about later life now abound. When should I retire? Have I saved enough money? Will my nest egg last as long as I do? Do I want to, or need to, work in retirement (the new oxymoron)—and if so, what jobs will be available? Can I continue to live at home? Will I need long-term care? And what about my spouse? Should both of us retire at the same time? Do we see later life and how to fill our days in the same light?

The pages that follow will speak to all these issues and more. To help simplify your planning, we divide retirement—and our chapters—into two parts. In Part One, we begin by talking about time: figuring out the life you want to lead in your fifties and beyond. Again, it's hard to pinpoint how much money you need in retirement unless you first have a good idea of how you want to spend your days. We'll also talk about working in retirement, volunteering, relocation and how to keep your mind and body healthy. In Part Two, we turn to finances: how to tap and preserve a nest egg, when to collect Social Security and how to create an estate plan (among other essential steps). Finally, we leave you with success stories—profiles of individuals who successfully made the transition into fulfilling retirements.

The good news is that retirement today, for all its changes and challenges, appears to be more gratifying than ever before. We know this first-hand. In almost a decade of reporting and writing about retirement for *The Wall Street Journal,* we have interviewed hundreds of retirees, would-be retirees and "former" retirees from all parts of the country. The lessons they have shared about life after age fifty have proved invaluable for the *Journal*'s readers. We trust that these insights and experiences will be similarly useful to you.

PART I

RETIRE TO THE LIFE YOU WANT

CHAPTER 1

How Do I Want To Spend My Time In Retirement?

It's one of the biggest mistakes that people make in the years approaching retirement: failing to consider how they wish to spend their time in later life. Yes, we all need a good-sized nest egg once we leave work, but when it comes to *time* and retirement, most people give almost no thought to what an average day might look like. One reason, of course, is that retirement seems . . . easy, welcoming. (What can be so tough about not working?) There's also the assumption that leisure activities will be just as fulfilling, if not more so, than work—a dangerous assumption for people who have enjoyed their careers. It's not that people can't see themselves in retirement. If you ask almost anyone what he or she plans to do in his or her sixties and beyond, the answers invariably involve some mix of travel, play and work. Specifics, though, are few and far between. As it turns out, vague answers to the question, "What will I do for twenty or thirty years?" can be just as debilitating as vague financial goals.

The best way to begin shaping your life in retirement is to look upon retiring itself as a *process,* not an event. With a dream, some planning and a bit of luck, your retirement might resemble that of Pam and Larry Satek.

Pam had recently retired as principal of a Chicago-area elementary school, and Larry was a few months away from retiring from his job as a research chemist. The couple—both in their late fifties at the time—had opened a winery in Fremont, a small town in the northeast corner of Indiana.

In the early 1990s, about ten years before the couple planned to retire, they began talking about what their future might look like. Rest and relaxation didn't hold much appeal. "Neither one of us is a sit-down-and-do-nothing type of person," Larry told us. A shared interest in wines seemed to hold some promise, but how could they turn that interest into a second career? To find the answer, the Sateks started educating themselves about the wine business. They took courses at Purdue University. They compiled articles and books. They collared experts and asked questions. (What varieties of grapes are best suited to Indiana's soil and climate? What makes a good site for a winery?) They even planted a small vineyard on a patch of family property and sold the grapes to existing wineries in the area.

Gradually, over the course of several years, a dream took shape: The Sateks would attempt to build and operate their own winery in retirement.

In June 2001, Pam and Larry opened the doors of Satek Winery. The first day, some 500 customers walked through the entrance. "It was just the two of us in the tasting room," Pam recalled, "and neither one of us had ever worked a cash register. It was nerve-wracking." In all, there were just three employees, including the Sateks. Production that first year totaled 1,000 cases. By the time the fifth anniversary rolled around, the winery employed fifteen people and was producing about 6,000 cases of wine annually. (You can read about the very real fruits of the Sateks' labors at www.satekwinery.com.)

Looking back to when he and Pam began talking about their hopes for retirement, Larry Satek recalled that the important thing was simply to set out. "We told ourselves, 'If we don't start doing this, it will always be a dream.' "

If the Sateks' story sounds encouraging, consider that your retirement—at least initially—is more likely to resemble that of Terry Culp.

Terry was just fifty-two years old when he received an offer he couldn't refuse to sell his five manufacturing businesses in Buffalo, New York. He and his wife climbed into their sport-utility vehicle and moved to an exclusive retirement community in Las Vegas, where he proceeded to golf himself silly. Eighteen months later, he was frustrated and bored.

"There was too much missing—including a sense of me," Terry told us. "A huge piece of my life was totally gone. I realized that going cold turkey [from work] . . . was having a much bigger psychological impact on me than I had ever imagined."

His decision "was totally impromptu." "We had a great opportunity to sell the companies, it made good business sense, and we simply said, 'Maybe it's time to try retirement.' I spent absolutely no time really planning for it."

Terry eventually returned to full-time work, joining— much to his delight—a program at the University of Nevada, Las Vegas, that provides technical assistance to small manufacturing, mining and construction businesses. Looking back, however, he offered a blunt assessment of how he jumped into retirement: "I give myself a 'D'—at best."

———

We've found that the retirees who are most satisfied with their lives are the ones who thought and talked about their hopes for the future—typically, several years before retirement itself—and then took specific actions to move closer to those goals. The Sateks are a good example. One of the most important steps Pam and Larry took was simply to begin talking about retirement—what it might look like and how they might want to spend their time. "We took it very seriously," Larry told us. "And it paid off."

Others, like Alice Ahlers, take a more organic approach, remaining open to new interests (whether before or after retirement itself) that, in turn, open doors to a more meaningful life. In 1996, Alice retired from the Department of Labor and signed up to take several trips with Elderhostel, the Boston-based educational program for older learners. One trip took her to Peru, another on a barge down the Seine River through France. Wherever she went, she told us, she found herself drawn to the area's folk art. Eventually, the experiences led to a new passion: "I wanted to be able to make beautiful things and have the skill to do it."

To that end, Alice took fifty-three courses—some a week long, some on weekends—at the John C. Campbell Folk School in Brasstown, North Carolina, in a wide range of crafts. (She told us that she was financing her education, as well as additional trips, by keeping the books for her son's antiques business.) At the time we spoke, she was drawing plans to turn her backyard patio into a home studio so she and her friends from the craft school, who often travel across several states to visit, would have more space for creating artwork together.

EXPANDING YOUR HORIZONS

Ronald Manheimer, executive director of the Center for Creative Retirement at the University of North Carolina in Asheville, has distilled seven questions you should consider before retiring:

1. WHAT IS MY IMAGE OF RETIREMENT? AND IS IT USEFUL AND ACCURATE?

Start with the basics by taking an inventory of your interests—those activities or hobbies that already occupy some of your time—and ask, Which of these deserve more of your time? If you value reading and education, perhaps you see yourself attending classes at a local college in retirement or volunteering in a reading program at an inner-city school. Do you enjoy the outdoors? The open road? If so, maybe you see yourself buying a recreational vehicle in retirement or becoming a search-and-rescue volunteer. Do you like to collect things? Perhaps retirement might involve opening an antiques shop. The first step is figuring out whether your interests will translate into daily activities. Whether the activities are doable and fulfilling is the second step.

We listened to the story of one man who had dabbled in art when he was younger and decided that retirement would be the time when he could indulge this passion. But in his first art class in retirement, he found the work to be much harder and more time-consuming than he had imagined, and he came to the realization that art wasn't his calling. The discovery was something of a shock; this person had *assumed* that art would fill his days.

The point is to do some "field-testing" of your retirement plans before you retire. If you think you want to pursue a career in art, wonderful. But take a few art classes while you're still working to see if the idea makes sense. If not, you can start exploring other interests.

2. WHEN IS IT TIME TO LEAVE MY JOB, AND DO I WANT TO RETURN TO PAID EMPLOYMENT, POSSIBLY IN A SECOND OR THIRD CAREER?

Often, people leave work when they reach a certain age, when their nest egg reaches some pre-determined size, or when they take advantage of a buyout. None of that is necessarily unwise. But if you leave work primarily because your bank account, or the calendar, tells you it's time, you could be using the wrong yardsticks.

Early retirement can be especially tricky. That's because busy careers don't offer much time to develop a vision for retirement.

John Wilson, an insurance executive, was fifty years old when he took early retirement. Faced with a move from his home in the Midwest to company headquarters in New York City and not wishing to uproot his family, he decided to retire. All too quickly, he told us, that decision proved flawed.

First came the shock of trying to figure out "what I was going to do for the ten hours between when I got up and when I had dinner with my family," he said. "I am not a mint-juleps-on-the-porch kind of guy." Then came the regrets. "[This] may sound like a stupid answer, but when people ask me what I miss the most, it's the stress of my old job," he told us. "When you have seventy people working for you and they're pulling at you all day long, and you're scrambling to meet deadlines, you think: 'I'm in charge; I can handle this.' Suddenly, nobody's hanging at your door anymore. And the only stress you have is the stress of being retired."

Compare John's experience with that of Irv Laddin, who took an early buyout from International Business Machines Corp. The difference is that three years *before* the buyout offer, Irv and his wife opened a small travel business—specifically as part of their plans for retirement. "I always had in the back of my mind the idea that I would like to be the captain of a ship, as opposed to the crew or first officer or whatever," Irv told us. "A lot of my friends had left IBM and started their own businesses and had done very well.

"As it turned out, the timing worked great. About three years [after the travel agency was started], IBM came up with an outstanding program for early retirement for certain people, and I was able—because we had the business—to look at it much more positively as an opportunity. Quite possibly, I would not have taken the early out had we not had the business, too. In fact, it was very much a going business at that point."

A SWING AND A MISS

No matter how well you plan for life after retirement, get ready for some withdrawal pangs.

That's what we learned from none other than Nolan Ryan, perhaps the most famous fastball pitcher in the history of baseball and one of the most admired athletes of his generation. Over the course of his twenty-seven years in the major leagues—several times the average tenure of professional athletes—he set some fifty records, including number of career no-hitters (seven) and strikeouts (5,714). In 1999, as soon as he was eligible after his 1993 retirement, he took his place among other legends in the National Baseball Hall of Fame in Cooperstown, New York.

As inspiring as the way Nolan Ryan played was the way he planned for retirement. The son of a local newspaper distributor, he founded a bank in his hometown of Alvin, Texas, as an investment and began fulfilling a child-hood dream of becoming a cowboy by building a ranching operation. When we met him, that operation included 1,500 head of cattle on three ranches (one of which covered 18,000 acres) and allowed him to enjoy an active out-door life in retirement.

Nolan, in other words, got the big picture. "I always had the attitude," he told us, "that there was life after baseball. And I tried to prepare for it."

But even when he was doing things, like traveling with his family or tending his ranch operations, activities that he had looked forward to in his first season off, "there was this feeling that I needed to be somewhere else," he said. What was missing was "the competition—the feeling of being a member of a team. It doesn't matter if you're the twenty-fifth player or one of the stars. When you walk in that clubhouse, when you put on that uniform, you are a member of that team."

The same complaints are frequently heard among retired executives. It's not that people miss their work; rather, they miss being part of a group and the excitement that comes from working on a team. If that describes you, you should allow yourself to do something that most people don't as-sociate with retirement: a bit of grieving.

"I didn't realize I was going to have such a tough transition emotion-ally," Nolan said. "It took two years."

3. How Do I Balance My Dreams and Goals with My Family and Societal Responsibilities?

People often look at retirement in isolation. They don't discuss their plans with other family members, including their adult children—and sometimes their spouses. And that can be a big mistake.

After Rosemary Ford retired as an attorney for the state of Massachusetts, she simply assumed that her husband would follow suit when he first became eligible for retirement benefits. As it turned out, Dick Ford, also a lawyer, kept right on working.

"She thought [my retirement] was a given, and I kind of thought it was a given, too," Dick told us. "But the fact of the matter is, when that [date] approached, Rosemary and I hadn't done any really hard discussion or planning [about retirement]." All of which meant that Rosemary Ford was left waiting to begin the rest of her life.

"I really had this vision that we'd just go and kind of travel wildly for a couple of years," she told us. "But it didn't work out that way."

If you're like many people approaching retirement, you probably have thought about doing some volunteer work. A recent survey by Civic Ventures, a San Francisco-based think tank, found that three out of five people in their fifties want to use the next stage of their lives to improve the quality of life in their communities. (We talk about volunteering in detail in Chapter Three.) Many retirees and would-be retirees are not only giving back to their communities, but going several steps further: identifying needs, forming organizations to meet those needs, raising money and creating (in effect) small businesses that can support and perpetuate themselves. The job title is "social entrepreneur."

After opening and running her own antiques store in Richmond, Virginia, for thirty years, Martha Franck Rollins

CAN RETIREMENT BE A SECOND HONEYMOON?

"The first year in retirement for almost all couples is rocky," according to David Arp, who with his wife, Claudia, founded Marriage Alive International, an education program for couples that's now in its third decade. During the years in which you're building your career and raising children, it's easy to put your relationship with your spouse on the "back burner," David told us. "All of a sudden you look around and the kids are gone; you have all this time—and you're not sure you know that other person."

Research shows rather than enjoying a second honeymoon, both spouses are adjusting to new routines and roles, and the kinks aren't necessarily worked out in the first weeks—or months. In many cases, it takes a year or two to sort things out.

The bad news is some couples won't make it. The rate of divorce among people age fifty-five and older now resembles that of the general population. But as tricky as passing through the door to retirement can be, marriages often emerge stronger on the other side.

That's because, Claudia explains, "the husband is focusing more on relationships and looking back home, and the wife is being a little bit more expansive—seeing there's a world out there. If you put them on a continuum, they're moving closer together toward the center. And most couples want that—a more personal marriage—at this stage."

Finally, think about timing: Will you and your spouse leave your jobs at about the same time, or will one of you keep working? For the most part, studies show that marriages do better when husbands and wives retire together.

turned over the reins to her husband and started Boaz and Ruth, a nonprofit group that helps rehabilitate former prison inmates. Today, the organization's side businesses include furniture restoration, a café, catering, home repair and moving— ventures that provide training and jobs and help revitalize surrounding neighborhoods. Martha told us that she began by asking herself a question: "I thought, how can God use an antiques dealer?"

4. CAN THE NEXT STEP IN MY LIFE BE TRULY REVITALIZING?

For some, retirement is an opportunity for a new beginning, a chance to transform one's life. It's worth taking time, then, to consider just how evolutionary—or revolutionary—you wish your retirement to be. Perhaps life after collecting a gold watch resembles life before the watch: still playing golf, still working with Habitat for Humanity or still visiting with the grandkids. And that's the way you prefer it. Or perhaps you end up reinventing yourself.

John Berkenfield, a thirty-year veteran of IBM, retired on a July afternoon. Thirty days later, he started work as the director of a small museum south of Santa Fe, New Mexico. There had been no specific plans for retirement until a friend, by chance, read a newspaper ad about an opening at the museum. John knew a lot about business and marketing, but nothing about running a museum. Still, he applied for, and got, the job. (The competition thinned considerably, he recalled, when aspirants learned about the pay and benefits—or virtual lack thereof.) During his watch, annual attendance rose to about 53,000 visitors from 15,000, and volunteers contributed more than 27,000 hours of their time compared with about 1,000 hours before his arrival.

"Spend your time [in retirement] learning and doing something very different from what you've done in your past life," John advises. You have a better chance of remaining "intellectually stimulated" if you do so, he said.

5. HOW WILL I STRUCTURE MY TIME?

For some people, the free time that comes with retirement produces anxiety about how to fill their days; thus, they take on too many responsibilities—volunteer work, school, a part-time job, etc. They become busier in retirement than when they were working.

As Ellen Graham, an award-winning reporter for *The Wall Street Journal,* put it: "I remember thinking about what I might enjoy in retirement: mentoring a child, perhaps, or acting in a little theater or returning to painting. Now, my days seem to evaporate in a haze of club activities and volunteer chores, most of which I wandered into by accident."

The point is to be discriminating. Ask yourself, What do I really care about? What do I want to do that's personally satisfying?

After three decades of working for companies like Sperry, Bendix and Control Data, Kirk Symmes wasn't sure what to do with his time. The best solution, seemingly, was to "join everything," he recalled. "I never really thought about what I was going to do in retirement." Fortunately, the flurry of activities led him to a local College for Seniors, where he ended up teaching a number of history courses and found himself being called upon as a guest lecturer at area schools and clubs.

"Originally, all I wanted to do was take some classes," Kirk told us. "But this opened a door."

Or as Ed Susank, a retired health-care benefits consultant who wants to become more proficient in a foreign language, said, "I like to have a few pegs around which the rest of it can kind of drape casually."

6. Does My Past Pattern of Dealing with Change Provide Me with a Good Model for Entering Retirement?

The challenge here is to get you thinking about how you have reacted to major turning points in your life: career choices, marriage, children, etc. It's a pretty good indicator of how you will approach the changes that come with retirement.

Perhaps you're impulsive; perhaps—looking back over your life—you think you should have spent more time reaching major decisions. Now in your retirement planning, it's time to slow down and get more facts, speak with more people and be more reflective.

This issue, of course, cuts both ways. Some people are hypercautious when it comes to change. Perhaps you are the kind of person who rarely takes risks or never goes beyond a "comfort zone." The danger, of course, is that you might miss out on some opportunities in retirement and come to regret it.

Fortunately, more groups and services—including classes at local colleges, mentoring programs, nonprofits, Web sites and business networks—are offering information and support for people making the transition to retirement. We write about these efforts and where you can find help in Chapters Two and Three.

7. What Is the First Step for Putting My Retirement Plan into Action?

It's all well and good to think about how you might spend your time in retirement. Equally important, though, is a plan for getting there. The best advice is think small.

Plans that are loose and open-ended accomplish little. Rather, make a list of specific actions and tackle them one at a time. Perhaps you want to start your own business. Fine. Enroll in a class on running a business. Sign up. Write the check. It doesn't have to be a big step. The hardest part is getting started.

Charlotte Tell, a former accountant, had always enjoyed taking pictures, but never took the idea of photography very seriously. Once retired, though, she found herself playing with the notion of turning this interest into something of consequence. Thus began a series of small, but important steps: taking more pictures in more locales (outdoor photography would become a specialty), affixing her photos to small note cards and showing them to local merchants, studying Impressionist painters and their use of light and learning about matting, framing and pricing. A breakthrough came when a prominent local gallery offered to showcase her work.

She would go on to create a successful business, with her work sold in dozens of shops. It was a new career, one born in fits and starts. No single step proved pivotal; each built upon the one before. "You have to understand: I knew *nothing* about photography," Charlotte told us. But, she adds, "When you can do exactly what you want to do every single day, what could be better than that?"

———

To these seven questions, we'll add an eighth:

8: How Do *You* Define "Retirement"?

Much has been made in recent years about "the new retirement" or the "changing face of retirement." This bright-and-shiny version of later life is one in which older Americans are more active and more "engaged." At the same time, though, there seems to be a certain . . . competitiveness creeping into retirement in America. Increasingly, educators, sociologists and marketers are urging us to be "productive" in retirement. And if you aren't being productive in later life—if you aren't "contributing"—well, perhaps you need to take a good, long look in the mirror—or so they would have you believe.

Consider, for example, a recent Morgan Stanley advertisement. We see an older adult—a man in his mid-fifties, by all appearances—sitting at his desk. The text that accompanies the photo reads as follows:

"Retire? I'm not dead yet. Who made 60 the magical number? I want to stay in the game for as long as I can. Maybe I'll start a company. Maybe I need someone to help me examine my options. After all, if I stayed home all day, my wife would probably divorce me."

The message to the reader is clear: Don't even *think* about retiring. (You lazy bum.)

Then there's the word itself: retirement. The Transition Network, a women's support group in New York, staged a contest to come up with a new name for retirement. (The winning word was "regeneration.") Residents at an assisted-living center in Chicago petitioned the good folks at Merriam-Webster to expand the definition of retirement in their dictionary; the residents felt the definition was limited to the notion of "withdrawing" from society, when it should include the idea of "engagement." (There's that word again.) Clearly, in some circles, retirement is a four-letter word.

We mention all this for one important reason: Whatever the current or popular image of later life, there is no "right" or "best" retirement. There is only *your* retirement, one that, ideally, will involve a good amount of planning on your part. If you wish to embrace what might be called a "traditional" retirement—if you want to golf every day, enjoy martinis at sunset and never "work" another moment in your life—more power to you. (As one labor expert asked the American Society on Aging, "Why is it so difficult for politicians, policymakers, academics and journalists to understand that people who have put in forty years as rank-and-file grunts, as they say in the armed services, are not eager to return to the world of paid 'gruntdom?'") Or, if you wish to climb the Andes in retirement, volunteer at a hospital, start your own kayaking business or save the whales, that's fine, too. Perhaps you don't want to "retire" at all; perhaps your work is your passion, and your idea of a happy ending is to die at your desk, working late on a Friday evening. Again, have at it.

All we ask is for you to spend some time thinking and talking about this. Especially with your partner. That process alone will increase your chances for a successful retirement exponentially.

Perhaps the best way to close this chapter is to tell you about those individuals who, from our reporting at the *Journal*, appear to enjoy later life more than most. They are a group who, through planning, experimentation and a measure of luck, experience what might be called an epiphany: a discovery of their life's work at the very moment when life could be seen as winding down. It could be the hobby that becomes a full-blown passion or the new interest that first consumes Monday (and then Monday through Friday) or the part-time volunteer work that becomes a full-time mission. Whatever the path, it's like finding the answer to the question, What do you want to be when you grow up? Some simply find the answer later than others.

Some common threads emerge among those who seem most fulfilled: a continuing search for challenges, a decision to immerse themselves in a wide range of activities and a firm belief that their best years are still ahead of them. One of these people is Jack Pizer.

In the mid-1980s, Jack had been retired for four years. His life in Massachusetts was equal parts tennis, charitable work and politics. "School issues, local candidates, that kind of thing," he recalled when we first met him. "I wasn't bored, but I wasn't that happy, either." One autumn, however, almost by chance, he enrolled in several courses at the University of Massachusetts in Boston. It was a decision, he told us, that "changed my life." Jack, as it turned out, had found his calling. The courses he took in gerontology and the problems of aging eventually steered him toward a series of posts from which he helped hundreds of people fight discrimination in the workplace. At age eighty-one, the "satisfaction of doing good," as he put it, was keeping him busy nine hours a day, four and sometimes five days a week. It was, he said simply, the "best time of my life."

When we asked Jack what advice he would offer to a person just entering retirement, he responded this way: Spend as much time thinking about how you might use your days as you do preparing your finances. Retirement could well "represent 25 percent of your life," he told us. "Why leave it to chance?"

CHAPTER 2

TO WORK OR NOT TO WORK?

Why are so many people suddenly working in retirement? Will you end up joining the crowd? And if you do, will you be able to get the job you want?

Those questions reflect one of the most startling changes in retirement during the past decade: At least 10 percent of retirees are going back to work, and the number of older Americans either holding jobs or looking for work has been rising for the past fifteen years or so after dropping steadily for decades. A number of studies also have found that an overwhelming majority of baby boomers expect to keep working in retirement—many into their late seventies or beyond.

Several key factors, including increasing life-expectancies, the curtailment of traditional pension plans, a jittery stock market and rising health-care costs, account for the change. One-third of working retirees, in a 2005 survey by Putnam Investments, said they need the extra income to make ends meet. Meanwhile, employers estimate that about half of workers in their fifties will be unprepared for retirement, according to Boston College's Center for Retirement Research. Only about half of all workers even participate in a retirement plan.

But people who *do* have large enough nest eggs are choosing to work, too—for pleasure. Two-thirds of the 1,700 working retirees whom Putnam interviewed said that they took jobs to help them stay healthy, energetic or mentally fit.

After decades of full-time employment, most retirees dream of more flexible, part-time work. But those jobs can be hard to come by, mainly because employers find it more expensive and inconvenient to manage two part-timers instead of one full-timer. In fact, the number of part-time workers between the ages of fifty-five and seventy barely budged from 1980 to 2004—while the percentage of older people working full-time increased. Let's not forget how many people you could be competing against, either, for this stagnant number of part-time jobs: If 80 percent of the boomers really do start beating the bushes, as they say they will, then 62 million job applicants could be looking for work, mainly part-time, in the next couple of decades.

There's also the problem of age discrimination. Despite a federal law enacted in 1967 to protect anyone forty or older in the workplace, 16,000 to 20,000 older workers bring age discrimination charges every year.

Perhaps you think you can sidestep these obstacles by hanging out your own shingle as a consultant. But that could be equally tough. Don Mayes, an experienced retiree-turned-consultant, warned us that unless you have specific, marketable expertise, you could wind up like a friend of his who printed up business cards he never used—or another who landed only one, small client after three years of soliciting work. Consulting requires perseverance, knowing your way around a computer, bookkeeping prowess and a willingness to stick your neck out to land your first customers. In the beginning, at least, those feats of nimbleness probably mean you won't be able to pick and choose your hours or much else about your working conditions.

There is a bit of good news on the horizon: Given the fact that the number of workers between the ages of thirty-five and forty-four is expected to drop by 7 percent by 2012, big companies are starting to think creatively about ways to keep at least

HOW TO FIGHT
AGE DISCRIMINATION

If you think you've been discriminated against due to your age, the first step is to discuss it with your employer directly, documenting those talks. If that doesn't work, you, or your lawyer, would start any claim by filing a charge with the Equal Employment Opportunity Commission (EEOC), which you have to do within 180 days of the alleged offense. Sixty days after that, you can file a lawsuit. (You can find your local EEOC field office at www.eeoc.gov/offices.html.)

a few seasoned veterans at the office. Often, individual bosses make one-on-one "phased retirement" deals with a handful of employees they are afraid to lose, meaning the employees gradually would get to scale back their hours or negotiate for lengthy, more frequent vacations while receiving some of their retirement benefits. If you're interested in such a deal, keep in mind that it requires walking a tightrope: First, you must persuade your boss that you're indispensable; then, you must find a way to keep making an impact without being around as much. And, realistically, you probably would have to make yourself available at times when you're not officially working.

So, how do you go about deciding for yourself whether to work in retirement? Helen Dennis, a gerontologist in Redondo Beach, California, who specializes in aging, employment and retirement, recommends that you ask yourself these six questions:

1. Do I Need to Keep Working, or Go Back to Work, for the Money?

If you're in good health and a paycheck could make it easier to pay the mortgage or the heating bill, then working may be the best way to improve or preserve your quality of life. This was the case for Dick Kiefer, a retired appliance salesman in Des Moines, Iowa, who took a sales job at age sixty-four at Home Depot Inc. to get access to medical coverage. But even after he turned sixty-five and qualified for Medicare, he kept the job—and upped his hours to forty a week from twenty-five—because the income made it easier to pay his bills. Indeed, half of the people in their fifties who are still working said they expect to *keep* working during retirement simply to cover basic expenses, according to a survey for Fidelity Investments.

Medical costs—both for younger retirees paying for their own health insurance and also for older retirees paying bills not covered by Medicare—are pushing some folks to return to work. Fidelity estimated that the average sixty-five-year-old couple who retired in 2007 without employer-sponsored health coverage would need $215,000 to cover medical costs for seventeen to twenty years. That staggering figure includes Medicare premiums, co-payments and deductibles and out-of-pocket prescription drug costs, but doesn't take into account over-the-counter drugs, most dental expenses or long-term care. We don't mean to scare you, but the average cost of a month's stay in an assisted-living facility in 2006 averaged $2,968 a month—that's $35,616 a year.

But even if your day-to-day bills aren't an immediate cause for worry, as they were for Dick, there's another part to the question you might want to consider: Would working help you feel more financially secure? If questions like, "What if I live to be 100?" are keeping you up at night, working could be a salve for those financial worries.

2. Would Work Make My Retirement More Worthwhile?

Only you can determine what's meaningful to you at this particular time in your life, and it may or may not be a job. Volunteering and taking some classes here and there may keep you busy and happy in retirement. Then again, it might not feel like enough. So, forcing yourself to answer a few pointed questions could help you cut to the chase: Do you want your life to continue to revolve around work? Or, do you want more time to do things you haven't had time for in the past?

Do you need to work to feel productive—to feel as if you're making a contribution—or could you successfully scratch those itches through volunteer work? After all, there are countless unpaid opportunities out there: retired teachers who combat illiteracy, retired doctors who staff clinics for the uninsured and retired lawyers who help entrepreneurs and fledgling legal systems in developing countries. (See Chapter Three for more ideas about volunteering.)

Then there's the social part: Do you still want to spend your days with co-workers? Or, at this point, would you prefer to do things on your own—perhaps finally reading the stack of books gathering dust on your bedside table or signing up for courses at a lifelong learning program? Do you want to feel like you're part of a team, or are you tired of being thrown together with colleagues who don't share the same interests?

For Norm Crampton, a grant writer in his seventies for an affordable-housing builder in Rockford, Illinois, it was a simple choice: "I just love being in the work community and having colleagues," he said. "I never learned to play golf or anything like that, and I had to find something to do with my time."

3. Would Working in Retirement Help, or Hurt, My Social Life?

As you consider when to retire, it's important to think about what's going on around you—particularly if you're a young retiree and most of your friends are still working. You might have a blast in retirement if some good friends are leaving their jobs around the same time. But if most of your social circle is still at the office, can you handle spending a lot of time alone?

When Patricia Breakstone retired at age sixty-two from her

state-government job, she was living alone and didn't have many retired friends. After a few months, she told us, "I didn't want to get up in the morning." An old friend finally prodded her into applying for a part-time job at a bakery near her home in San Diego, where she began spending a few afternoons a week behind the counter. Though it didn't provide much of a paycheck, the job brought structure to her days and gave her an easy way to socialize with people in her neighborhood.

It's also important to factor in your spouse: Is your husband waiting for you to retire so the two of you can take a cross-country RV trip? Alternatively, is your wife finally hitting her professional stride and reluctant to retire when you want to? With the first few generations of career-oriented women just starting to enter retirement, "there are no rules for negotiating this yet," said Helen Dennis, the retirement specialist in California.

Norm, the Illinois grant writer, told us that working in retirement made his marriage much stronger. "You both need private space and time," particularly after decades of going your separate ways during the day, he said. Plus, his time at work continued to provide good fodder for dinner conversation. Norm's wife confirmed his view: After the couple moved to Illinois to be closer to grandchildren, he was unemployed briefly. When he told his wife he had landed a new job, "She burst into song," he recalled.

4. If I Do Decide to Work, Should I Go Full-Time or Part-Time?

As we discussed above, you may not have much of a choice. But it's a good idea to decide, before you start a job search, whether you would prefer a part-time job with less responsibility or full-time work that's more consuming. A part-time job might be a good idea if you're looking for pocket money or a way to round out other commitments. But if you're intrigued by the idea of starting over with a new career in a profession

WORK OUT THE GROUND RULES

If you have a partner, chances are you'll be spending a lot more time together under one roof when you retire. That could lead to some stomping (albeit unintentional) on each other's toes. Ken Schumann found that within two months of his retirement as director of the North American agriculture business for Ciba Special Chemicals AG, his wife, Patty, came up with three rules for him: "Number one, I cannot fall asleep in front of the TV from Monday to Friday. Number two, I cannot follow Patty around and ask what she's doing next. Number three is, since I traveled so much and she wasn't used to cooking seven days a week, we needed an outside life, including dinners out. I now have a three 'A.' I must answer the telephone because the calls are for me for a change."

Ken talked about his new rules at an enrichment course on retirement at Emory University in Atlanta. His classmates agreed that negotiating personal space with your partner is one of the biggest hurdles in the first year of retirement. Among their recommendations are to shell out the bucks for separate phone lines, computers and e-mail addresses. Stake out space in your home that is yours alone. Robert Carpenter, another participant, said he has a "cave" with his own TV, computer and recliner.

that would require additional training, such as teaching or nursing, be honest with yourself about the time it would take.

Another idea for how to work is just starting to get some attention: You could try holding serial, full-time jobs in retirement with breaks in between for a few months, or even a few years, to travel, do a home project or otherwise recharge your batteries before diving back into the workforce. The experts call it "cyclical employment." Frankly, it's such a new idea that we haven't found anyone who has pulled it off successfully—yet. But other countries are doing things that the

JOB CYCLING

Many jobs and industries might be conducive to cyclical employment, particularly those in which employees work intensive, short shifts or those in which there are challenging short-term projects:

- Engineering

- Computer programming

- Health care (particularly nursing)

- Pharmaceutical research/testing

- Teaching

- Accounting

- Retail services

- Marketing/public relations/government relations

- Freelance writing

United States could use as a model. In 2001, Norway's "Competence Reform," for example, was introduced to provide older workers with a way to take time off to develop new skills and interests.

It's unclear whether U.S. employers will embrace the idea of revolving-door employment for older workers, but it might just be the way to keep many baby boomers in the workforce longer. "Change is not terrifying to us," said Ken Dychtwald, a San Francisco gerontologist and boomer. "We like the idea of evolving and growing and trying on new hats. Boomers are beginning to concoct all these fantastic notions of what they want work to be—eight months on and four off or part-time or three days on and two off."

In fact, the social scientists who study boomers are starting to draw a lot of parallels between the impact the generation could have on the workplace in later life with the impact women made in the 1970s, when working mothers pressured employers into offering child-care leave and flexible hours. "The next work revolution is going to be headed by older workers who reconstruct how they work," Ken Dychtwald predicts.

5. How Exactly Would I Go About Finding a Job?

If you liked what you were doing before you retired, or if you're still working, you might start with your employer. As of late 2005, about 11 percent of large employers were thinking about offering flexible work schedules to older workers or hiring back retirees as consultants or contractors, according to a study by accounting firm Ernst & Young LLP. About 10 percent of employers were looking at other options such as flexible benefits or phased retirement.

In the past, retirees were largely on their own as they figured out how to rewrite résumés, network and compete with thirty-year-olds. But so-called "life coaches" are starting to target boomers seeking direction, and a number of job-placement firms, mainly working through Web sites, are starting to match retirees with employers.

Civic Ventures, a San Francisco nonprofit urging retirees to embrace paid or unpaid work that gives back to society, is jump-starting a grassroots network of later-life career centers as a big part of what it calls the "Next Chapter" initiative. These centers offer a variety of programs to help people nearing or already in retirement figure out what to do next and how to execute their plans. Civic Ventures hopes its experiment will spark a network of specialized counselors with professional training and credentials, along with a new type of "student union for sixty-year-olds."

HOW TO FIND A JOB

Web Sites Matching Older Workers with Employers:

- **Action Without Borders**—www.idealist.org. Lists jobs and internships in nonprofit organizations, plus tips on finding work in the nonprofit sector
- **Bridgestar**—www.bridgestar.org. Listings of senior staff and board positions in nonprofit organizations
- **CharityChannel Career Search Online**— www.charitychannel.com/classifieds/cso/. An online position recruitment system dedicated exclusively to the nonprofit/non-government organization sector
- **The Chronicle of Philanthropy's Philanthropy Careers**— www.philanthropy.com/jobs. Job listings primarily in foundations
- **Community Career Center**—www.communitycareercenter.org. Searchable job openings in nonprofit organizations
- **Dinosaur Exchange**—www.dinosaur-exchange.com. One of the few senior job sites with an international focus
- **Employment Network for Retired Government Experts**— www.enrge.us. Focused on former federal employees who want to work in the private sector
- **ExecSearches.com**—www.execsearches.com/exec/default.asp. Executive, fundraising and mid-level jobs in nonprofit, government, health care, education and other not-for-profit sectors
- **Forward Group**—www.seniors4hire.com. Employers pay $65 to $125 a year to post openings that job seekers can browse at no charge
- **Monster.com**—www.careersat50.monster.com. Large general job site, including special section with advice and resources for older workers
- **National Organizers Alliance**—www.noacentral.org. Job listings in organizations that work for social, economic and environmental justice
- **OpportunityKnocks.org**—www.opportunityknocks.org. Search for nonprofit jobs by keyword or multiple criteria
- **The Phoenix Link**—www.thephoenixlink.com. Connects experienced executives and technologists with interim and full-time management positions

- **Retired Brains**—www.retiredbrains.com. Connects retiring or retired workers with employers and provides information on charitable organizations and nonprofits looking for senior volunteers

- **RetirementJobs.com**—www.retirementjobs.com. Database for employers seeking workers over the age of fifty

- **Senior Job Bank**—www.seniorjobbank.com. Job listings for older workers, including occasional, part-time, temporary, flexible and full-time opportunities

- **Score**—www.score.org. A nonprofit organization offering advice and training to small businesses. Volunteers are working or retired business owners, executives and corporate leaders who share their wisdom and lessons learned in business

- **Your Encore Inc.**—www.yourencore.com. Recruits retired scientists, engineers and product developers who are available to solve problems on a short-term basis

Sources: Printed with permission from Civic Ventures, www.civicventures.org and The Wall Street Journal.

6. What if I Decide Not to Work?

George Fulmore, who retired from a job in data processing and has no plans to return to paid employment—ever—explained his decision to us this way: "I'm adamant that my work career's over, and I've gone on to the third phase of my life that has all kinds of open ends and opportunities that I enjoy. I firmly believe that I have more money than time to spend it. If you feel that way and you live within your means, you don't worry about money." According to George, the key to retiring successfully without missing work is to "find enough things you enjoy to put into your calendar, but allow yourself some latitude to go with the flow."

George has found, as we described in Chapter One, that retirement activities often evolve naturally out of one's own interests. For his homeowners' association, he says that he has "become kind of a lay expert in the laws. For some reason, I get a lot of satisfaction out of that. I'm also researching Medicare now. I'm kind of intellectually independent. In retirement, I have time to . . . pick my own directions. The first year I didn't work, I went from reading two books a year to thirty books. I think people are finding joy in retirement that just isn't recognized often enough."

CHAPTER 3

VOLUNTEERING IN RETIREMENT

After winning a battle against breast cancer, Rita Vance retired to devote herself to full-time volunteer work. Her time felt more precious, and she wanted to spend it helping people in need in a hands-on way.

But her efforts didn't start out with the intended result.

Rita's first foray into volunteering found her sitting through meetings at an Ashland, Oregon, group focused on aging services. Those running the organization wanted her to serve in an advisory role and, because they believed such a position would fit her skills, they kept trying to persuade her to return to the full-time work she had just escaped. "But that's not what I wanted to do," she says. With her frustration mounting, she insisted on getting a chance to work face-to-face with the agency's clients and wound up dishing up cafeteria-style meals at a senior center, with little opportunity for interaction.

So, Rita decided to put together her own "volunteer satisfaction criteria" to screen other groups' volunteer opportunities. To come up with her personal requirements, she turned to resources including a well-worn copy of *What Color Is Your Parachute?*, the venerable self-help guide to finding a job, which she had used years ago while switching career paths.

EXPERIENCE CORPS

Experience Corps, a nonprofit group based in Washington, D.C., pays 1,800 older adults small stipends to tutor at least 13,250 schoolchildren in more than a dozen cities. The volunteers help teach children to read and develop the confidence and skills to succeed both in and outside of school. Research has shown that the group's work boosts the students' academic performance, helps schools and youth-serving organizations become more successful, strengthens ties between those institutions and surrounding neighborhoods and enhances the well-being of the volunteers in the process. Go to www.experiencecorps.org to see the places where Experience Corps works and to find contact information for local staff.

Eventually, through trial and error, she developed a meaningful portfolio of volunteer activities that felt like a good fit. And she even found a way to work with the aging agency: helping to organize workshops for caregivers of frail relatives.

As Rita learned the hard way, finding the right place to offer your time and services—even when you're doing it for free—sometimes requires great effort. "If you want volunteering to be a significant part of your life, then it's likely going to take some work to figure out the right fit," said John Gomperts, chief executive of Experience Corps.

Here's the advice we gathered from people who, like Rita, figured out for themselves how to find meaningful volunteer work:

Find a Cause that Matters to You

Start by asking yourself what really matters to you: Human rights? Homelessness? Education? Is there a cause that your day job has prevented you from championing? Could you rekindle any volunteer experiences you already found fulfilling or give something a second try?

When we last talked to Rita, she was doing the bulk of her pro-bono work for Jackson County's Court Appointed Special Advocate program, or CASA for short, a local chapter of a national group that tries to help abused and neglected children in the court system (www.nationalcasa.org). She was advocating on behalf of two families and their foster children. Rita also found other opportunities to round out her days, among them working at a child-care center, which gives her contact with small children, and providing books to homebound elderly.

Leslie Berry, a retiree in suburban Atlanta, yearned to relive the experiences she had enjoyed in Thailand and Kenya—learning about local art. She had spent thirteen years of her adult life overseas, during which she sought out volunteer work in museums and libraries, finding their peacefulness and beauty an antidote for her "chaotic" home life. A few years ago, she discovered that Atlanta's High Museum of Art was seeking docents, just at the moment she was reducing her hours at a party-supply store. Today, she spends at least two days a week at the High, taking classes from curators on Mondays, when the galleries are closed to the public, and leading fourth-graders on tours later in the week. Her latest goal is learning enough about so-called "found objects" used in folk art to help schoolchildren understand how they can apply the same principle to their own art projects.

IF NEED BE, HIRE YOURSELF

If you can't find a volunteer activity or position that interests you, you may want to consider creating your own.

Steve Weiner, a retired university administrator in Piedmont, California, described the first six years of his retirement as "trial and all errors—nothing painful, but just paths that I went down that I didn't want to stick with." After volunteering as a consultant for a nonprofit group and serving on a few boards, he decided that he "had to join with others to create entirely new enterprises" if he was going to "put together the pieces that I wanted to find at this particular point in my life."

In 2002, Steve and a colleague started the Campaign for College Opportunity, a nonprofit lobbying group sparked by the realization that college-bound Californians could be turned away from state colleges and universities due to lack of funding and limited classroom space—the reversal of access that had been all but guaranteed under state law since 1960. "The campaign has not solved the problem yet," Steve told us, "but it's mobilized thousands around the state."

On the East Coast, Jim Beaton, a retired vice president of corporate services and facilities for New England Financial Corp., became intrigued by a nonprofit venture called Dana's Field, which is starting a farm on Cape Cod, Massachusetts. The project, part of Housing Assistance Corp. in Hyannis, Massachusetts, aims to rehabilitate homeless people by teaching them the basic skills involved in running a small business, such as cooking, maintenance and using a computer. But it didn't really have a person to guide it through what proved to be a contentious approval process.

Jim, who "had gone through the rigorous process" of obtaining permits to build a large office building in Boston, offered to serve as head of a steering committee to get the farm off the ground. This time around, unlike with his former job, he didn't mind the obstacles. "It became kind of a mission for me," he told us. "We've managed to get to where we are with [almost] no funding, other than some grants from the Boston Foundation and pro-bono work, local churches' fundraising and a walk for the homeless. It's been a real bootstrap operation."

Make a Smooth Transition

Yes, it could be fun to try something completely different from your former day job when you first volunteer in retirement.

But tapping skills and knowledge from earlier jobs could help you settle into a volunteer role more easily and help you be more effective.

Bob Williams, for instance, retired as an investment banker with State Street Corp. after spending much of his career developing the firm's Asia business. He joined a volunteer project, coordinated by New Directions Inc., a Boston-based outplacement firm, where former executives help immigrants and low-income adults find jobs. There, he was able to translate his experience "looking for local people we could train to operate in a global market, but run our business in their own country" into doing much the same thing for the volunteer project. "I'm finding really capable immigrants who never bothered to put down on their résumé that they ran a restaurant in their home country. Somehow they get it in their minds that their experience back home doesn't matter here." For both Bob and the immigrants with whom he's worked, former job experience has opened doors to new and rewarding opportunities.

In addition, having an emissary who can connect you to a nonprofit and explain your skills often helps match you with a meaningful opportunity faster. Mary Westropp, who coordinates New Directions's volunteer programs, said the risk that retirees run is "not having their skills properly utilized" if they "show up at an agency just on their own without someone to usher them in. I want our partner agencies to understand how talented our volunteers really are." So, you might want to tap someone you know who has a connection to an agency you'd like to help, or network until you find such a person to make those introductions. Another place to find such a liaison may be the church, synagogue, mosque or other faith-based institution that you've attended for years. Most have a member who heads up missions work and often is a good contact with local social-services agencies.

Even if using your work-related skills isn't your ultimate goal, initially those talents might help you get involved with a group in which you're interested, especially if it can pick and

DOING WHAT YOU KNOW
DOESN'T ALWAYS WORK

There's a caveat to this idea of "do what you know": Volunteer work in your profession might not be as challenging as the paid work that you left. This was the case for Hazel Hutcheson, a former clinical nurse specialist who worked with patients immediately after surgery. Though the job was stressful, she found helping to relieve people's pain very satisfying. The volunteer roles she was offered in nursing—such as checking blood pressure, drawing blood for lab tests and giving immunizations—were important, but not challenging for her.

In that case, it's time for some introspection. What have you always enjoyed or wanted to learn more about, but didn't have time for while doing your day job? Hazel's answer was that she wanted to find a way to spend more time with children and to learn more about art because she always regretted not knowing more about it while visiting museums during her travels. So, she turned to the High Museum in Atlanta—and found a great fit working as a docent.

choose its unpaid help. Jeri Sedlar, a retirement-transition consultant in New York, put it this way: "A volunteer group might say, 'This is great: Jeri has this background in [human resources], so she can do all this HR stuff.' That may be the last thing I want to be involved with. But you may have to use a competency you have to get the door open."

PUT YOURSELF FIRST

The biggest incentive for volunteering may be what *you* get from the work: a chance to go behind the scenes at the local theater, pats on the back or friendships with fellow volunteers.

Marc Freedman, the chief executive of Civic Ventures, noted that, although people contemplating good works "tend to focus very heavily on the idealism of this phase of giving back," the volunteers he'd talked to said that "there are more immediate aspects that appeal to them—being part of a group or a team, giving themselves a reason to get up in the morning or a place to go or a schedule to live by. The relationships and a sense of purpose are just as important as some of the more lofty ideals in getting a satisfying experience."

Jeri Sedlar recalled joining the YWCA's New York board and saying, "This is what I want to give back." But when the group's leader asked her what she really wanted to get out of the experience, she realized it was "the leadership role and recognition. That's what keeps me committed and passionate about it."

Rich Yurman, a volunteer in San Francisco, gets to feed his desire to be a grandfather and compose poetry. For more than eight years, the writer and retired community college teacher has tutored young schoolchildren, mostly Asian immigrants, through Experience Corps, the program that taps older volunteers to work in urban schools. Rich turned to the organization after working with a counseling group for abusive men and seeing the impact their problems had on their children. His reason for volunteering was personal, too: "I hit age sixty, and this sudden surge of wanting to be a grandparent came out of who-knew-where. I have children who are not going to have children." In 2006, Rich was working one-on-one with a third-grader whom he called an "amazingly intense poet." She would jot down ideas to write about in a little notebook he persuaded her to carry around. Among her material were notes from her family's trips to Reno, Nevada. One day a week, they would get out the notebook, she would pick out a topic and they both would write about it. "It's just grand," he told us.

Many volunteers are also attracted to the learning opportunities that their work can provide. Lectures by museum curators, training on ways to work with children or seminars on retirement topics, such as how to enroll in the Medicare drug benefit, sometimes come as perks. When Hands On Network, an organization that connects volunteers to community needs,

VOLUNTEER TO IMPROVE YOUR HEALTH

Volunteering isn't just good for the people you're trying to help. Research has found that sharing your time and skills can improve your physical health.

Researchers at Johns Hopkins University in Baltimore followed 113 people who were fifty-nine to eighty-six years old. Fifty-nine were involved with Experience Corps, a nonprofit group that places older volunteers in elementary-school classrooms as mentors and tutors for fifteen hours a week and pays them a small stipend. The other fifty-four people were not involved in any volunteer work. The researchers found that volunteers who failed suggested U.S. standards for physical activity before they started volunteering *doubled* the calories they burned after volunteering for just one school year. (The Centers for Disease Control and Prevention recommends that all Americans be physically active for at least thirty minutes a day, five days a week.)

started recruiting volunteers in Atlanta for the Georgia Aquarium's opening in 2005, "it was amazing how many retirees were drawn to that," partly because of the training provided, said Michelle Nunn, the group's chief executive. Older volunteers also make up a large part of the audience for Hands On's Citizen Academy, where people can learn about such issues as sustainable development or fighting global poverty. The important thing for you to consider is what specifically you want to get out of volunteering and then where you might be able to get it.

FIND A PLACE THAT'S VOLUNTEER-CENTRIC

All nonprofit groups and social-service agencies are structured differently. A library, for instance, may have a few volunteers to shelve books, but it's not set up to offer frequent orientation, training, field trips and lectures solely for its volunteers. In contrast, groups organized to train and put volunteers to work tend to offer more educational opportunities, chances to mingle with fellow recruits, behind-the-scenes access to museums and theaters, social hours and recognition—all of which may take on increasing importance when volunteer work replaces a career. Something else to watch for is a place that wants to use you efficiently and that can work with you on a flexible schedule. (You're doing this at no charge, after all.)

For instance, Rita Vance in Oregon appreciated the formal recognition she received through the Court Appointed Special Advocate program, known in some communities as the guardian ad litem program, in which volunteers speak up for abused and neglected children in the courts. After forty hours of training, she and her colleagues went to a local court, where they were sworn in by a judge. "The judge thanks you in court, and you feel like you're a professional. That's different from some other volunteer places."

You Have to Start Somewhere

As in the business world, you may start in an "entry-level" volunteer position, but once you get a little experience, it's fairly easy to work your way up to the duties that you find most rewarding.

Rita wanted to volunteer at the library to select and deliver books to homebound readers, but "they didn't really need people to do that. They wanted me to come in and help with orientations, setting up coffee." She took the job—and worked her way into the role she wanted in about six months. Now, she works with five people who are homebound, often searching for large-print books from her home computer.

As with your early days in your work life, setting up volunteer "internships" can help you vet opportunities and get your foot in the door. You might consider trying out different roles and types of groups by rotating through two or three nonprofits that seem appealing. You could even use vacation time to do it while you're still working.

STAY FLEXIBLE

Unfortunately, volunteer work can be as fickle as any paid job: Leaders come and go, missions change and budgets expand and shrink. In the end, you might have to try something without knowing that it will be the right fit. And you may wind up working with a few different groups to satisfy your goals.

Take Patricia Weiner, a retired lawyer (she's married to Steve Weiner, the former college administrator we met earlier). Patricia tried three volunteer positions before finding one that suited her. While she was still working, she read a book about the Court Appointed Special Advocate program, in which volunteers work with abused and neglected children. "I really thought that CASA was going to be the one thing that I was going to want to do for years and years," she told us. But the foster child she was assigned to was moved to another county when they were "just about at the bonding point." Patricia was so frustrated by the move that she quit. CASA may have been the perfect fit for Rita Vance, but not so for Patricia Weiner. Next, after joining the board of the Family Violence Law Center, she realized she didn't want to attend meetings at night. She and her husband tried reading to the blind for an hour a week for two years, but they grew tired of the half-day commute involved.

Now, Patricia works with the first free-standing children's hospice in the country, leads school tours at the Oakland Museum and works in the book section of the museum's annual "white elephant" sale. "I do think there is some trial and error, and it is healthful," she told us. "I'm not sorry I did any of them." And they helped her narrow her focus to helping children. "It wasn't conscious—I just brought together things I cared about and where other interesting people were involved."

No matter where you settle in to volunteer, new opportunities may turn your head from time to time. When we last spoke with Rita, she was looking into the idea of "virtual volunteering"—writing grants, doing research and so forth, which are skills she honed during her career. An added benefit is that she can make these contributions while traveling with her husband in their camper. "We could still be helping while on the road," she said.

Help for Would-Be Helpers

United Way
www.unitedway.org
Local positions are posted under the "volunteer" button; some local United Way offices recruit volunteers to evaluate their community partners, which could help expose you to a variety of local agencies—particularly if you're a new resident.

Volunteer Match
www.volunteermatch.com
This popular Web site lists thousands of ways to volunteer, currently including many that involve Hurricane Katrina clean-up.

Hands On Network
www.handsonnetwork.org
This Web site has links to dozens of local clearinghouses of volunteer opportunities.

Next Chapter Initiative
www.civicventures.org/nextchapter
Here you will find a directory of Next Chapter projects around the country, many of which offer counseling services to help new retirees or people who are still working figure out how they want to spend their time in retirement, including how they might volunteer.

Newcomers Clubs

www.newcomersclub.com

Newcomers clubs, particularly in communities with lots of retirees, frequently invite guest speakers from nonprofit groups to talk about their organizations.

RespectAbility Initiative

www.respectability.org

Led by the National Council on the Aging, a Washington, D.C., advocacy group, the RespectAbility initiative currently is evaluating nonprofit groups that work well with older volunteers.

Out-placement firms

If you take a buyout from a large employer, chances are that out-placement counseling is part of the package. If you're planning to retire rather than looking for another job, such a firm may offer services to help you find meaningful pro-bono work.

CHAPTER 4

RELOCATION

P ete Lydens became familiar with many of the country's retirement hot spots while bouncing around the mid-Atlantic states and Southeast as a city manager and consultant for more than forty years. But he chose to retire to a hamlet where he worked in the 1960s—Mount Airy, North Carolina, population 8,454.

"It's almost mystical the way people here relate to friends and strangers," he told us, referring to the town that actor Andy Griffith memorialized on his 1960s TV show. "It's the ideal place to retire."

For Paul and Patricia Dravillas, the ideal retirement desti-nation is a bit larger: Chicago. The couple had always enjoyed city activities, especially using the sailboat they keep in Burn-ham Harbor on Lake Michigan. "But it was a pain to come down here with the parking and the traffic," Paul told us. Now, they ride their bikes to Chicago's Millennium Park and attend free concerts on weekends.

Small towns. Big cities. College communities. Co-housing developments. Even farms and ranches. Americans today ap-pear more willing to move in later life—and are exploring a wider variety of destinations—than ever before. Despite the popular image of seniors flocking to Florida or Arizona, about 90 percent of those over the age of sixty traditionally have stayed put in retirement for the simple reason that we like the familiar.

We enjoy being close to family and friends; we like knowing where to get our car fixed and how to reach our doctor.

Attitudes, though, are changing. Baby boomers, in particular, say they're more inclined than their parents to pull up stakes in retirement. Some surveys estimate that as many as one-third to one-half of retired boomers could be filling out change-of-address cards. Even if those figures prove to be exaggerated, the sheer size of this generation means that millions of Americans now in their forties, fifties and early sixties will end up relocating in retirement.

An individual's ties to the workplace tell a big part of the story. Historically, if you worked for the same company in the same town for thirty years, chances were good that you wouldn't venture far in retirement. Boomers, by contrast, are more likely to have worked for several different companies in several different locations; thus, their ties to any one community may not be as strong as those of their parents.

Along with changes in people's willingness to move, there's an appetite for different types of retirement destinations. Golf-course communities and so-called active-adult communities (like the popular Sun City developments) will always be part of the landscape. But many retirees are telling builders, developers and researchers that they are looking primarily for what Pete Lydens has found in Mount Airy: a destination where they quickly can make friends and connections—whether it's a small town or a walkable neighborhood in a big city. A close second and third on the what-I'm-looking-for lists are a home that's near grandchildren and a setting where one can indulge a post-work passion, such as a second career or even a newly adopted sport.

More retirees could also end up relocating because they *have* to—because their nest eggs are just too small for the lengthy retirements that lie ahead. For relief, people are turning to an asset that has jumped significantly in value: home sweet home. Selling your house and buying another at a lower price will be one way to reduce the strain on your savings and free up money in retirement. And don't think that strategy applies only to people of modest means; even individuals with healthy savings accounts are looking to the equity in their homes to meet expenses in later life. According to a recent study by the Spectrem Group, a consulting firm in Chicago, almost two-thirds of baby boomers with investments of $500,000 or more plan to finance their retirement by selling their primary residence.

Even if *you* have no intention of relocating in retirement, your *body* might have other ideas. The longer you live, the greater the likelihood that you'll need some kind of care or assistance. A recent study in *Congressional Quarterly Researcher* notes that nearly 70 percent of people who reach age sixty-five will need long-term care at some point in their lives, and 20 percent will need it for five years or longer. About 1.7 million Americans already are living in continuing-care retirement communities or assisted-living housing (see definitions on page 50); by the year 2020, an estimated 12 million older Americans will need long-term care.

So, where do you see yourself when it comes to moving in retirement? Do you stay or do you go?

Remember the math in later life is changing—as are the odds that your retirement will last longer than you think. As much as you might prefer to stay put, your budget or a change in your health could alter your plans. We recommend that almost all would-be retirees make the *possibility* of moving a part of retirement planning—just as you would consider the need for, say, an annuity or long-term care insurance.

If relocating becomes a strong possibility or a certainty, take a deep breath. Changing homes can be jarring in the best of times, and a move in retirement can be particularly unsettling when thrown into the mix of adjusting to new routines and new roles and ironing out new wrinkles in relationships.

The best way to start the process, even if the answers seem obvious, is to ask yourself, What would I gain (and lose) from moving?

WHAT WILL IT COST?

The number and types of living arrangements for older adults appear to be multiplying as fast as the population over the age of fifty-five itself. Here's a snapshot of relocation options and their costs:

Active-adult community. This is typically an "age-restricted" development where at least one member of a household must be fifty-five or older. It usually includes single-family homes, condominiums or townhouses, ranging in price from about $200,000 to more than $1 million. It is oriented toward an active lifestyle, with a fitness center, swimming pool, golf course and other amenities often found on-site.

Assisted living. This is a type of residence for people who need help with personal care, including bathing, cooking, dressing, eating or grooming. Residents live in rooms or apartments of a shared facility. Most facilities have between 25 and 120 units. Daily basic fees run as high as $200. Medical care is limited. Currently, about 1 million Americans live in about 39,500 assisted-living residences.

Board and care. This type of residence is similar to assisted living, but smaller in size. It may hold from three or four residents to two dozen. It is often a converted or adapted single-family home. Sometimes called a "group home" or "residential care home," some of these residences specialize in a specific type of care, such as early-stage Alzheimer's. Again, medical care is limited. Prices vary widely, from several hundred to several thousand dollars a month.

Congregate housing. This is a type of independent living, typically in separate apartments in a single building. Units may be owned or rented. Some custodial and medical care is provided. (Typically, more medical care is provided than in assisted living, but less than in a nursing home.) Again, prices range from several hundred to several thousand dollars a month.

Continuing-care retirement community (CCRC). Here, multiple levels of care and living arrangements are offered in a single location, starting with independent living and progressing to assisted living and skilled nursing care. Also known as a life-care community. Residences may include single-family homes, townhouses, cluster homes or apartments, often in a "campus" setting. (That said, CCRCs are also found in cities.) About 725,000 Americans live in CCRCs. They normally require an entry fee—ranging from about $20,000 to $400,000—in addition to monthly maintenance fees of about $200 to $2,500.

Residential living. Also known as independent living, this is a broad term that applies to a community of older adults, generally over the age of fifty-five, living in an apartment building or a collection of cottages or single-family homes. Generally, little or no medical or custodial assistance is available. Prices vary widely.

Skilled nursing facility. Twenty-four-hour care is provided at such a facility, normally for individuals with more serious medical problems. Residents, who occupy a private or shared room, generally need help with most or all daily activities of living, including bathing, dressing and eating. Forty-seven percent of residents are age eighty-five or older; 72 percent are women. About 17,000 nursing homes can be found in the United States. The average daily cost of a private room is $206, or about $75,200 a year.

Sources: American Association of Homes and Services for the Aging; Assisted Living Federation of America; www.Helpguide.org; MetLife

DO YOU REALLY WANT—
OR NEED—TO MOVE?

Most of us have fantasized about settling in "paradise" when we retire: the beach or hillside that we love or the vacation spot that never disappoints. But before you pull up stakes, here are four important issues to consider and how one couple handled each:

1. The Ties that Bind

What will you miss the most about the community you're leaving? What trade-offs—big and small—will you be making? Are you severing ties with a supportive church or other religious institution? Are you walking away from a great library? Most important, never underestimate the difficulty in leaving family and friends.

For Joe and Janet Sberro, the biggest "downside" of retiring from their jobs in Washington, D.C., and moving to the Southwest would be "leaving family behind—our children and grandchildren." The couple also would be saying goodbye to a support network in the Washington area built up over several decades. "Doctors, dentists, veterinarians—we had thirty years of bonds there," Janet explained.

But they ultimately decided that the advantages—a warm, mile-high climate; striking scenery; a thriving arts community; and a reasonable cost of living—outweighed the negatives. The Sberros made their new home just north of Albuquerque, New Mexico. And what about the family members and support network that were left behind? Today, the former pay visits (the city's International Balloon Fiesta, with hundreds of hot-air balloons, is a popular time to drop in), and the Sberros reciprocate, making trips to visit family back east. Meanwhile, the couple has built new ties to health clinics and other services in New Mexico. "Word of mouth steered us to the right people," Janet said. "This is a friendly place."

2. Becoming a Local

Be realistic about your chances for "fitting in" with your new surroundings, particularly if you're moving to a small town from a big city. While you certainly could become part of the inner circle, you're more likely to find yourself joining the ranks of *other retirees* in the area, especially those who have relocated from the same part of the country. Consider, for instance, this bumper sticker seen in Florida: "We don't care how you did it up North." You get the idea.

One answer, of course, is to join groups (religious institutions, social organizations, volunteer efforts, etc.) and meet people with similar interests. The Sberros, for their part, became involved with local theater, music groups, fellow anglers (Janet described her husband as a "fishing nut") and the main campus of the University of New Mexico, where Joe was taking classes three days a week for the grand total of $5 a credit.

3. CHARACTER TRAITS

At the risk of over-generalizing, retirees who relocate tend to be more assertive, more aggressive and more likely to have been managers or decision-makers. (After all, starting a new life in a distant locale isn't for the faint-of-heart.) However, a strong personality that might have been a big help in the business world may not work as well in a rural, unhurried environment with a population that has always done things a certain way.

Ask yourself if the "temperament" of a possible retirement destination is comparable to your own. Would you prefer the energy of a city or the serenity of a small town? Are you content living only a few feet from your neighbors or would you enjoy more privacy? The Sberros specifically decided *against* living in a retirement community and settled in the small town of Corrales, population 7,300, because they "wanted a *real* neighborhood," as Janet put it. "To just see people our own age would be pretty boring."

4. MONEY MATTERS

Finally, there's the issue of money. As part of your list of pros and cons, you will have to answer some fundamental questions: If my nest egg won't be big enough to support me down the road, will I need to tap the equity in my house to generate retirement income? If so, is a move to a new home the best way

RELOCATION TOOLS

Before you start packing, take a look at these "relocation calculators." Although most are designed to help people with moves connected to their work, these Web sites also can help would-be retirees.

www.factfinder.census.gov/home/saff/main.html

Here you'll find some of your tax dollars at work. This valuable Census Bureau site provides a wealth of information about cities and towns across the country, including dozens of social characteristics (i.e., the number of grandparents raising grandchildren), economic characteristics (including commuting times to work) and housing characteristics (such as the number of homes heated with solar energy).

www.monstermoving.monster.com/Find_a_Place/Compare2Cities/

Monster Moving, an extension of the popular job-listing Web site, has a good tool for comparing cities side by side. One interesting factoid is earthquake risk.

www.relocationessentials.com

After clicking on "Demographics," you can enter ZIP codes to compare various communities (to determine median home values, for instance, and average temperatures), the cost of living in those communities (including the relative tabs for groceries and health care) and local crime rates. The risk of robbery is "moderate" in Gainesville, Florida, for example, but "low" in Tucson, Arizona.

www.neighborhoodscout.com

The site's "Neighborhood Search Engine" provides community profiles, with information about housing costs, crime rates, the proportion of families with children and the ages of people in the area, among other statistics. Some data are free, but some require a subscription. For example, a seven-day subscription is offered for $19.95, or one year for $99.95.

www.retirementliving.com

Since money plays a large part in most people's retirement plans, make sure you check this Web site. It allows you to compare the overall tax burden in each state, including taxes on retirement income, property taxes, senior exemptions and sales taxes.

www.bestplaces.net

In addition to esoteric studies on the "worst cities for respiratory infections" (Greenville, South Carolina, takes the prize), users can compare features on 3,000 destinations. Let's say you live in Hawthorne, New Jersey, and are considering a move to Chapel Hill, North Carolina. The median age falls to 23.9 from 38.1, the number of physicians per 100,000 population jumps to 1,321 from 204 and the average yearly snowfall drops to five inches from twenty-three.

www.epodunk.com

This site is strange, but fascinating and exhaustive. Offers information about 46,000 communities across the country. Thinking about retiring in Savannah, Georgia? It's the "Turf Grass Capital of the World," home to the Sand Gnats (a minor-league baseball team) and has eight museums, fifty-eight cemeteries and a median air-quality index level of thirty-three (in 2003). Just in case you were wondering, 6 percent of residents report German ancestry and 7 percent report Irish ancestry.

to do that? And just how radical a move would I have to make in terms of downsizing and distance from my current address to free up sufficient equity? (We'll discuss other options for tapping the value in your home, including reverse mortgages, in Chapter Seven.)

The Sberros took steps well before retiring—including hiring a financial adviser—to get their finances in order. Janet had worked for the federal government, which meant that she and her husband had good health benefits after leaving their jobs. Even so, the couple had started scaling back some expenditures in retirement. "Just cutting a few luxuries," Janet told us. "So far, our finances are looking all right, but we want to stay ahead of the game."

DECIDING WHERE TO MOVE

All right. You think—or know—that a move is in your future. What follows are the Big Seven factors you should consider in finding a community that fits your needs.

1. **Climate**   Few questions will narrow your search for a place to retire faster than this one: What's the weather like? (Or lately, What are the chances this area will be hit by hurricanes?) Ideally, the destination you select will allow you to get outdoors almost year-round to pursue one of the most important activities in retirement: regular exercise.

   Hot and humid summers have discouraged many from retiring to the Gulf Coast region, while long, cold winters have deterred others from moving farther north. The more temperate climates of North Carolina, California and Nevada have made these states popular retirement destinations. Then again, you may not mind scurrying from one air-conditioned place to another or bundling up in multiple layers. The important thing is to find a climate that's right for your lifestyle. Speaking of which . . .

2. **Lifestyles and interests**   Is the community or destination you're considering a stimulating environment? Does it offer activities and opportunities—education, culture, outdoor pursuits, entertainment or volunteer work—that meet your particular needs?

   Dean Darling, an Ohio native, found happiness in Mountain Home, Arkansas, where he could fish the local rivers to his heart's content. "What we catch here in one day," he told us, "is what others catch in an entire season in places like Colorado or Montana or Wyoming." James Dobie settled in Kerrville, Texas, after retiring from Auburn University in Alabama where he taught biology. One big reason for his move was Schreiner University, a Presbyterian college in Kerrville. James still writes scholarly articles, and the school's biology staff helps him order the scientific-journal reprints he needs. "There's a recognition in this area that education is important," he said.

3. **Housing** The availability of quality housing at a reasonable price is the fundamental challenge in any move. You also should consider whether a home already has elements that will accommodate common needs of later life—a first-floor master suite, wide doorways, levered handles (instead of doorknobs) and task lighting—or whether such features can be incorporated into a house in the future. Ball State University in Muncie, Indiana, has a valuable resource called WellComeHome that addresses such modifications. You can find it at www.bsu.edu/wellcomehome/index.html.

4. **Safety** Beyond the obvious—feeling comfortable about walking through your new neighborhood at any hour of the day or night—you should check several sets of information, if available: property crime rates, violent crime rates and victimization surveys.

Start with the Federal Bureau of Investigation's report titled "Crime in the United States." (See www.fbi.gov/ucr/ucr.htm;nscius.) Here, you'll find information about violent crime (murder, rape, robbery and aggravated assault) and property crime (burglary, larceny, motor-vehicle theft and arson) in cities and towns with a population of 100,000 or more and some counties and metropolitan areas. Keep in mind that the statistics include only those crimes that were reported to the FBI by local law-enforcement authorities, but they still provide a good snapshot for large locales.

Next check with the police and sheriff departments in your target destinations. A growing number of departments are publishing crime statistics, and many of these statistics are available online. Again, it's difficult to know just how many incidents are actually reported to—or by—local officials. (Does a stolen bicycle make the cut?) Not surprisingly, some towns are reluctant to paint a detailed picture of misdeeds in their neighborhoods.

Several other questions to consider regarding safety: Would you feel comfortable leaving your new home for extended vacations? Is there a neighborhood watch program or a homeowner's association that makes safety part of its focus? And are there reasonable response times for emergency services?

5. **Affordability**   Take your budget for retirement and see what each item would cost in your new neighborhood. Most of the comparisons, such as food, cable-TV, telephone, insurance, gasoline, utilities, transportation, etc., should be straightforward. The one area where many people stumble is taxes.

Traditionally, people are quick to put states like Florida, Nevada and Texas at the top of their where-to-move lists because those states have no income taxes, but don't assume a guaranteed small tax bill. Washington state, for instance, has no income tax, but a combination of high fuel and sales taxes means that Washington ranks thirteenth among the fifty states for highest state and local tax burden, according to the Tax Foundation, a nonpartisan research group. Contact local and state tax departments and review *all* levies in a possible retirement destination: sales taxes, local and state income taxes, personal property taxes, real-estate taxes, taxes on pensions and Social Security and even estate taxes.

6. **Health care**   Not long ago, researching medical care in a retirement destination involved little more than making sure an adequate hospital was available, and, if needed, a spe-

TAXING TIMES

These states have the lowest tax burden* as a percentage of per-capita income:

Alaska	6.6%
New Hampshire	7.3%
Delaware	8.4%
Tennessee	8.6%
Alabama	8.8%
South Dakota	9.2%
Texas	9.4%
Nevada	9.5%
Montana	9.5%
Virginia	9.5%

*For state and local taxes in 2006   *Source: Tax Foundation*

cialist for a particular illness. But, as health care and health-insurance become more complicated and expensive, the research is getting more difficult. Increasingly, doctors are reluctant to accept new Medicare patients, and health maintenance organizations (HMOs) are closing their doors in unprofitable communities. Thus, it becomes imperative before moving to determine if you can find a family practice or an HMO able and willing to add you to its patient rolls.

Here is an additional consideration: If you have long-term care insurance, your coverage in all likelihood was based on the cost of care where you currently live. If you move and end up needing care, will your policy still be sufficient? Calls to a half-dozen assisted-living centers, nursing homes and home-care agencies in a target retirement destination can give you a quick idea about the cost of care in the area. Also, check out MetLife's annual surveys of the cost of long-term care in various markets. (Go to the insurance company's Web site, www.metlife.com, and search for "Mature Market Institute.")

7. **Transportation** You could be living in your new community for a long time. What happens if you're forced to cut back, or eliminate, your time behind the wheel? What kind of public transportation is available? Do volunteer organizations or local government agencies offer transportation programs for older adults? And consider the broader idea of accessibility. Will you be close to shopping, grocery stores and medical care? Where is the nearest airport? How easy, or difficult, will it be for friends and family to visit you without having to drive?

RANKINGS AND RESEARCH

These days, major bookstores are filled with books and magazines opining about the best places to retire. One might be heavily weighted toward statistics, with rankings of hospitals and the availability of part-time work; a second might favor lengthy descriptions of dozens of locales; and a third might take a more practical approach, limiting choices to sites where retirees can walk to a grocery store, take in a first-rate museum opening and end their day in a five-star restaurant.

"The more I delve into it, the more I realize how much guess, by-gosh suppositions, bias and plain bull goes into this business," John Howell, author of *Where to Retire—America's Best and Most Affordable Places,* told us.

The key is recognizing that no single set of parameters—however well thought out—will yield the "correct" answer. Charles Lockhart and Jean Giles-Sims, professors at Texas Christian University, realized this when they attempted to measure the ability of individual states to meet the needs of older Americans. Their 2005 study, "Variations in Elderly Friendliness," produced rankings of "state elderly friendliness," which, as it turned out, varied dramatically based on the need being measured. When it came to "recreational lifestyle," for instance, Florida and nine Western states (Alaska, Arizona, California, Hawaii, Idaho, Nevada, New Mexico, Texas and Utah) took top honors. But when the professors looked at "health and acute medical care"—presumably an equally important factor in most relocation decisions—only two of the "recreational lifestyle" winners (Hawaii and Utah) made the Top Ten. The others were Colorado, Iowa, Minnesota, New Hampshire, North Dakota, Oregon, Vermont and Wisconsin.

It's not that you should ignore lists of retirement hot spots. Most can provide good names to consider. Retirees we spoke with said they enjoy reading the lists, but they added that they were more likely to consider factors that aren't mentioned in the books before making a decision.

Esther Jennings, for example, moved to Hot Springs, Arkansas, because she had fond memories of vacations there with her family in the 1970s. The town's top ratings in some retirement guides weren't much of a factor. As she put it, "Those guides are mostly for fun."

Dale Appel, a food chemist, moved twice after retiring. Both times, he consulted a book that rated retirement destinations, but the deciding factor wasn't a number one ranking. He first moved to Clearwater, Florida, to be near his son. When the heavy traffic and humidity became too much to bear, he picked up stakes and moved to Kerrville, Texas, to be near his sister. Dale said Kerrville's high rating in the book he purchased helped him single out that city. But what really sold him were the smiling faces at the local chamber of commerce, the friendly people who gave him directions when he got lost and the beautiful town square.

"This is the kind of small-town life I was looking for," he said.

VISITS AND MORE VISITS— THE "EVEREST" APPROACH

At some point—once the list of possible destinations is narrowed to two or three finalists—it's time to visit each spot. The best way to do this is to think about Mount Everest.

Climbers who tackle Everest do so in stages. They will ascend to a particular height, spend a brief time there and return to a base camp. Then, they will climb to the previous height a second time and remain for a longer period. Climbers repeat this process at ever-higher altitudes, as they acclimate themselves to the mountain's thin air. We advise a similar process when considering possible retirement destinations:

The first trip might last a week. It will give you a chance to drive through neighborhoods, dine at local restaurants and get an initial impression. Assuming that the first visit is promising, the second trip should last two or three weeks and take place during a different time of the year. At this point, it helps to talk with prospective neighbors and real-estate agents. Finally, if you think you have found your retirement home, book a short-term rental and visit for two or three months. If you still like the community, put up the "For Sale" sign back home.

Yes, this is a lengthy and potentially expensive process. But few decisions in retirement are more painful than discovering you have settled in an area that proves to be something quite different from what you imagined.

Charles Longino, a professor at Wake Forest University and a leading expert on retirement migration, summed it up nicely for us: "Visit South Florida when the mosquitoes are out and the temperatures are high—not just in February. Or visit when tourists don't come—when the towns go back to their native residents. Some people will do that and decide this is not the place for them."

A RETIREMENT COMMUNITY SAMPLER

The idea of retirement living as a passive existence in some distant, sweltering setting is as dated as *Look* magazine. On page 50, we briefly describe the numerous types of relocation options and their costs. What follows is a closer look at some of the most popular choices today—and a few warnings:

EXPLORING A TOWN

What's the best way to quickly size up a town when exploring possible retirement destinations? Follow this guide:

- Head straight for the Chamber of Commerce to get its relocation package. This usually includes the community's basic demographic information, a thumbnail sketch of the economy, average temperatures, average snowfall, cost of living, taxes, available services, medical and educational facilities, crime rate, restaurants and a list of real-estate brokers.

- Pick up a copy of the local phone book. A thumb through the yellow pages will give you a good idea of what an area has to offer: the range of physicians and alternative-health practices, restaurants, book stores, theaters, service organizations, numbers of professionals, religious institutions and airline service.

- Skim the local newspaper and read its editorials and letters to the editor to get a sense of issues of local importance and local attitudes.

- Walk the downtown area to get a feel for the stores and restaurants and tour the residential areas. Drive twenty to thirty minutes on each of the roads leading out of town to see what the countryside looks like. Try to book into local bed-and-breakfasts; they offer a good chance to talk with the local citizenry.

- Finally, if your interest in a place is high, visit a local real-estate agent to get an idea of the properties available in your price range. In most cases, even if you explain that this is an exploratory look and that you might not settle in the area, real-estate agents can be generous with their time and can give you a good sampling of houses and property in different areas— plus plenty of food for thought.

College Towns

The attractions are evident: a bracing atmosphere, the chance for continuing education, diverse demographics and (often) lots of restaurants, shopping and cultural events. There are actually two ways to retire to a college community: simply settling in the town itself or moving into a so-called collegiate village—housing that a college or university builds or sponsors specifically for retirees. These "college-linked" communities can now be found on about seventy campuses nationwide—including Notre Dame, the University of Michigan and Cornell, among others—and more are on the drawing boards.

Before digging out your old letter sweater, however, recognize that not every college setting will give you the ivy-covered experience you may be seeking. In particular, if you want to attend classes or develop close ties to a school, you should look into the access—or lack thereof—to school resources and the quality and frequency of contact with professors and undergraduates. If a college or university isn't interested in working with local retirees, your proximity to a campus might not count for much.

BACK TO SCHOOL

To learn more about campus communities, visit the following developers' Web sites:

www.campuscontinuum.com

www.collegevillecommunities.com

www.collegiateretirementcommunity.com

www.kendall.org

"Grover's Corners"

That, of course, is the name of Thornton Wilder's mythical village in *Our Town* and what many retirees are seeking: a small, safe and picturesque town with a sense of community.

It's why Terry and Kathy Miller told us they moved to Southport, North Carolina, population 2,558. ("We would never consider retiring someplace big," Mrs. Miller said.) And why Carey Heckman retired to Hanover, New Hampshire, population 10,800. ("You can . . . do things and not have to make reservations a week and a half in advance," he said.) And why Jim Weiss settled outside Beaufort, South Carolina, population 12,950. ("It's not a gated, closed community," he noted. "That's part of the charm.")

These towns and many others used to be well-kept secrets, but when typing the words "retirement destination" into Google yields 75,000 results, the chances of any small, attractive community staying that way are increasingly slim. In Beaufort, for instance, town officials are trying to figure out how to build a transportation system that can reach the area's numerous islands without triggering gridlock. In Southport, more than 1,200 homes have been built in a neighboring development since the early 1990s; existing roads and services are having trouble keeping pace with the area's "explosive growth," as one official described it.

If you find your Grover's Corners, the best place to settle (even if you find yourself paying a premium) could be in a historic district, where future development likely will be kept to a minimum.

ACTIVE-ADULT COMMUNITIES

The Sun Cities of the world typically come to mind: sprawling developments with thousands of homes in states like Florida and Arizona. Of course, these age-restricted communities long ago dropped or minimized most of the activities (like sing-alongs and shuffleboard) that conjured up images of "rest homes." Today, multimillion-dollar fitness centers are the big selling point, along with enough activities—in-line skating, hiking, cooking classes, investment clubs, bicycling, kayaking, etc.—to satisfy even the most kinetic personality.

More recently, builders of active-adult communities have made two big changes: moving to colder climes (on the theory that retirees "up north" like to remain close to family and friends) and creating smaller, "cozier" developments, with hundreds, instead of thousands, of homes. (That decision also reflects the higher cost of land in markets like the Northeast and Midwest.) While these new communities are attracting their fair share of buyers, the question for many retirees remains: Do I wish to live in an age-restricted community (typically open to those over the age of fifty-five) or in a neighborhood with families of various ages?

In truth, the frequently heard complaint "I don't want to live with a bunch of old people" overlooks the fact that many retirement communities today are hives of activity, with relatively low taxes and tranquil streets. Conversely, in a town that skews young, schools and related services might take priority over programs for older adults, which means taxes could be high. And youthful neighborhoods can be (how to put this?) a bit boisterous.

CONTINUING-CARE RETIREMENT COMMUNITIES

CCRCs are some of the most specialized and costly retirement communities on the market. These developments offer assurances of care from the day you first move in until the day you die. A single CCRC, with a staff of hundreds, typically includes independent-living quarters (detached homes or apartments), assisted-living facilities (for residents who require help with tasks such as preparing meals or dressing) and skilled nursing care (for those who need more comprehensive medical care). A resident who grows more dependent over time can move from his or her independent-living site to an assisted-living apartment to a nursing home all within the same community— typically for a predetermined cost.

Getting in the door can be difficult, though. Some people wait until they're in need of substantial amounts of care to seek entrance, but most CCRCs want residents to be able to live independently when they first enter the community. Waiting lists are also growing faster than the pace of development: While a free-standing assisted-living facility can be built in as little as six months for as little as $7 million, according to industry estimates, some CCRCs take a year or more to develop and carry price tags in the tens of millions of dollars.

Finally, the pricing options can be numbing: a small deposit coupled with monthly fees in some instances or a much larger deposit—with a chance for your heirs to inherit a portion of that down payment—in others. A third option is an "equity CCRC," in which residents can sell their independent-living unit and apply the proceeds to the cost of future care (in an assisted-living or nursing-home setting). In short, a significant amount of homework is required.

Co-housing

These neighborhoods, in which residents live in private homes but share a central "common house" with a kitchen and other service facilities, were designed originally for anybody interested in living communally or conserving resources, such as environmentalists. But they are becoming increasingly popular with older residents, and several developments specifically for people age fifty and older are now under construction. A large part of the appeal is the "idea of aging in a community," according to Neshama Abraham, a co-housing consultant in Boulder, Colorado. The hope is that residents will be able to receive much of their medical needs on site and help one another more easily through crises.

The ElderSpirit Community project in Abingdon, Virginia, is designed for older adults interested in living in a faith-based setting. Spearheaded by a group of former nuns, the development will offer companionship and care from the early years of retirement through death. It will offer a mix of "spirituality and mutual support," said Dene Peterson, one of Elder-Spirit's founders.

CCRC RESOURCES

More than 2,000 communities across the country identify themselves as continuing-care developments, but most have differing ownership models, fees, services, housing, activities, management styles and entrance requirements.

The following resources offer some of the best information available about CCRCs:

The American Association of Homes and Services for the Aging
Washington, D.C.
800-508-9442
www.aahsa.org

This organization offers a comprehensive handbook on the subject, *Continuing Care Retirement Community: A Guidebook for Consumers,* which answers frequently asked questions about CCRCs and contains checklists for comparing amenities and services. Visit the bookstore on the group's Web site or order by phone. Publication No. CC001.

California Department of Social Services
Sacramento, CA
800-952-8348
www.calccrc.ca.gov/facilityquestions.html

An excellent list of questions for would-be residents of CCRCs is on offer here. The list includes queries about contracts, health care and a community's financial status.

CarePathways
Kitty Hawk, NC
877-521-9987
www.carepathways.com

Information about senior care and housing options is available here. The organization offers an extensive checklist for evaluating CCRCs. It is available at www.carepathways.com/checklist-ccrc.cfm.

Commission on Accreditation of Rehabilitation Facilities
Washington, D.C.
866-888-1122
www.carf.org

This is the accrediting body for continuing-care communities. It offers an online search of accredited communities, with links to those communities.

CHAPTER 5

FITNESS
AND
HEALTH

Life expectancies are increasing as our health improves: On average today, men who reach age sixty-five can expect to live an additional seventeen years, and women could live an additional twenty, according to the National Center for Health Statistics. Now, the goal isn't just to live longer, it's to make sure you spend all those decades in retirement in the best health possible. Americans are making some strides in the right direction: The disability rate for people sixty-five and older fell significantly between 1982 and 1999 to one in five people from one in four. But that meant 14 million folks were still disabled, many from chronic conditions including heart disease, diabetes and arthritis. Adult children, increasingly called on to help disabled parents while heading into their own retirements, are paying attention, and many list staying— or getting—fit as a top priority in later life.

Freelance writer Carol Daus, for example, decided to delve into her family's health history after her mother was diagnosed with breast cancer. Carol discovered that her family's other demon is cardiovascular disease: Her father died at age fifty-nine of a ruptured aneurysm, her brothers have high blood pressure, and her grandmother suffered a debilitating stroke at age forty-nine. Once that health history was staring her in the face, Carol started exercising much more regularly, spending at least thirty minutes every day either at a gym or on her treadmill at home. She read *Fast Food Nation,* which delves into the origins of American junk food, aloud to her children, "and they won't even set foot in a McDonald's," she said proudly.

It's not just a matter of your health. Combating chronic conditions with more physical activity and fewer drugs could save you money. As we mentioned already, Fidelity Investments has predicted that a sixty-five-year-old couple retiring in 2007 would need $215,000 in savings just to cover their basic medical costs in retirement, including premiums for Medicare's doctor and drug coverage (Parts B and D); co-payments, deductibles and other expenses not covered; and out-of-pocket drug costs. That estimate doesn't even include long-term care, over-the-counter medicine or most dental work. It also assumes that the husband and wife would die at ages eighty-two and eighty-five, respectively.

Motivated to exercise yet? The first step is measuring your fitness now.

MEASURING UP

After decades of wear and tear on muscles and bones, many people are unsure of their fitness level. But knowing where you stand could help motivate you to get or stay active and to do it safely. Researchers at the Cooper Institute, a well-known medical research foundation in Dallas, put nearly 10,000 men through two treadmill fitness tests about five years apart. They then monitored the men for another five years. The findings were dramatic for the men who took their initial poor fitness level to heart: Those who improved enough to qualify as fit five years later were able to cut their risk of premature death *nearly in half!*

CRUNCHING NUMBERS

Here are some online calculators to help you do the math involved with assessing your health.

Body Mass Index (BMI)

BMI calculators gauge your weight relative to your height.

www.webhealthcentre.com (click on "Health Calculators")

www.xenical.com

Exercise and Nutrition

www.webmd.com (enter "dessert wizard" as search term)

www.primusweb.com/fitnesspartner

www.caloriesperhour.com

www.netnutritionist.com

Heart and Cholesterol

www.webmd.com (enter "heart rate calculator" as search term)

www.healthatoz.com (click on "Tools" tab)

Assuming that you don't have sophisticated testing equipment at home, how do you gauge your own fitness? One way is to do some simple math. Walter Ettinger, a doctor and an author of a book on fitness and aging, shared his method with Tara Parker-Pope, our colleague at *The Wall Street Journal*: Count the number of hours each week that you take part in physical activity—and don't forget the little things, such as taking the stairs, working in the garden or walking through a huge parking lot. (Any activity helps. Older adults who have high levels of daily activity, as mundane as working in the yard, holding a part-time job or climbing stairs, expend more energy and have a lower premature death rate compared to less-active groups, according to a 2006 study by National Institute on Aging scientists.)

Have you added up your hours? Here's where you rank:

- If you spend at least five hours a week engaged in a moderate level of physical activity (equivalent to a brisk walk) your fitness level is high.

- If you spend three hours a week on moderate physical activities, your fitness level is medium.

- If you don't do much moving (an hour or less each week engaged in moderate activity) your fitness level is low, and you're five times as likely to die from cardiovascular disease as someone in the high-fitness-level group.

Based on these rankings, it's easy to see just how many hours of activity you need to add on a weekly basis if you want to improve your overall health.

If you'd like a more specific, in-depth analysis, you might want to get a professional fitness assessment. We talked to an adventure-travel writer, Margie Goldsmith, who was no shirker, with several marathons under her belt by age fifty-eight. But when she started finding it tough to work out with the same vigor as in the past, she signed up for a $100 assessment at Red Mountain Spa in St. George, Utah. There, she was outfitted with a heart monitor, mouthpiece and breathing tube. As she walked on a treadmill, a computer analyzed the exchange of oxygen, carbon dioxide and other gases at different heart rates. She learned she was exercising above her target heart rate and quickly wearing herself out. She slowed her power-walking pace, increased her endurance and went on to complete her first triathlon.

You can also get a comprehensive assessment at most health clubs to help you figure out how much you need to push yourself both with aerobic exercise and conditioning. An assessment should include a mini-workout where you ride a bike or

THE JOCK TEST

If you'd prefer a test that's more precise, the American College of Sports Medicine's fitness guidelines identify people of excellent to superior fitness, good fitness, and fair to poor fitness using several types of exercise tests. After you finish the tests, compare your scores to the benchmarks. In each case, the first number is for people between the ages of fifty to fifty-nine, while the number in parentheses is for people sixty and older. One caveat: If any of these tests seem like something you shouldn't do, don't. Or, at least ask your doctor first.

Aerobic Fitness

THE BENEFIT:
Aerobic exercise (swimming, running and the like) can strengthen your heart and increase your ability to use oxygen.

THE TEST:
Time yourself on a 1.5 mile run.

SCORECARD:
Excellent: Your time is less than 14:03 minutes (15:19) if a man or less than 16:51 (17:29) if a woman.

Good: Your time is 14:24 to 15:08 (15:29 to 16:27) if a man or 16:58 to 17:29 (17:46 to 18:31) if a woman.

Fair to Poor: Your time is 15:26 or more (16:43 or more) if a man or 17:55 or more (18:44 or more) if a woman.

Strength Fitness

THE BENEFIT:
Resistance training makes bones stronger, improves balance and increases muscle strength and mass.

THE TEST:
Do as many push-ups as you can without stopping. Men should start in the standard "up" position: hands shoulder-width apart, back straight and head up. Lower your chest to within a "fist" reach of the floor, and then push up

to a straight-arm position. Women can start in modified knee push-up position: ankles crossed, knees bent at a 90-degree angle, back straight, hands shoulder-width apart and head up. Press down as far as you can and push up to a straight-arm position.

SCORECARD:

Excellent: You are able to complete at least 20 (20) push-ups if a man or 18 (13) if a woman.

Good: You complete 14 to 19 (12 to 18) push-ups if a man or 13 to 17 (6 to 12) push-ups if a woman.

Fair to poor: You complete fewer than 13 (10) push-ups if a man or 12 (5) push-ups if a woman.

Muscular Endurance

THE BENEFIT:
Strength-developing exercises help improve musculoskeletal health and maintain independence, allowing you to perform the activities of daily life as you age and help relieve back pain and reduce the risk of falling.

THE TEST:
Count the number of sit-ups you can do in a minute. A traditional sit-up is fine for the purposes of the test, but not recommended because of the strain it can put on your lower back. The American College of Sports Medicine recommends a modified crunch-type sit-up, in which you lie on your back with your knees bent. Place your hands, palms down, under your lower back to support it. Flex your abdominal muscles to pull your head and shoulders toward your knees, and then go back to the floor in a controlled motion.

SCORECARD:

Excellent: If you can do 30 (24) or more sit-ups if a man or 21 (12) if a woman, you have fab abs.

Good: Men doing 25 to 28 (19 to 22) sit-ups and women doing 16 to 20 (8 to 11) have healthy stomach muscles and strong backs.

(continued)

Fair to poor: Men completing 24 (19) or fewer sit-ups, and women doing 14 (6) or fewer.

Flexibility

THE BENEFIT:

Stretching and exercise helps delay a loss of elasticity in the muscles and thickening of tissues around your joints, which limits your range of motion, by preventing them from becoming short and tight.

THE TEST:

Sit on the floor and reach toward your feet. Start by placing a yardstick on the floor and attaching a piece of tape, about two feet long, across the 15-inch mark on the yardstick (so it looks like a big "plus" sign). Next, sit on the floor with your legs on either side of the yardstick, about shoulder-width apart, and your heels resting on top of the tape. Keep your legs straight. Slowly reach forward with both hands, keeping them parallel. Stretch as far as you can, and record the number. The score is the most distant point reached on the yardstick with the fingertips.

SCORECARD:

Excellent: Call yourself "Gumby" if you can stretch 16 (15) inches or more if a man or 19 (17.5) inches or more if a woman.

Good: Men stretching 14 to 15.5 inches (13 to 14.5) and women stretching 17 to 18.5 (16.1 to 17) are loose and limber.

Poor: You're probably pretty stiff if you can stretch only 13.3 inches (12.5) or less if a man or 16.8 inches (15.5) or less if a woman.

walk on a treadmill long enough for the trainer to help you figure out your maximum aerobic capacity. With that information, you can figure out just how fast your heart should be beating when you exercise.

SWIM, BIKE, RUN—REPEAT

Climbing off the couch is difficult enough for most people. But a growing number of older adults are participating in one of the most grueling athletic competitions imaginable—the triathlon.

Today, almost 12 percent of nearly 84,000 members of USA Triathlon, the sport's governing body, are fifty or older. The toughest of these three-stage races, the Ironman, stretches for 140 miles of swimming, biking and running. Others, including the Olympic triathlon, cut that distance by half or more.

What makes people take on the challenge? We asked Sandy Bainbridge in Denver to tell us her story.

In late 2002, I remember feeling kind of blue—not feeling quite together. My husband and I had sold the home we had been in for fourteen years and moved from Minneapolis to Denver. Our kids had graduated from college and had found significant others, and my father had passed away. There was quite a void in my life. I was an empty nester, and all of a sudden the fast pace slowed down.

I went to see my physician and said I needed something to do. She told me about Danskin Triathlons, a series around the country to encourage women to get into endurance sports. These triathlons are "sprint triathlons," half the Olympic distances. I cooked on the idea for a couple of months, and then in the fall of 2003, I started training on my fifty-fifth birthday.

In July 2004, I was one of 3,500 women in the Danskin Triathlon in Denver. I placed twenty-ninth out of the sixty-five people in my age group, which was fifty-five to fifty-nine. It took me over two hours to swim half a mile, ride a bike 12 miles and do a 3.2-mile run. Not great times, but I finished running and smiling. Then I did my second sprint triathlon a month later.

For a woman at midlife, triathlons have really been an upper. I am so much happier when I have had a workout. I have taken off twenty pounds, dropped almost two sizes, and have so much more capacity to do my job and live my life. And I have made a ton of new friends. My kids, in their mid-twenties, brag about their athletic mom, and my husband of thirty-four years introduces me as a triathlete to anyone who will listen.

I used to think I would retire at fifty-five—that I would need the break from work. But now I feel as though I could go forever. My goal is to be a triathlete at least until age sixty-five. I would love in my retirement to be some sort of a senior-citizen fitness coach. It's all about beginnings.

GET OFF THE COUCH

Now you should know where you stand. If your fitness level is less than you'd like, it's up to you to do the rest—especially as you gain more control of your time and have the freedom to make physical activity a higher priority than it was when you worked dozens of hours a week.

One of the first tools you may want to buy is a heart-rate monitor that can be worn on your wrist like a watch. Richard Grunsten, a Chicago catalog-industry consultant, told us he had been using one for a decade to challenge himself while running or taking a spinning class (aerobics on an exercise bike). If he was tempted to exercise at a slower, more-comfortable pace, the monitor would beep, pushing him on. Trusted brands include Polar, LifeSource and Mio, and they've fallen in price like computers and calculators in recent years, with good ones costing under $100. Look for three features: a chest strap to measure your heart rate, a large display that's easy to read while exercising and an alarm that beeps when your rate is out of your target range.

Your computer could be a valuable piece of home-exercise equipment as well. A slew of online personal trainers and fitness programs are making it easier to get expert advice without the expense of a personal-training session. A typical session

COMPUTER WORKOUTS

Here are some online training programs:

www.jeffgalloway.com ($249/6 months)
Personal e-mails from an Olympic runner

www.markallenonline.com ($102 to $162/6 weeks)
Triathlon training from an Ironman champion

www.workoutsforyou.com ($48–$180/6 months)
Various training options

www.cardiocoach.com ($15–$70)
Coached workouts and music to download

costs $5 to $10 a week compared with $50 to $75 an hour with a trainer. Online training involves one-on-one contact with a trainer by e-mail, in which exercisers update the trainer on their progress and injury status and get feedback.

If you'd like to try strength training without hanging out at a gym, you can get started at home with some low-cost equipment. Physical trainer Keli Roberts recommended this assortment of equipment, which totals $100 or so:

- A yoga mat for stretching and floor work

- An inflatable ball that can be used in place of a weight bench and for body-stability training

- Stretchy tubes (light and medium resistance) for squats and lunges

- Rubber rings (light and medium resistance) to strengthen hips and thighs

- Three pairs of neoprene dumbbells in five-pound, eight-pound and twelve-pound increments

Worried that you won't know what to do with a stability ball and the other equipment? You can buy manuals and DVDs, often as part of a package deal, that show you how to exercise with them. Claire Kopp, a Los Angeles psychologist, has worked out at home with a stability ball several times a day to combat back problems, doing eight different exercises that take about fifteen minutes altogether. "I see a difference," she told us. "My back is not getting worse."

If you decide to buy one big piece of equipment to use at home, there are three reasons to consider a treadmill: Walking is the most natural movement for your body, so it's one of the easiest ways to start exercising if you're out of shape. You can burn more calories working out on a treadmill than on other exercise machines, according to a 1996 study in the Journal of the American Medical Association. And even if you prefer to walk outdoors, a treadmill can keep you moving in bad weather. Prices range from $300 to more than $4,000; plan on spending at least $1,000 for a decent model to use for walking. The best way to shop is to put on your sweats and sneakers and go for a combined walk and jog for at least ten minutes on a range of models. A two-horsepower engine should be plenty, and a five-year warranty on the motor is a plus. You should also lift up the belt to see if there's a layer of plastic between it and the deck. That plastic may make the treadmill quieter, but it isn't considered good for long-term wear.

Another beneficial activity you may want to try is yoga, particularly if you're dealing with chronic pain. One study showed that for people with osteoarthritis in the hands, the discipline significantly reduces pain and tenderness while increasing range of motion in the fingers. To get yoga's full benefits, you would need to take at least one class a week and practice at home at least ten minutes a day. The Yoga Alliance, a trade group in Clinton, Maryland, has a directory of certified instructors at www.yogaalliance.org who have had at least 200 hours of instruction.

A novel way to have fun working out with your partner, several retirees have told us, is pedaling a tandem bicycle together. Many couples with differing cycling endurance turn to tandems as a way to stick together, according to Jack Goertz, owner of Tandems Ltd., a bike retailer in Birmingham, Alabama. "The person in the back [called the stoker] doesn't have to fight the headwind, and fighting the headwind zaps a considerable amount of your effort. So that person can put more power into the bicycle than he or she could on a single bike." New tandems range in price from roughly $1,000 to $7,000, depending on the material used for the frame and the quality of the gears, brakes and other parts, tandem purveyors told us. But $5,000 will get you a tandem that's "coupled," meaning it is bolted together and can be taken apart to fit into a suitcase small enough to check as airline baggage, said Mel Kornbluh, owner of Tandems East LLC, a Pittsgrove, New Jersey, retailer. "My wife and I have traveled over twenty times" with a tandem, including to New Zealand. When you arrive at your exotic locale, it takes about ninety minutes to put the bike back together. "But the nice thing is that you already have the proper seat, tires, gearing—everything is right," Mel told us. The Tandem Club of America's Web site, www.tandemclub.org, can help you find local tandem enthusiasts and dealers.

EATING RIGHT

To make eating meals chock full of fruits and vegetables and light on the meat and fats more interesting, you could experiment with new recipes. Cookbooks that emphasize veggies and fiber, using meat as more of a flavor accent than an anchor for the meal, are a good bet. One example is *Eat, Drink, & Weigh Less*, by Mollie Katzen and Walter Willett, a Harvard University doctor and nutritionist. Ms. Katzen wrote a classic vegetarian cookbook called *Moosewood Cookbook*, but as a baby boomer who travels and has had to adjust her menus for her family, she has returned to eating meat, poultry and fish in moderation.

If money is no object, the most luxurious strategy may be to hire a personal chef. Sharon Esche-Irving and her husband

MORE YEARS, FEWER CALORIES

According to the updated food pyramid that the U.S. Agriculture Department unveiled in 2005, people over age fifty generally need about 200 fewer calories a day than those in their thirties and forties. So, for example, if you are a moderately active fifty-one-year-old woman, meaning you walk 1½ to three miles a day or do equivalent exercise, you need to consume 1,800 calories a day rather than the 2,000 calories a day you needed for the past twenty years. Men doing the same activity at the same ages would drop to a range of 2,200 to 2,400 calories from 2,400 to 2,600. For more age-related details, refer to the government's 2005 dietary guidelines, available at www.mypyramid.gov/guidelines.

Whatever your age, the guidelines say, you're generally supposed to be eating more fruit and vegetables—five to thirteen servings a day, up from the five to nine servings that the government recommended previously. The new rules also cut back the recommended amounts of grains and set limits on salt and sugar.

Several specific recommendations for older eaters are sprinkled throughout the guidelines:

- Many people over age fifty have a reduced ability to absorb naturally occurring vitamin B12, so they should eat fortified cereal or other foods with the vitamin added or take B12 supplements.

- Older adults should consume extra vitamin D.

- People who suffer from hypertension, along with all middle-aged and older adults, should try to consume no more than 1,500 milligrams of sodium per day.

- The same group of folks also should get the recommended 4,700 milligrams per day of potassium through food (because potassium can lower blood pressure and blunt the effects of salt).

- Older adults also should choose foods rich in fiber.

Another nutritional goal to keep in mind is variety, which the government is hoping to encourage with its multi-hued pyramid, in which each color represents a different food group.

managed to get an exercise regime going, but they found themselves sabotaging their efforts with their eating habits, specifically the after-the-gym junk food rewards. So she hired a personal chef. Jessica Leibovich would show up at Sharon's home in Oceanside, California, once every two weeks with pots, pans and ingredients. Four hours later, the freezer would be stocked with ten dinners for two, featuring such entrees as seafood Newburg and apple meatloaf with garlic mashed potatoes. Total cost: $350. "We get the nutrition and taste we want when we want it at a price that we found is no more expensive, and in some cases less, than buying your own food," Sharon told us. "You really have nothing to lose except weight." When you first hire a personal chef, he or she will probably interview you in your kitchen, asking what you like to eat and whether you have food allergies or any other restrictions on your diet. The American Personal & Private Chef Association has a nationwide directory of personal chefs on its Web site, www.personalchef.com. Find out whether a chef has taken the National Restaurant Association's "safe food handler" course. Don't worry about your favorite skillet or paring knife—these cooks generally have their own tools in tow.

An all-round jump-start to a healthier lifestyle could come from a relatively low-cost fitness spa. We talked to Dana Ferrigno, a faithful visitor to Tennessee Fitness Spa near Waynesboro, Tennessee, who said she typically sheds five pounds in a week from walking, stretching and water aerobics. After one visit, she took home the chef's recipes and stuck with the program for an entire year. A referral service, Destination Spa Group, offers online information for about two dozen such resorts at www.destinationspagroup.com.

BODY WORK

So you know your goals, you've started moving and you're eating better. That's it, right? Not quite. By the time you reach your early fifties, you should be getting prostate screenings, colonoscopies, mammograms and so forth. But a lot of us probably have a better idea of when our pets need tests and shots than when we need our own. Only half of all Americans over age sixty-five are getting tested for colon cancer, for example, at the appropriate intervals, according to the Centers for Disease Control and Prevention in Atlanta. And 20 percent of women in their late sixties don't get mammograms regularly, even though Medicare pays for them.

Figuring out just what illnesses you should be poked and prodded for, and when, is one of the most important ways you can take care of yourself. You should start paying close attention to preventive screening tests in your fifties, said David Atkins, the former preventive-services coordinator at the U.S. Agency for Healthcare Research and Quality, or AHRQ, a Rockville, Maryland, arm of the U.S. Department of Health and Human Services. He advised this because "it's the age when women go through menopause, and there are many [tests] that start then, like colon-cancer screening."

Don't assume that your doctor will keep track of these tests for you. Few health-insurance plans, including Medicare, adequately reimburse physicians for the time they spend counseling patients about such preventive measures—even though such tests are typically inexpensive. Plus, by the time you're in your late fifties or early sixties, you're probably seeing a handful of specialists who are paying more attention to specific conditions than to your overall health. So you need to do your homework. Start with the screening guidelines developed by the U.S. Preventive Services Task Force, a panel of medical experts overseen by AHRQ. The group's Web site (www.ahrq.gov) includes suggested screening tests for men and women, and also has a guide for adults who are fifty or older.

You'll probably want to research other guidelines as well, because the task force's guidelines are conservative. They mainly include tests for which there is firm scientific evidence that screening makes a big impact on preventing or treating the disease in question. Guidelines from groups that focus on a particular disease, such as the American Heart Association and the American Diabetes Association, tend to include a number of tests not recommended as strongly on the AHRQ list. The American Cancer Society (www.cancer.org) says all adults forty and older should get a cancer-related checkup every year that includes examinations for cancers of the thyroid, testicles, ovaries, lymph nodes, mouth and skin. But you should consider that the group might be biased toward having you take all of those tests, even though some of them may not be necessary for you. Your own medical and family history should be factors when deciding whether you want to get one of those yearly checkups.

We gathered the guidelines developed by major medical organizations across the country, starting with the U.S. Preventive Services Task Force's checklist, and then added recommendations from geriatrics groups, such as glucose measurement for diabetes. Finally, we hunted down advice from more-specialized medical groups, such as the American Cancer Society, and added, for instance, annual skin-cancer checkups. We wound up with about twenty tests or recommended procedures. Don't panic. Some measures, such as pneumonia shots, usually are required only once in a lifetime. And we listed which groups recommend which tests to help you make decisions depending on your own health. A few technical notes: These recommendations apply to people in average health. And you're supposed to start some of the tests, like mammograms, at an earlier age. If you have a family history of a disease or other risk factors, be sure to check with your doctor to find out whether you should be screened more often or with additional tests. Finally, if you need help figuring out what the risk factors are for a specific disease, there's almost always a nonprofit advocacy group that can provide a good starting point.

Not surprisingly, the test at the top of most general lists of preventive guidelines is a simple blood-pressure check, using a cuff, which can help detect the beginnings of heart disease.

Most of the other screenings involve cancer checks: mammograms and Pap tests for women and, for both genders, annual fecal occult blood testing and a sigmoidoscopy every three to five years, both used to detect colorectal cancer. (You could instead choose to have a colonoscopy or a barium enema every five to ten years.) Further down the list, but still worth thinking about, are a blood-glucose test for diabetes, which tends to strike in middle age, and a cancer-related checkup that includes one recommendation few people know about—the check for skin cancer from head to toe, typically done by a dermatologist.

For women, geriatricians say the clinical breast exam and mammogram should be done as long as you're in good health because the risk of breast cancer increases with age. Some doctors don't recommend performing the tests on women suffering from dementia or the later stages of Alzheimer's because they can traumatize such patients. As for testing for cervical cancer, most doctors recommend ending Pap smears in the mid to late sixties. Women should also have their level of thyroid-stimulating hormone (TSH) measured every five years because they become more likely to develop hypothyroidism as they age. If left untreated, the condition can lead to coronary-artery disease or a life-threatening coma. Finally, women should discuss with their doctors whether they need a bone-density test to detect osteoporosis.

Men age fifty and over should consider having their prostate checked on a regular basis. The American Cancer Society and other groups have said you should get a digital rectal exam and prostate-specific antigen test every year as long as you have a life expectancy of ten years. High-risk patients should get checked annually starting at age forty.

One caveat: The preventive steps above are conservative and scientifically documented to save lives. There's no similar proof that you'll get your money's worth by seeking out a doctor who practices in the controversial field of anti-aging medicine—treating aging more like a disease than an inevitable consequence of being human. Still, increasing numbers of older people are flocking to such doctors, and their ranks are growing. The American Academy of Anti-Aging Medicine had 15,000 members in 2006, up from 8,500 in 2001. Proponents of anti-aging medicine often swear by their increased energy; critics have said that some treatments involved are potentially dangerous, such as the use of human growth hormone, and that the academy's conferences include vitamin companies making unscientific claims.

SLEEPING YOUR WAY TO BETTER HEALTH

Beyond getting poked and prodded by the doctor, you'll be glad to know that there's one way to stay healthy that takes no exertion at all: sleeping. But there's a catch: By the time we turn sixty-five, we have a fifty-fifty chance of suffering from a chronic sleep complaint. Fortunately, scientists are getting a better idea why that happens and how to treat it. One important point: It's a myth that sleeping less is part of growing old. As Sonia Ancoli-Israel, a psychiatry professor at the University of California, San Diego, explained to us: "It's not the need for sleep that changes. It's our ability to sleep well."

Take Shirley Homer, a Chicago retiree who enjoyed spending her afternoons at Art Institute lectures. "My trouble is, I would fall asleep constantly," she told us. By a fluke, she found help through one of her volunteer activities, participating in research studies at the Chicago campus of Northwestern University's Feinberg School of Medicine. She took part in an experiment in which subjects sat for two hours a day in front of a "light box," a tabletop display that uses fluorescent bulbs to mimic natural sunlight. The goal of the experiment was to find out if light could normalize the timing of the circadian rhythm, or body clock, which in turn could improve sleep and daytime performance in older people. As we age, there are natural

DOING YOUR HEALTH HOMEWORK

Screening tests recommended for people by age fifty-five

FOR MEN AND WOMEN

Test	Condition to be detected or prevented	Recommendation (Frequency or suggested age if higher than 55)	What's involved	Who recommends it
Blood pressure	Hypertension	Every medical exam, at least every 1 to 2 years	Measured with a cuff; should be less than 140/90	a, b, g
Height and weight	Obesity, malnutrition	At least once a year	Part of regular checkup	a, b
Cholesterol	Heart disease	At least once every 5 years	Low density lipoprotein (LDL, the "bad" cholesterol) should be less than 160 mg/dL	a, b, g
Fecal occult blood test	Colon cancer	Annually	Stool samples collected three days in a row and examined for blood	a, b, c
Sigmoid-oscopy/colon-oscopy	Colon cancer	Every 3 to 5 years/Every 10 years	Viewing instrument inserted into the rectum and colon	a, b, c
Problem-drinking assessment	Alcoholism	First visit and periodically	Screening questionnaire	a, b, d
Vision screening	Eyesight loss	Merck Manual recommends annually, starting at age 65	Done with an eye chart or Snellen acuity testing	b, d
Hearing assessment	Hearing loss	Merck Manual recommends annually, starting at age 65	Doctor assesses and refers to an audiologist if needed	b, d

DOING YOUR HEALTH HOMEWORK

Screening tests recommended for people by age fifty-five

FOR MEN AND WOMEN *(continued)*

Test	Condition to be detected or prevented	Recommendation (Frequency or suggested age if higher than 55)	What's involved	Who recommends it
Glucose	Diabetes, type 2 diabetes, pre-diabetes	Every 3 years	An overnight fast followed by blood tests	b, e
Bone-density measurement	Osteoporosis	Routine screening every 2 years for all women 65 and older, and for men and women taking glucocorticoids	There are several types of machines that measure density, either in the hip and spine, or the finger, wrist, kneecap, shin bone and/or heel	a, b
Other cancer screening	Cancer	Annually	Exams of skin, mouth, thyroid, testicles or ovaries and nodes	c

FOR MEN ONLY

Test	Condition to be detected or prevented	Recommendation (Frequency or suggested age if higher than 55)	What's involved	Who recommends it
Digital rectal exam/ prostate-specific antigen test	Prostate cancer	Digital rectal exam annually/ PSA test if life expectancy is at least 10 years	Doctor checks prostate gland for enlargement, nodules and other abnormalities; blood test measures prostate-specific antigen (PSA)	b, c, f

DOING YOUR HEALTH HOMEWORK

Screening tests recommended for people by age fifty-five

FOR WOMEN ONLY

Test	Condition to be detected or prevented	Recommendation (Frequency or suggested age if higher than 55)	What's involved	Who recommends it
Clinical breast exam	Breast cancer	Annually	Doctor checks breasts for lumps	c, d
Mammogram	Breast cancer	Every 1 to 2 years through age 69; every 1 to 3 years after age 70, depending on overall health	Breast X-ray often done at special clinic	a, b, c, d
Pap test	Cervical, uterine cancers	At least every three years; can be discontinued at 70	Cell sample from cervix is examined	a, b, c, d
Thyroid-stimulating hormone measurement	Hypo-thyroidism	After age 65	Blood test	b, d

OTHER MEASURES

Test	Condition to be detected or prevented	Recommendation (Frequency or suggested age if higher than 55)	What's involved	Who recommends it
Influenza vaccination	Influenza	Annually for people 65 or older	Get before/ during flu season	b, d
Pneumo-coccal vaccine	Pneumonia	Once at age 65	Once immunized, you need 10-year booster shots	b, d

DOING YOUR HEALTH HOMEWORK

Screening tests recommended for people by age fifty-five

OTHER MEASURES *(continued)*

Test	Condition to be detected or prevented	Recommendation (Frequency or suggested age if higher than 55)	What's involved	Who recommends it
Tetanus booster	Tetanus	Every 10 years	Revaccination recommended every 6 to 8 years for patients with chronic diseases	b

Note: These recommendations apply to people without risk factors. Where different groups disagree on recommendations for frequency of testing, we list the most aggressive schedule. Your specific circumstances may require a different testing schedule. Also, these tests may not be appropriate for people who have limited life expectancies.

Recommendations from: a) U.S. Preventive Services Task Force; b) Merck Manual of Geriatrics; c) American Cancer Society; d) American Geriatrics Society; e) American Diabetes Association; f) American Urological Association; g) American Heart Association

changes in our circadian rhythm: The hour when we feel the need for sleep can get pushed ahead earlier and earlier. Eventually, this can start to conflict with everyday life and effectively narrow the window of time when we can get a solid, eight-hour stretch of sleep. For example, if your body clock is telling you to go to sleep at 8 P.M. and wake up at 4 A.M., you may have to struggle to stay awake until 10 P.M. And then you may not be able to sleep a full eight hours; your body could wake you at the earlier hour that it now considers your wake-up time. The point of the experiment was to see whether adding more natural light to a person's day could push the circadian rhythm toward later sleep so that the test subjects wouldn't have to fight to stay up and could thus increase their chances of getting a full eight hours of sleep.

The study's upshot is that a little sunning helps us sleep

better. The other planks of good "sleep hygiene" that scientists are confirming through their work also make sense: Go to bed at the same time every night, and get up at the same time in the morning. Avoid alcohol and caffeine. Exercise, but not too close to bedtime. If you lie awake more than ten minutes, get up and do something quiet until you get sleepy. Set aside fifteen minutes a day to worry so you don't do it in the middle of the night. Turn the alarm clock around so you don't obsess over the time you're awake. If you get up to go to the bathroom, turn on the dimmest light possible—light triggers your body to stop producing melatonin, a substance that helps you sleep. The problem is, we get so locked into routines that work against our snoozing that we no longer can pinpoint exactly what's hindering our sleep. For some people, the answer may be going to a sleep-disorder center for a medical diagnosis. To locate an accredited center, go to the American Academy of Sleep Medicine's Web site at www.sleepcenters.org.

There are two kinds of sleep: rapid-eye movement, or REM, sleep, when we have our most vivid, emotional dreams, and non-REM sleep, which is divided into four stages from dozing to deepest slumber. For reasons no one's fully figured out yet, the two deepest stages of non-REM sleep are the toughest to achieve as we grow older. During these stages, collectively known as "slow-wave sleep," your body secretes human growth hormone and does a lot of healing. So, if you're missing out on these two stages, you are losing health benefits in addition to feeling tired.

Scientists don't think aging itself is the culprit, but rather all the problems that pile up as we grow older. First, there's the change in circadian rhythm. Second, when sleep disorders do develop, they frequently go undetected. Examples include sleep apnea, where your breathing stops and you wake up repeatedly, or period-limb-movement disorder, where you get the urge to shake your legs frequently. The incidence of insomnia also goes up as people deal with disease and the loss of loved ones. And menopause can cause disturbing night sweats. Then there are chronic medical problems and the drugs used to treat them; some asthma medications, for example, are full of stimulants, which keep you awake. Finally, changes in your own behavior as you age—less structure in your days and nights or decreased physical activity—can hurt your sleep.

Ignoring the warning signs—daytime sleepiness, crankiness and having a tough time concentrating—may help you meet short-term deadlines, but long-term sleep deprivation could have dire consequences. A study in the *Journal of the American Geriatrics Society* found that insomnia made men sixty-five and older 50 percent more likely to suffer from serious cognitive decline. Losing deep sleep can increase your risk of a heart attack, too, because deep sleep gives your cardiovascular system a break.

Some cures have their own problems. Only about half of all apnea patients use recommended masks, which blow air through their nostrils to keep their throats open, often enough to get any benefit. Grogginess from traditional sleeping pills could lead to falls in the middle of the night, though a newer group of drugs called nonbenzodiazepines leaves patients less woozy. Melatonin, which may help people avoid waking up in the middle of the night, is an unregulated supplement, leaving quantity and quality in question. Then there's hormone-replacement therapy, the silver bullet for night sweats, which has so many risks that a national study of the therapy was cut short. But scientists are taking their first round of discoveries back to the lab in hopes of finding more sophisticated treatments. At Northwestern and the University of Utah in Salt Lake City, researchers are mapping genes that regulate circadian rhythm so they eventually can pinpoint proteins to rejigger the body clock. In San Diego, Dr. Ancoli-Israel is treating apnea in patients with mild dementia to see whether it slows their memory loss. And at the University of Washington in Seattle, scientists have found that sending a chemical signal to the brain that triggers the production of growth hormone and slow-wave sleep helped the study's subjects lose around 8 percent of their body fat.

WHEN DEMENTIA IS TREATABLE

Before you or a loved one accepts a diagnosis of dementia, you may want to get a second opinion. Odds are, your doctor is right. But other neurological conditions—among them normal pressure hydrocephalus, epilepsy and essential tremor— often share symptoms with Alzheimer's or Parkinson's disease, particularly in older patients. The signs of the lesser-known disorders present themselves more subtly as people age, making it tougher to distinguish among them. Other barriers to a correct diagnosis include the fact that some physicians are quicker to attribute any memory loss in an older patient to dementia and any tremor to Parkinson's. Still other doctors, and often patients themselves, simply chalk up the problems to "old age." But there's a big incentive for families to avoid such resignation and make sure the diagnosis is accurate: There are effective treatments for these three problems.

Normal pressure hydrocephalus (NPH) is a slow accumulation of excess fluid in the brain, mostly affecting people sixty or older. The buildup swells the brain's ventricles, which can stretch nerve tissue, leading to symptoms of dementia. The cause usually can't be pinpointed. The most common symptoms are mild dementia, difficulty walking and impaired bladder control. Granted, "if you go into a nursing home, everyone will have one or all three of those things," said Mark Luciano, a neurosurgeon at the Cleveland Clinic who treats NPH. But NPH patients, he said, often appear as if "their machinery has slowed down. Their memory is worse, they don't initiate as much speech and they are slower and inattentive." In contrast, Alzheimer's patients "may seem quite sharp, but they just don't recognize you." The best way to confirm an NPH diagnosis is a brain scan that shows the characteristically enlarged ventricles, he told us. To treat NPH, a neurosurgeon typically implants a shunt, made from flexible plastic tubing, in the brain to divert excess fluid to another part of the body. But shunting isn't a guaranteed success, and, particularly in older patients, there's always the possibility that they are suffering from NPH in addition to another type of dementia.

NPH isn't the only treatable disorder masquerading as dementia. Epileptic seizures in older people can disguise themselves as gaps in conversation, confusion or blank stares. The image many people have of epileptic fits is one "of convulsions, where you're shaking all over, falling down or biting your tongue," said R. Eugene Ramsay, professor of neurology and psychiatry and director of the International Center for Epilepsy at the University of Miami. But seizures in older people can be much more subtle, with "periods where they stop what they do and stare off into the distance." Epilepsy is far more common among older people than was once believed—six to eight times as common in patients over age sixty as in any other age group. The main difference between epilepsy and dementia is that epileptic seizures can cause confusion that lasts for a few hours or for several days. Seizures are typically controlled, at least partially, with drugs. There is an older and a newer class of antiepileptic medication. The older type, which includes carbamazepine, is more commonly prescribed and has cheaper, generic versions. But the older medicines have more side effects in some patients. The newer type, which includes levetiracetam, is more easily tolerated by some older patients.

Essential tremor is another common disorder, estimated to afflict 10 million people, typically starting around age forty-five. Once called senile tremor, it is often mistaken for Parkinson's, particularly in older patients. It's tough to distinguish the two diseases in their early stages. Parkinson's has become so common that many family physicians are diagnosing it and treating it themselves rather than referring patients to a neurologist, noted Catherine Rice, executive director of the International Essential Tremor Foundation in Lenexa, Kansas. But as the tremors worsen, it's easier for a specialist to distinguish between the two conditions: With essential tremor, the person typically shakes—often in the hands—when the body is active; with Parkinson's, the shaking often happens when the body is otherwise still. In essential tremor, the shaking can get worse over time, but the disorder doesn't progress into other debilitating conditions, as Parkinson's can. Treatments include beta blockers and antiseizure medications or, in severe cases, a device implanted in the brain.

BRAIN GAMES AND OTHER HIGH-TECH HELP

No drugs have been proven to reverse dementia so far, but your computer might wind up providing some help. At least half a dozen companies have developed software and Web sites selling memory-building computer exercises. One, Posit Science Corp. of San Francisco, claims that hundreds of older people using its software in preliminary tests have the mental acuity of someone five to ten years younger. Within a decade, the company hopes to kick-start "brain gyms" as well as online "cognitive-fitness centers," where older people looking for social reinforcement could play the games in a group environment.

Companies such as Intel Corp., Philips Electronics NV and Accenture Ltd. are developing technological tools for the home that try to be as unobtrusive as possible while keeping people safe and connecting them to the outside world. With health-care budgets stretched to the breaking point—and with health-care workers in short supply—improved use of technology is widely thought to be a solution to meeting the growing needs of an aging America. These new tools would help people live in their homes longer, rather than being institutionalized, and could help make monitoring conditions like diabetes and heart disease more affordable and efficient.

Intel's team of social scientists, for instance, has developed computerized memory aids. One gadget, tested in two dozen households in Las Vegas and Portland, Oregon, was designed to help people ease their fears of not recognizing a face or voice when answering the door or telephone. Intel used wireless sensor networks to collect data for four months about who visited, called and e-mailed the participants (and how often they did so). The data were used to create a "solar-system display" on a TV or computer screen. Circles representing friends and family orbit around you; when you move the mouse over those circles, you see photos of the people they represent along with the last time you spoke to them and what you talked about. Similarly, Intel developed what designers dubbed "caller ID on steroids." When the phone rings, a nearby digital photo frame displays a picture of the caller and lists what you talked about during your last call. The "presence lamp" was also a big hit among test subjects. One of these lights is placed in the parent's house and one in the child's. When the child returns home after a visit, the light automatically goes on in the parent's house and vice versa. The gadget lowered depression among the older adults with Alzheimer's disease by showing them their kids had gotten home safely. It also alerted a few boomers when their parents got lost on the drive home after they had dinner together.

Philips Electronics has released a product called Motiva, a broadband-based platform that delivers health information through a TV. The system can send personalized educational information, such as videos about health conditions. Patients also can monitor their weight, heart rate and blood pressure using Philips's wireless devices and get feedback through the television system about how they're doing. Another example of remote health care comes from robotics company InTouch Health Inc., which has developed what it calls a Remote Presence robot. The robot stands 5½ feet tall and has a computer screen where a person's head would be; the screen broadcasts the face of a physician, who controls the device remotely.

Then there are the monitoring systems: HomeFree Systems Ltd.'s Personal Watcher wristwatch can track its wearer by beaming signals back to a wireless network. It also can show the person's temperature and indicate whether the device is being removed. ADT Security Services Inc., a unit of Bermuda-based Tyco International Ltd., has a line of digital devices that monitor medication compliance, track vital signs and send reminders for healthy behavior. Cleveland-based Eaton Corp.'s Home Key, which looks like a key fob with a small screen, can be paired with sensors to help older adults living on their own make sure they have closed a garage door or turned off the kitchen faucet.

Various companies are testing different versions of online medicine cabinets. Accenture's device uses face-recognition capabilities and a female robot voice. Instead of a mirror, one door of the cabinet is outfitted with a computer screen. If you have allergies, the screen would show the day's pollen count and recommend taking a pill if necessary. If you chose the wrong pill bottle, sensors in this "smart appliance" would pick up the mistake, and the robot voice would tell you.

PART II

MONEY
MECHANICS

CHAPTER 6

BEFORE YOU OPEN THAT NEST EGG...

I t's time to talk about money, which for many people elicits the most common and most vexing question in retirement planning: "Have I saved enough?" Whether you realize it or not, you've probably asked similar questions in the past: Have I saved enough money to buy a house? Have I saved enough money to put the kids through college? Usually, the answer is, It depends. It depends on the size of the house you wish to buy and where it's located; it depends on whether the college is Yale or a public university. Yes, other factors certainly can affect the health of your savings accounts: inflation, taxes, investment returns, life expectancy and withdrawal rates from holdings. We'll address each of these. But unless you have a good idea about what you want to do in retirement and what that lifestyle might cost, questions about the size of your nest egg are beside the point.

POTENTIAL CRACKS IN YOUR NEST EGG

Once you've determined the particular life you want to lead in retirement and you're ready to begin your calculations, you need to know how to avoid the biggest mistakes Americans make with their nest eggs:

1. **Timing**   Many people dip into their retirement savings at age sixty-two—the age when you can first file for Social Security benefits. But as appealing as early retirement might sound, it could put considerable strain on your savings. For example, Do you still have a mortgage? Most financial planners recommend paying off as much debt as possible before tapping a nest egg. What about health insurance? Medicare, unlike Social Security, isn't available until age sixty-five for most people. What kind of medical coverage—if any—do you have for the gap between ages sixty-two and sixty-five, and how much will it cost?

   The point is that delaying retirement for just two or three years could make a big difference in the size and stability of your nest egg. You could also give your retirement savings additional breathing room if your employer offers, or is willing to consider, a "phased-retirement plan" in which you reduce the number of hours you work but still draw a paycheck. A study at Cornell University found that 73 percent of employers were open to phased retirement, primarily on an informal basis.

2. **Life expectancy**   The big risk, of course, is that your savings will expire before you do. Combine several rough years in the stock market—particularly early in your retirement—with an aggressive rate of withdrawal from your investments and the nest egg you spent thirty years building could be gone in half that time.

   Several tools can help you estimate your life expectancy. (See, for instance, www.livingto100.com.) But you often end up with an *average* life expectancy (an imprecise figure), and these tools don't usually consider *joint* life expectancy—the odds that one partner in a couple will live considerably longer than the other.

Want a quick number for planning purposes? Expect to live to age ninety, at the very least; ninety-five is even better. According to the Society of Actuaries's mortality tables, a healthy sixty-five-year-old man has a 25 percent chance of reaching age ninety-two, while a healthy sixty-five-year-old woman has the same chance of reaching age ninety-four.

3. **Taxes and inflation** One million dollars in a 401(k) is really more like $800,000 because of the 20 percent or so that might go to taxes. And don't assume that taxes will go down when you retire; when Social Security, pensions, 401(k)s and other savings are factored in, you might find yourself in the same or nearly the same tax bracket as when you were employed.

Inflation, too, will chip away at your nest egg—faster and with greater effect than most people realize. Consider that a $1 million nest egg, with an annual rate of inflation of 3 percent, will have a value of only $737,000 after ten years. And some expenses, like health care, are rising *faster* than 3 percent. (Hospital costs alone have been increasing almost 6 percent a year.)

In short, you must factor inflation (and ideally, different rates of inflation for different expenses) into your retirement budgeting. We'll discuss this in more detail in Chapter Seven.

4. **Health-care expenses** When most of us think about threats to our retirement savings, we think primarily about investment losses—damage from a tumbling stock market, for instance. But hazards such as big medical fees or the need for long-term care can cause as much harm to your nest egg as a volatile market.

Keep in mind that you'll likely be responsible for all your dental, hearing and vision expenses in retirement, as Medicare covers almost none of that. As noted, studies by Fidelity Investments indicate that Americans without employer-sponsored health coverage will need an estimated

$215,000 to pay their medical bills in retirement. It's also important to know that Medicare and private insurance don't pay for most long-term care. A recent study by the Lewin Group (a consulting firm) and professors at Pennsylvania State University and Georgetown University projects that 37 percent of all sixty-five-year-olds will need long-term care in a nursing home or assisted-living facility. The good news is that most stays will be less than two years. The bad news is that about 11 percent of patients will be hit with costs of between $100,000 and $250,000; about 5 percent will face bills exceeding $250,000. The key here is to incorporate such projections into your household budget.

5. **Working in retirement**   If you're counting on continued employment to help pay the bills in retirement, you could be in for a nasty surprise. What if you *can't* work in retirement or can work only for a few years? What if your health prevents you from working? What if you can't find the type of job you want? If 70 percent of boomers want to work in retirement, that means about 55 million people at some point will be scanning the help-wanted ads! And you thought the rat race was over.

Though working in later life can be an emotionally and physically rewarding experience, don't *assume* that the opportunities—and a paycheck—will be there.

6. **Saving money**   Even in retirement—and especially early in retirement—you must *keep* saving. No, the numbers probably won't be as big as in the past, which is nice. But think about it: Emergencies have no respect for retirement; crises will continue to crop up. (A son or daughter loses a job, for instance, and looks to you for financial help.) And some expenses never go away: maintaining your house, paying for new appliances, looking after your car, etc.

Speaking of which, lots of people buy a new car before retiring, thinking that that vehicle will see them through their final years. Remember, there's a good chance you will live long enough to buy *three or four* cars. All of which means that you need to keep saving.

7. **Withdrawals from nest eggs** Many people think they can pull as much as 7 percent or more from their retirement savings each year. The rationale is that if withdrawals are equal to the average return on investments, then the size of the nest egg will remain fairly constant. But that thinking is flawed.

For starters, annual returns are seldom "average." You probably have heard that the stock market returns about 10 percent a year, on average. That's true—if the calculations begin with the 1920s. But if you were a new retiree in 2000 and had pulled 10 percent from your nest egg each year, your savings—if any remained—would now be on life support.

A more realistic rate of withdrawal is about 4 percent. That figure is based primarily on research by William Bengen, a certified financial planner in El Cajon, California. In other words, if your retirement savings total $500,000, you could withdraw $20,000 the first year. Assuming that a good chunk of your nest egg (about 40 percent to 60 percent) remains invested in equities (to help your savings keep pace with inflation), a 4 percent rate of withdrawal means your nest egg has a good chance of lasting as long as you do.

We'll discuss withdrawal rates and strategies in much more detail in the next two chapters to help you avoid withdrawing too much too soon, which is the single biggest financial mistake a retiree can make.

8. **Asset allocation** People tend to stay fully invested in stocks until "R Day" approaches, at which point there's a

mad scramble to move into bonds and related investments. Instead of waiting until the last minute to diversify
your holdings, do so gradually in the years leading up to
retirement to avoid sudden or prolonged downturns in
the market. (For more on how you should allocate your assets, see Chapter Eight.)

FIVE STEPS TO FINDING THE RIGHT FINANCIAL ADVISER

For retirees, in particular, finances can be daunting. There are
the questions and concerns that bedevil investors of any age,
such as, "What's the best mix of stocks, bonds and cash?" There's
a good chance you have more investments than you know what
to do with (individual retirement accounts, 401(k)s, insurance
policies, real estate and taxable savings accounts, among others). And there's a new set of rules: After thirty or forty years
of building a portfolio, retirees are compelled—eventually, by
the Internal Revenue Service—to begin tearing it down.

That's why, as you approach retirement (if at no other
point in your financial life) it's worth spending time with an
adviser. Even two or three visits with a professional can help
you figure out whether you and your money are heading in the
right direction.

Jonathan Clements, our colleague at the *Journal* who writes
the paper's "Getting Going" column, offers a good five-step
plan to help you find a knowledgeable, honest and (relatively)
affordable expert:

1. **Titles matter** Ideally, you want an adviser with broad
   training in the financial-planning field. The most widely
   recognized designation for a generalist is a certified financial planner, or CFP, a title held by some 50,000 people
   nationwide. A CFP's training covers everything from taxes
   and insurance to investing and estate planning. Before
   earning the designation, an individual must have three

years' experience, pass a ten-hour exam (the coursework takes about two years) and have a bachelor's degree. Other highly regarded designations are the ChFC (chartered financial consultant), PFS (personal financial specialist) and CFA (chartered financial analyst). The coursework and exams for these specialties generally are as comprehensive as the CFP program. A ChFC often will have an additional interest in insurance. The PFS is sought by certified public accountants who want to broaden their training into financial planning. Though a title alone isn't a guarantee of sound financial advice, it does mean the holder has made a commitment to the financial-planning business and combines knowledge with experience.

You also should be aware of the differences among "brokers," "investment advisers" and "financial planners" (or "financial advisers"), distinctions that can have a big effect on your rights as an investor (in the event of a dispute with a financial adviser) and on your nest egg. Generally, brokers recommend to clients which investment products to buy and sell and earn commissions on their trades. They must be registered with the National Association of Securities Dealers and licensed by their state securities agency. Investment advisers (including CFPs, among others) provide broad guidance about investing and financial planning and recommendations about specific products. They must register with the Securities and Exchange Commission or their state securities agency (depending on how much money they manage).

Financial advisers or planners (as opposed to "certified" financial planners) are generic terms used to describe people who offer advice about money and investments. The problem is that there's nothing to stop your neighbor, your uncle and the kid who cuts your grass from calling themselves "financial advisers." There is no registration or licensing requirement, no investment firm or governing body to turn to in the event of a dispute and no guarantee that the "adviser" is acting in the best interests of you or your nest egg. Needless to say, it's essential to check the professional background of any would-be financial consultant.

2. **Think small.**   Some of the best and brightest advisers are found in small three- and four-person offices in your own town. They normally work on a "fee-only" basis (as opposed to commissions), and a good number are willing to charge by the hour. Start your list of candidates with these individuals. Several organizations can point to professionals in your area: the National Association of Personal Financial Advisors (www.napfa.org), the Certified Financial Planner Board of Standards Inc. (www.cfp.net), the Financial Planning Association (www.fpanet. org), the Garrett Planning Network (www.garrettplanningnetwork.com) and Cambridge Advisors (www.cambridgeadvisors.com).

   Friends and family, of course, can be a good source of referrals. But err on the side of considering only those planners with long-standing ties to your buddies or relatives—at least four or five years.

3. **The interview**   Once you have a list of a half-dozen candidates, it's time to call these advisers and begin narrowing the field. Scratch any adviser who suggests he or she will deliver high returns; that person is promising something he or she can't deliver. (Financial advisers don't move markets.) Be wary, too, of planners who indicate a lot of trading might take place in your portfolio or who inform you that their services are "free." That probably means they make their money from selling you financial products you may not need.

   After these initial phone interviews, visit your two or three best candidates in person. Remember, retirement planning involves a host of issues: taxes, estate planning, long-term care, Social Security, withdrawal strategies for your nest egg and insurance, so you want to establish that an adviser is interested in more than just investments.

Before any visits, you should take time to complete the worksheets in the next chapter and to read the remaining "money" chapters in this book. Doing so will make it easier to explain your needs to an adviser and to interpret his or her language.

4. **Whose interests come first?**   Unfortunately, not all financial advisers place your needs and interests above their own—a point you must establish early in any interview.

The biggest difference arises between "brokers" and "investment advisers." Brokers, who fall under the direction of the National Association of Securities Dealers, are required, according to the association, to have a "clear understanding of each customer's financial condition . . . [and] investment objectives" and to make "suitable" recommendations. But in recent years, to cite one prominent example, some brokers have been selling variable annuities to older clients—even though such products are generally regarded as a poor fit for retirees' portfolios. The reason is that these "suitable" investments can generate hefty commissions. While brokers have an obligation to their clients, generally their first loyalty is to their firms.

Investment advisers, for their part, have a "fiduciary responsibility" to their customers, meaning they must put the interests of their clients ahead of their own. Let's say an investment adviser and a broker both believe that a client needs an international stock fund to help diversify his or her portfolio. The investment adviser, ideally, will canvass the marketplace for quality funds with the lowest annual expenses. A broker, however, may simply turn to the international stock fund recommended by his or her brokerage firm, regardless of performance or expenses.

So . . . Does this mean all brokers are "bad" and all investment advisers are "good"? Not at all. There are brokers

BACKGROUND CHECKS

Before hiring brokers or investment advisers, check whether they are licensed and whether they have faced consumer complaints or disciplinary actions.

BROKERS

Start with state securities regulators, who can tap what's called the Central Registration Depository, a database with background information on more than 650,000 current and former brokers and more than 5,000 registered firms. The background information includes a broker's registration and licensing status, former jobs and disciplinary actions, if any. (The depository itself isn't open to the public.) You can find contact information for state regulators at the North American Securities Administrators Association. The telephone number is 202-737-0900, or visit the Web site at www.nasaa.org.

The National Association of Securities Dealers (NASD) also provides a way—usually quicker—to access much of the same information. On the home page of the organization's Web site (www.nasd.com), click on "NASD BrokerCheck." Here, you can simply type in the name of a broker or firm and, several minutes later, receive an e-mail with the appropriate background information. (As with state regulators, the Central Registration Depository is the source of information for BrokerCheck.) You also can call a BrokerCheck "hotline" at 800-289-9999.

Why call state officials first? As the Securities and Exchange Commission (SEC) states, "Your state securities regulator may provide more information from the Central Registration Depository than NASD, especially when it comes to investor complaints."

INVESTMENT ADVISERS

In the eyes of the SEC, investment advisers are divided into two groups: those who manage $25 million or more in client assets and those who manage less. The former generally must register with the SEC itself; the latter are required to register with state securities regulators.

When registering, investment advisers fill out the two-part "Form ADV." Part one includes general information about the adviser's business and—importantly—any run-ins with customers or regulators. Part two provides details about services, fees and investment strategies. The advice here is simple: Always ask for and read both parts of the ADV before hiring an adviser.

In the best of all worlds, an adviser will simply hand you his or her Form ADV. (You might have to ask.) Otherwise, depending on the size of the adviser's client assets, you can get the information from state officials or the SEC. Again, you can find contact information for state officials at the North American Securities Administrators Association. If the adviser has filed his or her registration electronically with the SEC, you can visit the SEC Web site www.sec.gov/investor/brokers.htm and click on "Investment Adviser Public Disclosure." Otherwise, you can request paper copies of Form ADV by calling the SEC at 202-551-8090 or by e-mailing the agency at publicinfo@sec.gov.

One final note: Some brokers are investments advisers and vice versa. In that case, make sure to check both the Central Registration Depository and Form ADV.

who make prudent recommendations, sell worthwhile investments and are upfront about their compensation. And there are investment advisers who make terrible mistakes with clients' money. The onus is on you to ask about and understand an adviser's responsibilities and obligations— and how he or she gets paid. Which brings us to . . .

5. **Ask about fees**   Generally, financial advisers get paid in one of two ways: fees or commissions. A CFP who is a "fee-only planner," for instance, will bill by the hour or set a flat fee (say, $3,000 for a financial plan) or collect a percentage of "assets under management." A financial adviser working on commission will collect a payment for each financial service or product (like insurance and annuities) he or she sells. In recent years, fee-only planning has become more popular because of its supposed transparency. But fee-only planners aren't completely immune from potential conflicts of interest.

WHAT TO ASK

When interviewing prospective financial planners, start with these questions:

How long have you been offering financial advice to clients?

How many clients do you currently have?

Briefly describe your work history.

What are your educational qualifications? Where did you go to school?

What financial planning designations or certifications do you hold?

What financial planning continuing-education requirements do you fulfill?

What licenses do you hold?

Are you a broker or an investment adviser or both?

Are you personally licensed or registered as an investment adviser with the state or federal government?

Is your firm licensed or registered as an investment adviser with the state or federal government?

Will you provide me with the appropriate form (Form ADV, parts one and two) that shows you are properly registered?

Have you ever been disciplined by any government regulator for unethical or improper conduct or been sued by a client who was not satisfied with your work?

Will you provide me with a written disclosure detailing any disciplinary history for you or your firm?

Describe the amount of experience you have, if any, and the number of years you have been providing advice in the following areas: retirement planning, investment planning, tax planning, estate planning and insurance planning.

What are your areas of specialization?

Describe your approach to financial planning.

How might you address my particular needs?

How often will my financial plan be updated?

Will you show me several financial plans that you have developed?

Who will work with me? You? An associate?

Will the same individual review my financial situation?

What type of clients do you serve?

Do you have a minimum net worth or income requirement for clients?

Will you give me references?

What services do you offer? What kind of services can I expect?

How are you paid for your services (fee, commission, fee and commission, salary, other)?

What do you typically charge (hourly rate, flat fee, percentage of assets under management, etc.)?

If you are paid by commission, identify the approximate percentage of the investment or premium you receive on stocks and bonds, mutual funds, annuities and insurance products.

Do you have a business affiliation with any company whose products or services you are recommending?

Is any of your compensation based on selling products?

Do professionals and sales agents to whom you may refer me send business, fees or any other benefits to you?

Is the account that you are offering an "advisory account" or is it a "brokerage account" exempt from investment adviser registration?

If it is a brokerage account, are you required under law to act as a fiduciary by always placing my interests first?

Will you be able to tell me when you are acting as a sales agent of your brokerage firm and when you are acting as an investment adviser?

Regarding any brokerage account that I may open, what are the potential conflicts of interest that you have when recommending certain products for sale to me, and how will you disclose these to me prior to the purchase—including any special cash payments or incentives that you receive?

Sources: Financial Planning Association; Certified Financial Planner Board of Standards; Securities and Exchange Commission

For example, if a fee-only planner is advising you how and where to allocate your investments, his or her bill for those services might take the form of a percentage of the assets under his or her direction. A customary figure is 1 percent. So, if your nest egg totals $800,000, a planner might charge $8,000 a year ($800,000 × .01) to manage those savings. Now, let's say you're about to retire. Your nest egg is worth $800,000, but you still owe $200,000 on your mortgage. You hire a certified financial planner, whose fee is a percentage of assets under management, and you ask, "What should I do? Should I start retirement with $200,000 in debt or should I pay off the mortgage in full?" If your CFP says, "Yes, let's pay off the mortgage," he or she ends up managing $600,000 in assets and collecting a fee of $6,000. If he or she says, "No, let's keep the nest egg intact," he or she ends up managing the full $800,000 and collects a fee of $8,000. Either choice could be correct, based on the circumstances. It's important, though, that you understand the math—and how financial advisers can be reimbursed.

Financial guidance, of course, can be expensive. To keep things simple and relatively affordable, first try sitting down with a financial adviser who charges by the hour. Ideally, several visits (at a cost of, say, $150 to $250 an hour) will help you determine whether you want to manage your retirement finances on your own, whether you want a financial adviser or whether you want a financial services company or mutual-fund company to handle the job. Firms like Vanguard Group Inc., Fidelity Investments and T. Rowe Price are more than happy to manage your retirement savings. If you end up working with a financial planner, his or her annual fee certainly should be no more than 1 percent of the assets under management.

A very wise financial adviser once told us that individuals debating whether to manage their retirement finances on their own should ask three questions: Do I have the interest in doing this myself? Do I have the expertise? Do I have the time? If the answer to any of those is no, you might want some help.

CHAPTER 7

BUDGETING FOR RETIREMENT

Research shows that almost half the people who put numbers on paper—who actually take the time to estimate how much money will be coming in the door during retirement and how much will be going out—end up changing their savings plans. And yet, most of us don't make the effort. First, there are the emotional aspects. For most of our adult lives, we've had the "right" to spend our money as we wish. Suddenly, in retirement, we have a finite amount of resources. Second, retirement has many unknowns: life expectancy, health costs and inflation, among others. How are you supposed to know what your expenses will be?

What follows are two of the most straightforward tools to estimate how much money you'll need in retirement and to determine whether your nest egg is sufficient. The first takes about one minute and gets you in the ballpark. The second approach takes a bit longer and gets you a seat behind home plate.

ONE-MINUTE DRILL

This method, developed by Charles J. Farrell, an investment adviser in Denver, is based on the idea of replacement ratios. First, to calculate your annual budget, multiply your current gross income by the replacement ratio of 0.8. This means we're estimating that you will need a "salary" in retirement that amounts to 80 percent of your pre-retirement income. Then, to calculate the size of the nest egg needed in later life, multiply your current gross income by twelve.

Let's see what this math would look like for a couple—we'll call them Andrea and Scott—who are a year or two away from retirement and are making about $80,000 (combined) a year:

Salary needed in retirement	Savings needed for retirement
$80,000	$80,000
×0.8	×12
$64,000	$960,000

It's important to note that we start with a big assumption: that the average American can, in fact, live comfortably on 80 percent of his or her pre-retirement income in retirement itself. While the rule of thumb has long been that most of us will need about 70 percent to 80 percent of our pre-retirement earnings once we leave work, this assumes that about 20 percent to 30 percent of our money while we're working goes to things like taxes, transportation and savings and that all those bills will drop off in retirement. In recent years, though, some financial planners have begun arguing that we actually need 100 percent—or more—of our pre-retirement income in later life because, if anything, expenses *increase* in retirement: for travel, home improvements and health care, among other items. (As one financial planner told us, "I have yet to see a client who, the day he or she retired, started living on 30 percent less than the day before.")

As you might imagine, research supports both sides of the argument. The Employee Benefit Research Institute found that more than half of current retirees (55 percent) had replacement ratios of 100 percent or more in retirement. Conversely, some of the best research on replacement ratios, done by Aon Consulting and Georgia State University, has found that the "average" retiree (making about $60,000 a year before retirement) needs about 75 percent of that income after leaving the workplace.

For his part, Charles Farrell, the Denver adviser, reasons that if individuals entering retirement have paid off their major debts, including a mortgage, and if they already were saving about 10 percent of each paycheck during their working years (as almost all financial advisers recommend), then 80 percent of pre-retirement income should suffice in later life. For the moment, let's accept that figure and finish examining his math.

So now you know what your yearly "salary" should be, but where does that money come from? Again, we need to make some assumptions: first, that your nest egg will earn between 4 percent and 5 percent a year in retirement (after inflation) and, second, that you can safely withdraw 5 percent of your savings each year. So, let's return to our couple—Andrea and Scott—who are making $80,000 a year before retiring. If they have managed to build a nest egg totaling $960,000, a 5 percent withdrawal yields $48,000. Add to that figure a minimum of $16,000 that our retirees will collect each year from Social Security (that's a rough calculation from the Social Security Administration) and—voila!—you get $64,000, or 80 percent of pre-retirement income.

The numbers above, as you may have already figured out, don't account for pensions, annuities or other sources of income. Most important, the math doesn't account for *your particular* needs and expenses. In order to figure in these elements more precisely, let's turn to a framework developed by T. Rowe Price, the Baltimore-based mutual-fund company.

PLANNING MADE EASY

In an article in the *Journal of Financial Planning* in early 2006, Charles Farrell laid out some of the best and simplest tools we've seen to help people gauge where they stand in their financial preparations for later life. The numbers in the following chart—involving relationships among salary, savings and debt—serve as a roadmap to a very specific goal: retiring at age sixty-five with no debt and a nest egg equal to twelve times one's annual salary.

Age	Savings-to-income	Debt-to-income
35	0.9	1.50
40	1.7	1.25
45	3.0	1.00
50	4.5	0.75
55	6.5	0.50
60	8.8	0.20
65	12.0	0.00

To use it, multiply your gross salary by the numbers in the columns, corresponding to your age. For example, a person age fifty has a gross salary of $80,000, a mortgage of $100,000, two auto loans totaling $20,000 and savings—such as a 401(k), but not the equity in a home—of $250,000. Using Mr. Farrell's ratios, we arrive at the following:

Salary:	$80,000		Salary:	$80,000
Savings ratio:	×4.5		Debt ratio:	×0.75
	$360,000			$60,000

So, our fifty-year-old making $80,000 should already have a nest egg totaling about $360,000, and should have no more than $60,000 in debt. Instead, he or she has only $250,000 in savings (equal to just 3.13 times his or her salary) and $120,000 in debt (equal to 1.5 times his or her salary).

BUILDING A BUDGET

To begin, let's take a closer look at Andrea and Scott and their finances.

Scott is sixty-four years old and works for a manufacturer of agricultural equipment, making about $50,000 a year. His wife, Andrea, age sixty, is a teacher in a private school and earns about $30,000 a year. They plan to retire in about two years. In the past year, they made the last mortgage payment on their thirty-five-year-old home. They are in good health and have good genes. Andrea's parents died in their late eighties; Scott's mother and father are still going strong at ages eighty-five and eighty-eight, respectively. Scott and Andrea's plans for retirement are starting to take shape. They know they want to do a lot of traveling; in particular, they have fallen in love in recent years with cruise vacations. In fact, the two are toying with the idea of setting up their own, small travel business in retirement, in which they would lead group tours. They want to devote more time to their favorite volunteer organizations (him, the county fire and rescue squad; her, the Red Cross), and they want to contribute, if possible, to their two grandsons' college education.

Scott and Andrea's assets run along traditional lines: a 401(k), an individual retirement account and some personal savings. They also have some icing on their retirement cake: a small pension from Andrea's work and a small rental property—a one-bedroom apartment—that they inherited from Andrea's parents.

With all that in mind, Scott and Andrea want to know where they stand financially. Will their nest egg allow them to travel as much as they wish, help their grandchildren and still meet their basic household expenses? We'll start with expenses.

EXPENSES

Expenses can be broken down into as many categories as you wish. Our framework has five: essentials, discretionary, special,

THE "LAYER CAKE" APPROACH

In the past decade, the idea of 4 percent as an optimal withdrawal rate has come to be widely accepted in the financial planning business, primarily because of pioneering studies by William Bengen, a certified financial planner in El Cajon, California. Looking back at how stocks and bonds have performed since the late 1920s, Mr. Bengen found that portfolios with about 60 percent of their assets invested in large-company stocks and about 40 percent in intermediate-term U.S. bonds could sustain withdrawal rates of about 4 percent almost indefinitely; a person could pull that figure from his or her nest egg each and every year and almost never run out of money. But the same historical data show that once withdrawal rates begin to *exceed* 4 percent, portfolios run the risk of drying up. Note the caveat: A good chunk of your savings—about 60 percent—should remain invested in stocks to help your nest egg keep pace with inflation.

However, new research published by Mr. Bengen in mid-2006 allows for the fact that "one size" may not fit everyone when it comes to withdrawal rates. What if a retiree, for instance, adds some small-company stocks to the investment mix and is willing to accept a 94 percent chance of success (versus almost 100 percent) that his or her portfolio would last thirty years? In that case, the retiree could adopt an initial withdrawal rate of 5 percent. And what if a second retiree, whose parents and grandparents all died at relatively young ages, thinks his or her portfolio needs to last only twenty years (versus thirty) and is content with an 80 percent chance of success? In that case, he or she could choose an initial withdrawal rate of about 7 percent.

Mr. Bengen calls this a "layer-cake" approach to identifying an appropriate withdrawal rate—showing an investor how different variables can increase or decrease withdrawal rates and then layering these variables on top of one another to reach a final figure. (You can read the research itself in the August 2006 issue of the *Journal of Financial Planning* at www.fpanet.org/journal/. Click on "Past Issues & Articles.")

debt and reserves. Essentials are fairly self-explanatory (housing, food, transportation), as are discretionary (travel, entertainment, gifts). "Special" would include major purchases (like a recreational vehicle) or major investments, like Andrea and Scott's desire to help with their grandsons' college education. Debt includes mortgage payments, car payments and the like. And reserves (a critical but often overlooked category) include savings for future purchases, like a car, new furnace or new roof on the house.

Here are Andrea and Scott's projected expenses, with space for your own figures:

1. Essentials

Note two expenses in particular: $600 a month for health care and $360 a month for long-term care insurance. You might think that $600 a month for health care—including supplemental insurance, drugs and other out-of-pocket expenses—sounds high. If anything, it might be conservative. For instance, if Andrea and Scott have no health-care benefits beyond Medicare in retirement, they should be budgeting at least $500 or $600 a month for out-of-pocket expenses, according to the Fidelity study we mentioned in Chapter Six. What's more, Andrea and Scott have purchased long-term care insurance in anticipation of living well into their eighties and possibly beyond. Yes, such insurance is expensive and ridiculously complex. But the possible purchase of such coverage should be part of every family's discussions about retirement finances. We talk about long-term care insurance in detail in Chapter Eleven.

2. Discretionary

The item to note here is travel. Again, our couple enjoys cruise vacations and would like to make at least two such trips a year. They figure that each trip will cost a total of $3,000. For other shorter trips, they have allotted $1,800 a year, for a total annual travel budget of $7,800, or $650 a month. Yes, it can be difficult

HOUSING (MONTHLY)

Water	$30	_____
Gas	$125	_____
Electric	$125	_____
Cable	$60	_____
Internet	$40	_____
Telephone	$80	_____
Cell phone	$50	_____
Insurance	$80	_____
Maintenance/repairs	$150	_____
Property taxes	$350	_____
Total:	**$1,090**	_____

FOOD (MONTHLY)

Groceries for home	$600	_____
Dining out	$200	_____
Total:	**$800**	_____

TRANSPORTATION (MONTHLY)

Car insurance	$135	_____
Gasoline	$140	_____
Maintenance	$25	_____
Total:	**$300**	_____

PERSONAL CARE (MONTHLY)

Clothing	$210	_____
Dry cleaning	$50	_____
Personal care (haircuts, etc.)	$100	_____
Total:	**$360**	_____

MEDICAL (MONTHLY)

Health care	$600	_____
Long-term care insurance	$360	_____
Total:	**$960**	_____
Essential expenses (monthly):	$3,510	_____
	× 12	
Essential expenses (annual):	**$42,120**	_____

to estimate such expenses, but you probably can do a better job than you think. Look back at earlier vacations and earlier expenses; look at the prices of travel packages online and in magazines. Your numbers won't be perfect, but simply getting some figures on paper will make a big difference in your planning.

Travel	$650	_____
Charity	$200	_____
Gifts	$150	_____
Entertainment/hobbies	$300	_____
Education	$50	_____
Memberships/subscriptions/dues	$50	_____
Discretionary expenses (monthly):	$1,400	_____
	× 12	
Discretionary expenses (annual):	**$16,800**	_____

3. Special

This is where Scott and Andrea are budgeting for college tuition bills for their grandsons. They don't anticipate that they will be able to pay such bills in full, especially if the boys attend private schools. But Andrea and Scott want to help if they're able. To start, they budget $500 a month.

Special expenses (monthly):	$500	_____
	× 12	
Special expenses (annual):	**$6,000**	_____

4. Debt

As noted, Andrea and Scott already have paid off their mortgage. They have no credit card debt; they pay the balance in full each month. There are few better gifts you can give yourself than to start retirement debt-free. In its most recent survey of consumer finances, the Federal Reserve Board found that, among families in which the head of the family was age sixty-five to seventy-four, almost one-third (31.9 percent) carried credit-card debt and almost one-third (32.1 percent) still carried a loan secured by their primary residence.

Debt expenses: $0 _____

5. Reserves

Saving money *in* retirement is just as important as saving money *before* retirement. Major expenses—for your home and transportation, in particular—will continue to be part of your life. But how to account for this? Henry K. "Bud" Hebeler—a former senior executive at Boeing and author of one of the most informative Web sites about retirement planning, www.analyzenow.com—offers a simple solution. Make a list of all the big-ticket items in your household (new and future) with their expected life spans. Divide the current cost by the expected life span, and the resulting figure is the amount of money you should budget or "hold in reserve" each year to replace these items as needed.

Let's say you have a new $2,000 furnace that you think will last fifteen years. Dividing $2,000 by fifteen, we get $133.33. That's the amount of money you should set aside each year (or $11.11 each month) for a future furnace.

Here's what Andrea and Scott came up with:

Item	Cost	Useful Life	Reserve
Car	$25,000	8 years	$3,125
Roof	$5,000	20 years	$250
Carpeting	$4,000	12 years	$333
Furnace	$2,000	15 years	$133
Air-conditioning	$4,000	15 years	$266
Water heater	$1,000	10 years	$100
Exterior painting	$3,500	6 years	$583
Interior painting	$5,000	6 years	$833
Washer and dryer	$1,200	10 years	$120
Computer	$1,500	4 years	$375

Reserve expenses (annual): $6,118 _____

That does it for annual expenses. Here's what Andrea and Scott have estimated for their budget in retirement:

Essential	$42,120	_____
Discretionary	$16,800	_____
Special	$6,000	_____
Debt	$0	_____
Reserves	$6,118	_____
Total Expenses:	**$71,038**	_____

Remember our discussion of "replacement ratios"? Andrea and Scott's figure of $71,038 works out to almost 89 percent of their pre-retirement income of $80,000, and it represents *their* specific situation with *their* specific figures.

Now, let's see what our couple has in terms of income.

SOURCES OF INCOME

Most retirees have two sources of income: "benefits" income (which involves relatively predictable payments, like Social Security and pensions) and "income from assets" (money withdrawn from individual retirement accounts, personal savings and the like). Identifying the former is fairly easy; calculating the latter will take a few extra minutes.

1. Benefits Income
Here are the most common sources of benefits income:

a. Social Security
Each year, the good people at Social Security mail you a Statement of Benefits that shows what your monthly check will be in retirement. Don't have one? You can go to www.ssa.gov and request a copy. You also can use calculators at the same site to estimate your benefits. In the case of Scott and Andrea, Scott plans to file for Social Security at age sixty-five and ten months, when he becomes eligible for his full retirement benefits. Andrea plans to collect benefits at age sixty-two; her payout will

be almost 30 percent lower than if she waited until age sixty-six (her full retirement age). Their expected annual payouts, estimated by Uncle Sam, are as follows:

Scott:	$15,744	_____
Andrea:	$8,280	_____
Social Security:	**$24,024**	_____

b. Pension

As with Social Security, your employer can give you an estimate of your monthly or annual payout and your payout options, which we'll discuss in Chapter Nine. Scott doesn't have a pension; Andrea will collect $9,500 a year.

Pension:	**$9,500**	_____

c. Annuities

Annuities—fixed, immediate, deferred, variable—are playing an increasingly important role in Americans' retirement plans. We'll discuss these products in more detail at the end of this chapter. For the moment, Andrea and Scott have no payments from annuities.

Annuities:	**$0**	_____

d. Dividends and interest

You might have investments—including stocks and bonds—that aren't allocated specifically for retirement, but are still a source of annual income. Scott and Andrea don't have any such investments outside their retirement accounts.

Dividends and interest:	**$0**	_____

e. Income from property

As noted, our couple owns a small rental property, which generates $6,000 in income each year. This investment represents both an opportunity and a potentially difficult decision: Andrea and Scott would like to leave the property to their children as part of their estate, but they also recognize that they might have to sell it at some point to help finance their own retirement.

Income from property: **$6,000** _____

f. Other income

This might include income from the part-time business that our couple envisions starting or payments from a trust. For the moment, Andrea and Scott have no miscellaneous income.

Other income: **$0** _____

That does it for benefits income. Here's the total:

Social Security	$24,024	_____
Pension	$9,500	_____
Annuities	$0	_____
Dividends and interest	$0	_____
Rental income	$6,000	_____
Other	$0	_____
Total benefits income:	**$39,524**	_____

Now, let's turn to the couple's second major source of income.

2. Income from Assets

Here, we're going to add up Andrea and Scott's retirement accounts—their personal savings, 401(k), IRA and any other assets—and determine just how much money they wish to pull from those combined accounts each year (their rate of withdrawal).

a. Taxable investments

These are personal savings (certificates of deposits, mutual funds, cash, stocks, etc.) _outside_ your tax-deferred savings (like an IRA) that are set aside specifically for retirement. Andrea and Scott have saved $110,000 in these accounts.

Taxable investments: **$110,000** _____

b. Tax-deferred investments

These are the backbone of most retirement plans today: 401(k)s, 403(b)s and various IRAs. We'll talk about these in more detail in Chapter Nine. Here are Scott and Andrea's holdings:

IRA	$120,000	_____
401(k)	$550,000	_____
Tax-deferred investments:	**$670,000**	_____

c. Other investments

Here, you could include a business or property that could be sold or converted to cash. Because Andrea and Scott have decided to catalog their rental house as a source of benefits income, they have no miscellaneous investments.

Other investments:	**$0**	_____

Now, let's add all these savings:

Taxable investments	$110,000	_____
Tax-deferred investments	$670,000	_____
Other investments	$0	_____
Total income from assets:	**$780,000**	_____

The next step is a crucial one: selecting a rate of withdrawal —how much money Andrea and Scott wish to pull from this $780,000 each year. To make the decision easier, we can use a technique called Monte Carlo analysis, which has nothing to do with the European resort city and everything to do with "probability theory." This analysis (made with various software programs) gives us a probability that our savings will last as long as we do, given tens of thousands of potential economic, market, mortality and spending possibilities. Here are some withdrawal rates and their chances of success, as calculated by T. Rowe Price. In this case, "success" is defined as having at least $1 in your savings at the end of each time period:

So, if you expect your retirement to last thirty years and your investment mix is 60 percent stocks and 40 percent bonds,

		Stock/bond mix (percent)			
		80/20	60/40	40/60	20/80
Years in Retirement	Withdrawal rate	Likelihood of success			
	4%	97%	99%	99%	99%
20	5%	89%	92%	95%	97%
	6%	74%	75%	75%	71%
	4%	91%	94%	97%	98%
25	5%	77%	78%	78%	73%
	6%	57%	53%	44%	25%
	4%	84%	87%	89%	89%
30	5%	65%	63%	57%	40%
	6%	45%	38%	24%	7%

there's an 87 percent chance that your savings will last for those thirty years at a withdrawal rate of 4 percent. Increasing the withdrawal rate to 6 percent lowers the likelihood of having at least $1 at the end of thirty years to just 38 percent.

These numbers simply represent the "likelihood" or the "probability" of a particular outcome, and Monte Carlo analysis does have its detractors; some financial planners argue that the results can give clients a false sense of security. Many financial advisers, though, agree that such calculations—because they consider variability—are superior to those built around averages.

At this point, you may ask, "Well, why not just pick a rate of withdrawal that offers, say, a 90 percent chance of success? Wouldn't that be . . . safe?" It depends on the person. When it comes to withdrawal rates, you might need a 95 percent chance of success to sleep well at night while your neighbor is just fine with 75 percent. Again, the key is doing the math—*getting the numbers on paper*—so that you can see the possible repercussions and decide what degree of risk is comfortable for you.

Which brings us back to Andrea and Scott. Their asset allocation is 60 percent stocks and 40 percent bonds (more about that in Chapter Eight), and they have decided to use a 4 percent rate of withdrawal based on a retirement lasting twenty-five years—at least to start. That allows us to complete our income calculations:

Total income from assets	$780,000	_____
Withdrawal rate	×.04	_____
Annual income from assets:	**$31,200**	_____

Then, we add that figure to our annual benefits income (from Social Security, etc.) and get our total annual income:

Annual income from assets	$31,200	_____
Annual benefits income	+$39,524	_____
Total annual income:	**$70,724**	_____

TAXES

We're almost done. Now that we know how much annual income Andrea and Scott are counting on in retirement, we can calculate the size of their tax bill. Of course, we could simply pick a figure; 20 percent is a reasonable estimate for many families and takes into account both federal and state taxes. We can get a more accurate figure by calculating Andrea and Scott's effective, or average, tax rate. We do this by taking the sum of all taxes they paid last year (federal, state and local) and dividing that figure by their taxable income (after exemptions and deductions). All these figures can be found on their tax returns.

Andrea and Scott calculate their effective tax rate to be 15 percent. This allows us to calculate how much income tax they will pay in their first year of retirement:

Total annual income	$70,724	_____
Tax rate	×.15	_____
Tax bill:	**$10,608**	_____

The Result

We now have all the pieces: projected income for the first year in retirement, taxes and expenses. Let's see where Scott and Andrea stand:

Total annual income	$70,724	_____
Tax bill	− $10,608	_____
Expenses	− $71,038	_____
Surplus/shortfall:	**(− $10,922)**	_____

Ouch. That projected shortfall amounts to about $900 a month—hardly the way any couple would wish to start retirement. But here's the good news: Andrea and Scott are no longer operating in the dark. With all these figures clearly in front of them, they can start making some decisions. What follows are several strategies for turning a shortfall into a surplus in retirement planning or simply for getting the most out of your savings.

REVISE YOUR BUDGET

As with budgeting during our working years, two of the best ways to bolster household finances in retirement are to cut expenses or find new sources of income. With that in mind, let's make two quick changes in Andrea and Scott's budget. Sorry, but we're going to eliminate the $6,000 a year set aside for the grandkids' education. At the same time, we'll increase the withdrawal rate from savings to 5 percent from 4 percent. As a result, annual expenses fall to $65,038, and income increases to $78,524. That means the tax bill ($78,524 × .15) is now $11,778. Here's the new result:

Total annual income	$78,524	_____
Tax bill	− $11,778	_____
Expenses	− $65,038	_____
Surplus/shortfall:	**+ $1,708**	_____

APPLYING YOUR WITHDRAWAL RATE

You can budget for inflation and other external forces that might affect your nest egg by choosing a particular method for applying your withdrawal rate. Here are the most common approaches:

Fixed Percentage

You pull a fixed amount from your savings (a steady 4.5 percent, for instance) each and every year. The amount withdrawn will depend on the size of your nest egg, which will change in value over time.

Adjusted for Inflation

Here, you set an initial withdrawal rate (say, 4 percent) and increase the withdrawal each year by the amount of inflation. So, if your nest egg totals $400,000 and inflation stands at 3 percent, you withdraw $16,000 the first year, $16,480 the second year and so on. This is probably the most popular approach among retirees.

Start High, Finish Low

You can withdraw large percentages from your savings early in retirement—perhaps as much as 6 percent or 7 percent a year—and then reduce withdrawals late in life, perhaps to as little as 3 percent. The thinking here is that people early in retirement are healthier and will want to do more (travel, remodel a home) and spend more. As you age, however, your lifestyle and spending will likely slow down, meaning your withdrawals can be smaller. Or so the theory goes.

Floor and Ceiling

In this case, you set an initial withdrawal rate, a dollar amount above that initial rate (a "ceiling") and a dollar amount below the initial rate (a "floor"). The actual amount of money withdrawn from your nest egg each year varies with market performance: If markets climb, your withdrawals climb as well, but never beyond the original "ceiling." If markets fall, withdrawals fall, too, but never below the original "floor."

Each of the first three approaches has drawbacks. If returns on stocks are below average and inflation is above average (which happened in the

1970s), pulling a steady 5 percent from your nest egg or rewarding yourself with annual increases in your withdrawals could be a recipe for emptying your savings in less than twenty years. Meanwhile, the "front-loaded" method sounds appealing, but excessive withdrawals early in retirement can lead to disaster if you happen to enjoy a very long life—with very big medical bills toward the end of that life.

With that in mind, your best bet might be "floor-and-ceiling" withdrawals. Based (again) on research by the industrious William Bengen, floor-and-ceiling withdrawals offer the best of both worlds and allow you to start retirement with a relatively aggressive withdrawal rate—as much as 5¼ percent—and with a high probability (more than 90 percent) that your nest egg will last at least thirty years.

The math does get complicated. For instance, you need to calculate the "nominal" and "real" values of withdrawals each year (adjusted for inflation) and monitor (again, each year) where your withdrawals might fall within predetermined limits. The floor-and-ceiling method also requires a good measure of discipline on your part; if markets fall, you have to be prepared to cut back on your withdrawals.

All of this argues for seeking help from a financial adviser. Again, choosing a rate of withdrawal from savings ranks among the most important financial decisions people make in retirement. We discuss withdrawal rates and withdrawal strategies in more detail in Chapter Eight.

Quite a difference. We go from a deficit of about $900 a month to a surplus of about $140. Does this, then, become the "approved solution" for Andrea and Scott? Maybe. Maybe not. That 5 percent withdrawal rate (again, assuming a twenty-five-year retirement) could be unsettling. The probability that their nest egg will survive now drops to 78 percent from 94 percent. So . . . Perhaps they split the difference and choose a 4.5 percent rate of withdrawal. Or perhaps they take one cruise each year instead of two. Or perhaps they sell the rental property (instead of leaving it to their children) and use the proceeds to supplement their nest egg. Each calculation could be done fairly quickly. The point is that they are able to consider—and see the consequences of—each option because they *took the time in the first place to estimate their expenses and sources of income.* It's essential that you do the same.

Ideally, you should reexamine your budget *annually* in retirement, including your expenses, sources of income and withdrawal rate. The markets, your investments and life itself (with all its exigencies) are far too volatile for retirement by rote.

To be more precise, long-term estimates of expenses should also take inflation into account—including different rates of inflation for different expenses. (Again, health costs are rising faster than other costs.) And when it comes to calculating reserves, few of us start retirement with all "new" possessions, which means we should have a reserve fund up and running *before* we enter retirement. (Note that Henry Hebeler—whom we mentioned earlier during our discussion of the need for cash reserves in retirement—has some excellent tools on his Web site, www.analyzenow.com, that account for inflation, reserves and other variables.)

In the end, there's a simple way to tell if your retirement budget is reasonable: Try living on that budget for a full year *before* you retire.

BRIDGING THE BUDGET GAP

KEEP WORKING . . . OR START WORKING (AGAIN)

One option for any couple or individual in the face of a budgetary shortfall might be to keep working and drawing a paycheck. As we mentioned in Chapter Six, delaying your retirement just two or three years gives you additional time to save and additional time for your nest egg to grow. And it's increasingly common: In 2005, about 5.3 million men and women age sixty-five or older in the United States were working, according to the Bureau of Labor Statistics. Labor-force participation rates among older Americans have been climbing steadily since the mid-1980s. Equally important, staying active as we age—whether it's working, volunteering, traveling, returning to school, etc.—promotes physical and mental well-being.

A second option is to retire and launch a second career. Among workers age fifty or older, 16 percent are self-employed, and fully one-third of those, according to a study by AARP and Rand Corp., made the jump to self-employment after turning fifty. Andrea and Scott, for instance, are thinking about opening their own travel business.

DELAY SOCIAL SECURITY

As with delaying retirement itself, delaying the start of Social Security benefits can boost your income in retirement. Many people are unaware of just how large the reduction in benefits can be at age sixty-two—a 30 percent cut for those born after 1960. Others worry that they might die before their full retirement age, meaning that Uncle Sam gets to keep all their Social Security dollars. In fact, a sixty-two-year-old man has a 93 percent probability of reaching his full retirement age, while a sixty-two-year-old woman has a 96 percent probability, according to the Social Security Administration.

Perhaps most important, a primary breadwinner who decides to collect benefits early could leave his or her spouse in a tight spot. Let's take a sixty-two-year-old who retires today with a monthly benefit from Social Security of about $1,400. At age eighty-one, that person's annual benefit (including cost-of-living adjustments) would total about $24,700. If the primary breadwinner dies at that point, the surviving spouse would receive the same annual benefit. But if that primary breadwinner had waited until full retirement age to begin collecting Social Security, his or her annual benefit at age eighty-one would total $33,360. In other words, the decision to take benefits at age sixty-two eventually could cost the surviving spouse $8,660 annually.

In our example, Andrea isn't the primary breadwinner, but if she were to wait until age sixty-six to collect her full benefits, her payout would jump almost $3,000 a year to about $11,700. Not bad.

Many financial planners do agree that a person in poor health at age sixty-two—or one who isn't confident about living beyond his or her early eighties—should take the money and run. But too many people opt for early benefits without taking a hard look at the potential downside.

Buy an Annuity

One way of generating a steady stream of income in retirement is to buy an immediate-fixed annuity. Though an annuity might have seemed very safe and very dull a few years ago, today that security is what makes the product appealing and helps explain why you should consider making an annuity a part of your portfolio.

With an immediate-fixed annuity, you give an insurance company a lump sum in exchange for monthly payments for the rest of your life. (Contracts are also available for a specified period of time, generally between five and twenty-five years.) The amount of the payments depends on the interest rate at the time you sign the contract and on your life expectancy. For instance, a sixty-five-year-old man who lives in New York and puts $100,000 into an immediate annuity today would receive an average of $698 a month for as long as he lives, according to www.immediateannuities.com, a Web site that calculates annuity payouts. Compare that with a seventy-year-old New Yorker who puts in the same amount. His shorter life expectancy means that he would get $772 a month for life.

Traditionally, an annuity meant the insurer got to keep your original investment when you died. So if you bought a

$100,000 policy on Monday and had a fatal heart attack on Tuesday, your insurer, and not your estate, would get to keep the $100,000. But today, there are options you can add to annuities that will allow you to leave something to your heirs in exchange for a lower payout. For instance, let's say you're married and you want a "joint and last survivor" annuity, which would pay out as long as either you or your spouse is alive. For $100,000, a sixty-five-year-old man with a sixty-year-old wife could get an annuity paying $586 a month even after one spouse dies.

If you wish, you can also ensure that your children will receive some of the payout if you die before a certain time. Or, if you want to ensure that your payouts rise with inflation, you can ask for inflation protection. (Indeed, given the length of many retirements today inflation protection should be part of most annuity purchases.) But ask yourself whether the cost of these extras is worth the benefit and if you actually need them. For instance, if you have life insurance, you might already have adequate financial protection for your spouse. Also keep in mind that if you have Social Security payments as well as a traditional pension plan, you may not need an annuity as much as a person who has only one or none of these income streams.

If you do take the plunge, most advisers recommend tying up no more than 20 percent to 25 percent of your portfolio in an annuity. You'll want the rest of your money in a diversified portfolio of stocks, bonds and alternative investments for continued growth. To figure out how much you'll need to invest upfront to get the monthly income you want, go to calculators like www.immediateannuities.com. Then, compare quotes from a number of different companies, making sure to check providers such as TIAA-CREF, Vanguard Group and Fidelity Investments, which have annuities with consistently high payouts because of low built-in expenses.

To spread out risk among annuities, you could limit your investment to, say, $100,000 with any one insurance company. You could also try "laddering" annuities to protect against bankruptcy and inflation, meaning you invest in immediate annuities that have shorter payout periods and that mature at different times. That way, if interest rates climb higher, you aren't locked in for too long and can move your money to a higher-paying annuity.

We're likely to see even more products and offerings in the annuity business as they become an increasingly popular solution for people who haven't saved enough for a long retirement or don't have a stream of income. One of the latest twists involves "longevity protection" for people who think there's a good chance they'll make it to their late eighties and perhaps to their nineties. For about $165,000, a sixty-five-year-old man could buy an annuity from New York Life Insurance Co. (with what the company calls a "Changing Needs Option") that provides an annual income of $10,000 until age eighty-five, at which point the annual payments would jump to $50,000 until he dies. (That compares with a premium of about $126,000 for a fixed annual payment of $10,000 for life.)

Annuities, to be sure, have their drawbacks. The fees can be steep, and the products themselves can be maddeningly complex. To get the biggest benefit, you would want to be fairly confident of living well into your eighties. Still, if you want the predictability of a pension as part of your income in retirement, you can, in effect, buy one with an annuity.

CONSIDER A REVERSE MORTGAGE

As we noted earlier in these pages, your home can serve as a safety net in retirement. If you trade down to a smaller place, you'll cut monthly costs (for utilities, insurance, taxes, etc.) and free up equity to fatten your nest egg.

But what if you can't trade down? What if you're already living in a small house or what if you settle in a smaller place and still need additional cash? In that case, you might consider a reverse mortgage, one of the fastest-growing products in the mortgage industry. These tools allow homeowners age sixty-two or older to essentially sell their house back to a bank in ex-change for monthly payments, a lump sum or a line of credit. (Money received from a reverse mortgage is tax-free.) You keep control of the house and don't have to pay back the money as long as you live there. Then, when you die or move out, the house is sold, the loan is paid off and any money left over goes back to you or your estate.

Several variables—your age, current interest rates and the value of your house—will help determine how much money you can get. The older you are, the larger the loan, typ-ically; you can also expect a larger loan if interest rates are low or if your home is appraised at top dollar. Then there's the type of reverse mortgage itself; an applicant can select from three basic models. The first is a federally insured reverse mortgage, also known as a Home Equity Conversion Mort-gage. This is backed by the Department of Housing and Urban Development, or HUD. You can also apply for what's known as a single-purpose reverse mortgage, which originates with nonprofit groups or local government agencies. Finally, there is a proprietary reverse mortgage—a private loan issued by a company that creates and markets such a product.

The federal program is often the best bet and accounts for the bulk of all reverse mortgages (about 85 percent) because interest rates tend to be lower with Uncle Sam and you may be able to apply for a bigger loan than with other programs. The downside is that the upfront costs are steep because of the mort-gage insurance. A calculator at the Web site for the National Reverse Mortgage Lenders Association (www.reversemortgage. org) can give you some ballpark figures on just how big a loan you might be able to get and how much it might cost. For in-stance, a seventy-two-year-old living outside Atlanta who's paid off his or her home—valued at $300,000—is eligible to borrow $132,185 with a Home Equity Conversion Mortgage (HECM) loan. But the key word is "eligible": After $16,313 in closing costs and a set-aside for service fees, the actual amount is $115,872.

Steep fees are just one potential drawback with reverse

RETIREMENT CALCULATORS AND TOOLS

There are tools that can help you wade through some of the more complicated parts of retirement planning, and some Web sites offer worksheets that can help simplify your calculations. Here are a few of the better ones:

AARP Retirement Calculator
www.aarp.org/bulletin/yourmoney/
> Click on "Retirement Calculator" to learn if you're saving enough.

BankSite
www.banksite.com
> This site requires registration. Click on "Calculators." Features include a retirement payout calculator and IRA calculators.

Financial Calculators
www.fincalc.com
> Click on "ConsumerCalcs." Eleven calculators dedicated to retirement can be found at this site.

Kiplinger's
www.kiplinger.com
> Click on "Tools and Calculators." You'll find thirteen retirement tools.

The Motley Fool
www.fool.com/calcs/calculators.htm
> This site features more than a dozen retirement tools.

Principal Financial Group
www.principal.com/calculators/retire.htm
> Various calculators and tools are offered here.

SmartMoney
www.smartmoney.com
> Click on "Personal Finance" and then on "Retirement." Various retirement tools and worksheets can be found.

T. Rowe Price Retirement Income Calculator

www3.troweprice.com/ric/RIC

This calculator looks at a wide range of potential market scenarios.

Vanguard

www.vanguard.com

Click on "Personal Investors," then on "Planning and Education" and then on "Retirement Planning." Various planning tools and calculators can be found here.

mortgages. If you fall behind on your property taxes or fail to maintain your house, the mortgage could be called or the lender could cut your monthly check (if that's the payment option you've chosen) to pay the delinquent taxes. A reverse mortgage also means that, in all likelihood, you can no longer hand down a major asset—your home—to the next generation.

Remember, the equity in your home could be the best safeguard you have in retirement. If you decide to apply for a reverse mortgage, be very careful that you're using the money for your needs and not just your wants.

CHAPTER 8

ASSETS AND BUCKETS

Diversification—making sure you always have a healthy variety of investments in your nest egg—will help your retirement savings last as long as you do. Studies have shown that the allocation of your assets (how your investments are balanced and blended) largely determines how your portfolio will perform. And yet, many investors continue to stumble when it comes to this critical step. The following pages address common mistakes and how to avoid them and the importance of asset *location:* which types of accounts should hold which types of investments.

In this chapter, we'll also discuss how to create a steady paycheck in retirement, often referred to as a "withdrawal strategy." Knowing which assets or accounts to tap first can make a big difference in the long-term health of your nest egg and the size of your tax bill.

ASSET ALLOCATION

In recent years, the most valuable lesson about asset allocation was also the most painful: the bear market of 2000–2002. The decade immediately preceding that period had been one of spectacular growth in most portfolios; between October 1990 and March 2000, the S&P 500 climbed 385 percent. Increases in productivity and advances in technology appeared to herald a "new economy," in which investors put all their money in "large-cap growth stocks" and Internet companies and could ignore asset allocation. That strategy actually worked well for a few years, until large-cap growth stocks and Internet companies went over the cliff in early 2000, taking investors' nest eggs with them.

Again today, many investors, including people approaching or already in retirement, are making the same fundamental errors involving asset allocation: People who haven't saved enough money for retirement are playing catch-up by creating portfolios top heavy with "hot" investments like gold or real estate. At the opposite end of the spectrum, fears of another market crash lead to portfolios with too much money in fixed-income investments (like bonds, for their presumed safety) and not enough in stocks. Unfortunately for those people entering retirement, if you still don't understand or appreciate the importance of asset allocation, you can't rely on time or a paycheck to help compensate for any shortfalls.

THE FUNDAMENTALS

Rather than focusing on one or two investments (like tech stocks in the 1990s), diversifying means we spread our dollars among several complementary asset classes, like stocks, bonds, cash and so-called alternative investments. (We'll define "alternative investments" in just a moment.) We also diversify among investments *within* each of these broad categories, buying domestic *and* international stocks, for instance.

For the most part, asset allocation serves two purposes: to reduce risk and help investors achieve their financial goals. In retirement, asset allocation has a third, equally important, objective: to make your financial life boring. That's right, boring. If you take time to allocate your assets properly (to diversify your holdings across and within asset classes), it really shouldn't matter to you what Wall Street is doing on any given day. If markets are zipping along nicely, your holdings in stocks will give your nest egg the growth it needs; if stocks are taking a beating, your investments in bonds and cash will help you weather the storm.

So, what's the "best" mix of investments at age fifty-five? How should that mix change at age sixty-five or seventy-five? Should you lean toward "passive" investments (like index funds), should you have actively managed mutual funds or should you have some of both? Which vessels (taxable accounts? tax-deferred accounts?) should hold which investments? How will your asset allocation affect your taxes? And how often should you rebalance all these pieces?

We tackle all these questions in the following pages. But again, we urge you to spend time with a financial adviser. As we suggested in Chapter Six, even two or three meetings can help determine if your nest egg is on the right track. If you choose to manage your own nest egg, you may wish to invest in a single "life-cycle" or "target-date" mutual fund, an increasingly popular product that contains a mix of stocks, bonds and cash and, thus, is nicely diversified from the start. What's more, these funds are adjusted automatically to become more conservative (read: more bonds, fewer stocks) as you age.

THE NUMBERS

The first step in allocating assets in retirement is to establish a "cushion," or cash reserve to supply your spending money (the cash you need to pay the electric bill, grocery bill, etc.). Ideally, this reserve will hold three to five years of living expenses. The money in your cash reserve should be invested in products—like money-market funds, short-term bonds, Treasury bills or certificates of deposit—that earn interest but that side-step most market gyrations. These highly liquid investments are sometimes called "cash equivalents" because they usually can be sold quickly with little or no loss of value.

Why three to five years? Since the late 1920s, the five longest bear markets on record have lasted about three years. The longest, between 1946 and 1949, lasted thirty-seven months; the debacle of 2000–2002 lasted thirty-six months. Ideally, you want to avoid a situation where you're forced to replenish your reserve at a time when stock prices are falling; a cushion of at least three years of living expenses (and safer still, one of five years) means that you should be able to ride out virtually any downturn in the markets without having to hold a fire sale in your stock positions. Later in this chapter, we'll discuss how to tap this reserve—and how to keep it filled—when we tackle withdrawal strategies.

At first, the numbers might seem daunting. Three to five years! Andrea and Scott, our couple in Chapter Seven, determined that their annual budget in retirement would be about $65,000. Does that mean they need to set aside a five-year cushion of $325,000? Not necessarily. Remember, part of Andrea and Scott's income each year comes from Social Security and a pension. (Yes, Social Security could have problems in the future, but for the moment, benefits will be paid in full through 2040.) So, we first *subtract* these guaranteed figures from their annual budget; the resulting shortfall helps determine the needed "cushion."

In the case of Andrea and Scott, they expect to get about $33,500 each year from their two known sources of income, Social Security and a pension. Subtracting that number from their annual budget ($65,000 – $33,500) gives us $31,500. *This* is the number we multiply by five to calculate their cushion: $157,500. (To be more precise, we could take the first-year shortfall ($31,500) and increase that figure by a projected rate of inflation for each subsequent year.)

But that reserve accounts for only 20 percent of Andrea and Scott's nest egg. How should they invest the remaining 80 percent? We recommend two strategies. First, they could divide their money among stock funds, bond funds and so-called alternative investments. We recommend mutual funds instead of individual stocks and bonds, and we prefer index funds to "actively managed" funds. Index funds are simply a collection of stocks that resemble the makeup of a particular market index—like the Standard & Poor's 500 (a collection of 500 large-company stocks) or the Wilshire 4500 (a collection of 4,500 medium- and small-size company stocks). As a second strategy, after setting aside a cash reserve, they could take about 20 percent of their nest egg and buy an immediate-fixed annuity (or annuities) in order to guarantee a stream of income for life. Then, the balance of their portfolio could be invested in stock and bond funds. Again, as we mentioned in Chapter Seven, one of the best ways to invest in annuities is to "ladder" these products; that means buying a series of annuities over time that have shorter payout periods and that mature at different dates.

Each strategy is illustrated on the next page.

Why these percentages and why these particular pieces? Again, we start with our cash cushion. (In our portfolio with an annuity, which gives us an additional guaranteed stream of income, we reduce the cushion to about three years of living expenses.) After setting aside a reserve, some people might turn to an old rule of thumb: subtract your age from 100 to calculate the percentage of assets that you should hold in stocks. But now, with many people spending thirty years in retirement, we need a heftier position in stocks well into later life to help our nest egg keep pace with inflation. Thus, we want to keep at least 40 percent to 60 percent of our money in stock funds in retirement. That leaves us (depending on the size of our cash reserves) with about 20 percent to 40 percent to divide among bond funds and alternative investments or to purchase annuities.

ASSET ALLOCATION WITHOUT AN ANNUITY

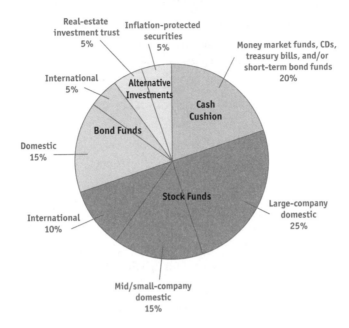

ASSET ALLOCATION WITH AN ANNUITY

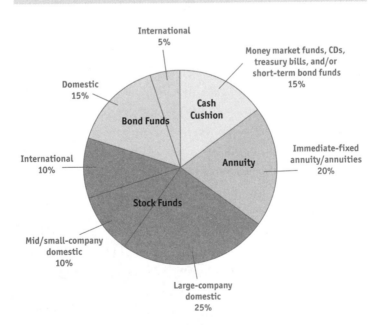

AS TIME GOES BY . . .

One common financial question among retirees is, "How should my asset mix change as I age?" David Darst, author of *The Art of Asset Allocation,* suggests the following:

IN YOUR FIFTIES . . .

Domestic and international stocks—45 percent to 60 percent

Domestic and international bonds—20 percent to 30 percent

Alternative investments—20 percent to 30 percent

Cash—5 percent to 10 percent

IN YOUR SIXTIES . . .

Domestic and international stocks—35 percent to 60 percent

Domestic and international bonds—25 percent to 40 percent

Alternative investments—20 percent to 30 percent

Cash—10 percent to 15 percent

IN YOUR SEVENTIES . . .

Domestic and international stocks—30 percent to 50 percent

Domestic and international bonds—35 percent to 50 percent

Alternative investments—15 percent to 20 percent

Cash—10 percent to 15 percent

Remember, we want to diversify our assets both among and *within* different asset classes. So within stock funds, we might want a large-company fund, a mid- to small-company fund and an international fund. We could refine that further by including, for instance, a large-company *growth* fund and a large-company *value* fund. (The former tends to focus on companies where earnings are growing faster than the norm; the latter seeks out stocks that are underperforming the market or have fallen out of favor with investors.)

A note about "alternative investments": Many financial advisers recommend including these products in your portfolio. Such investments—which include real-estate investment trusts and "inflation-protected securities" (i.e., government securities designed to provide a return that always beats inflation)—are said to have a "low correlation" with more traditional investments. That means that their value doesn't always move in the same direction as stocks and bonds, which can help reduce volatility in your portfolio. Ten percent of your assets in alternative investments is a reasonable allocation.

Remember, our numbers are guidelines. In the end, you have to be comfortable with the allocation you choose. But we've provided you with a good starting point.

The following pie charts give you an idea of the kinds of mutual funds you might select. They are based on research done in mid-2006 from Morningstar Inc., a provider of investment analysis. We aren't saying you should run out and buy these funds; rather, they are examples of how to assemble different portfolios based on asset allocations that meet your needs.

If making these decisions proves overwhelming, you may opt to place all your money in a life-cycle or target-date mutual fund, but there are some caveats. First, a life-cycle fund is designed to be a stand-alone investment containing all your savings; it's not something you buy to *add* diversity to a nest egg. If you have a life-cycle fund as one part of a bigger portfolio, you're probably saddling yourself with extra fees. (As with most investments, life-cycle funds carry a charge. If you have investments above and beyond the life-cycle fund, you'll be paying fees on them, as well.)

A second caveat: All life-cycle funds are not created equal. Of the 140 or so funds on the market, most have a different mix of assets, fees, investment strategies and returns. Perhaps most important, some life-cycle funds can get quite conservative quite quickly: One prominent financial-services company—at the point where investors in each of its life-cycle funds hit retirement—has only 30 percent of the funds' holdings in stock.

MUTUAL FUNDS WITHOUT AN ANNUITY

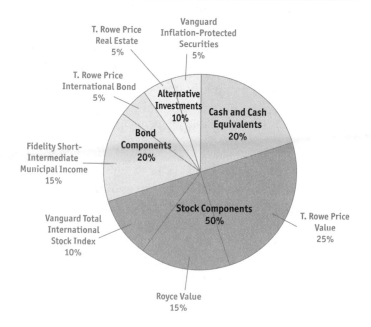

T. Rowe Price
Real Estate
5%

Vanguard
Inflation-Protected
Securities
5%

T. Rowe Price
International Bond
5%

Alternative
Investments
10%

Cash and Cash
Equivalents
20%

Bond
Components
20%

Fidelity Short-
Intermediate
Municipal Income
15%

Stock Components
50%

T. Rowe Price
Value
25%

Vanguard Total
International
Stock Index
10%

Royce Value
15%

MUTUAL FUNDS WITH AN ANNUITY

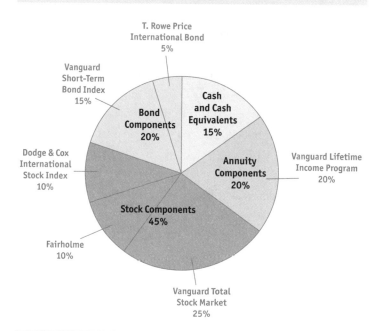

T. Rowe Price
International Bond
5%

Vanguard
Short-Term
Bond Index
15%

Bond
Components
20%

Cash
and Cash
Equivalents
15%

Dodge & Cox
International
Stock Index
10%

Annuity
Components
20%

Vanguard Lifetime
Income Program
20%

Stock Components
45%

Fairholme
10%

Vanguard Total
Stock Market
25%

Again, many financial advisers (as well as other fund companies with life-cycle products) would argue that retirees need at least 40 percent to 60 percent of their nest egg in stocks.

The lesson is that as attractive and apparently simple as target-date funds appear, you have to do some homework before picking a product. At a minimum, ask three questions: Am I comfortable with the fund's objectives? (Perhaps the target allocation for stocks at your retirement date is too conservative for you.) How are the fund's assets allocated? (Are there too many investments in the fund? Is there enough international exposure? How are the individual pieces of the fund rated?) And what are the costs involved? (The fees for a good target-date fund should total 1 percent or less of your investment.)

LOCATION — AND REBALANCING

So far, we've been talking about asset allocation, or how to spread your dollars over a number of investments. Equally important is asset *location*—deciding which assets should be in tax-deferred accounts, like 401(k)s and IRAs, and which should be in taxable accounts. The way in which you divide stocks, bonds, real estate and other assets between these accounts can have a big effect on your tax bill and the performance of your holdings. A much-cited study published in 2004 in the *Journal of Finance* found that investors, over a lifetime, could lose as much as 20 percent of their nest egg's after-tax returns simply by placing selected investments in the wrong type of account.

The (very) general guidelines are as follows:

- Stocks go in taxable accounts.

- Bonds go in tax-deferred accounts.

- Cash reserves (like the cushion we discussed) go in taxable accounts.

We called them "very general guidelines" for a couple of reasons. First, Congress keeps changing the federal tax code from one year to the next. Second, the length of time you hold an investment, as well as your tax bracket, could have an effect on the best location for a particular asset. For the most part, though, the guidelines above should serve you well.

What's behind these recommendations? Primarily, the federal government's Jobs and Growth Tax Relief Reconciliation Act of 2003. That measure cut the top tax rates on dividends and capital gains to 15 percent, from 35 percent and 20 percent, respectively. Since stocks (we hope) produce dividends and capital gains, keeping such investments in a taxable account means you can take advantage of the lower tax rates. If stocks, however, are sitting in a retirement account—where withdrawals are taxed at *ordinary* rates—the resulting dividends could be hit with federal levies as high as 35 percent. Conversely, fixed-income investments—like bonds and real-estate trusts—pay interest, which can be taxed at ordinary rates of as much as 35 percent. Consequently, the best way to shield those profits is to keep them in a tax-deferred account.

Jeff Opdyke, our colleague at *The Wall Street Journal*, has provided guidelines regarding where to hold various investments, which are located on page 158. Again, these are rules of thumb; it's always wise to check with a financial planner or tax attorney for advice on your particular situation.

Finally we need to spend a moment talking about rebalancing, the practice of buying *and* selling investments to keep your allocation levels at or near their original targets. Most investors hate to sell "winners" (assets that have increased in value) and are reluctant to buy "losers" (assets that have deceased in value). But that is precisely what rebalancing is all about: selling or reducing your position in investments that have risen in value and using those gains to buy assets that have gone through hard times. Again, we can turn to the bear market of 2000–2002. In the years leading up to that downturn,

Investment	Taxable account	Tax-deferred account	Comment
Annuities	✔		Annuities already are tax-deferred
Corporate bonds		✔	Generally, income is taxed at higher ordinary income rates
Growth stocks/ small-cap stocks	✔		Long-term capital gains are 15%, which are lower than most ordinary income rates
High-yield stocks	✔		Dividends are taxed at 15%, lower than the ordinary income rates you would pay pulling the money later from a tax-deferred account
Municipal bonds	✔		Free from local, state and federal taxes
Real-estate investment trusts (REITs)		✔	Normally, dividends don't qualify for the 15% rate. Thus, REITs should grow tax-deferred
Treasury bonds	✔		Free from local and state taxes

most investors' portfolios had become fat with large-company and technology stocks. But instead of taking some of those gains off the table and investing in assets that had been beaten down, investors stuck with stocks—and lost their shirts when the markets collapsed.

The process of rebalancing is straightforward enough. Let's say your desired allocation (for the sake of simplicity) is 60 percent stocks and 40 percent bonds and a good year in the stock market has left your allocation standing at 68 percent stocks and 32 percent bonds. You would sell 8 percent of your stocks and use that money to buy additional bonds—enough to get you back to the 40 percent level. The problem is that we don't do this. A number of studies have shown that Americans rarely make any trades in their 401(k)s and IRAs, which means we aren't rebalancing. The good news is that additional research has shown that it doesn't matter tremendously when you rebalance (be it every six months or once a year) or how you rebalance (perhaps you stick with precise targets or perhaps you're more comfortable keeping you allocations within some pre-determined boundaries). Rather, it matters only that you do, in fact, rebalance. With that in mind, pick a date—your birthday, the first week of the New Year, April 15 (taxes!)—and rebalance your portfolio at least once a year.

WITHDRAWAL STRATEGIES

Your goal is to tap your nest egg in a sequence that will allow you to (1.) meet your expenses, (2.) minimize taxes and (3.) extend the life of your savings as long as possible.

Let's take a simple example. You have just retired. You have filed for Social Security, but those funds alone won't cover your expenses. You have rolled over your 401(k) into an IRA, where you have carefully allocated your assets among stocks and bonds. You also have a taxable savings account, which holds stock and bond funds and a separate money-market fund, where you are keeping (as you were told!) about three to five years of cash for living expenses. Finally, you have a Roth IRA, which you have been funding for six years. This raises questions: How do you create a stream of income from all these pieces? Which accounts do you tap—and in which order—so that you can continue to buy groceries and go to the movies and visit your grandchildren?

Perhaps you sell a small part of the stock holdings in your IRA, but money withdrawn from an IRA is taxed at ordinary rates, which can mean paying as much as 35 percent. So, perhaps you sell a tiny part of your taxable account—but which part? The bonds? The stocks? Each could result in tax bites of different sizes. Of course, you could make life simple for yourself and withdraw the needed funds from your Roth IRA, where no taxes are due. But the Roth—among all these assets—is the best to leave to your children because they could make tax-free withdrawals from the account for decades.

One answer to all these questions, of course, is to turn to a financial adviser or a mutual-fund company. The Vanguards and T. Rowe Prices of the world are more than happy (for a fee) to allocate your assets and send you a check each month in retirement. We also outline our preferred approach below.

BRING OUT THE BUCKETS

The withdrawal approach favored by us and many financial advisers is called the buckets strategy: You divide your nest egg into several accounts, or buckets, each with a different level of risk. Three buckets is a good place to start. In this case, we'll have the following:

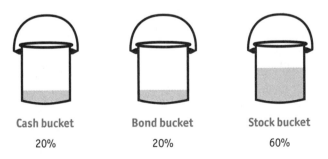

Cash bucket	Bond bucket	Stock bucket
20%	20%	60%

The cash bucket, of course, will hold your cash reserve or cushion—the three to five years of living expenses we discussed earlier. You'll siphon money from this bucket to pay your bills. Over time, of course, the level of cash in this bucket will fall. That's where your bond and stock buckets come into play. The specific *contents* of the bond and stock buckets will reflect the asset allocations we discussed earlier. So, each bucket might contain the following:

Cash bucket	Bond bucket	Stock bucket
Money-market: 20%	Domestic: 15%	Large-company: 25%
	International: 5%	Mid/Small-company: 15%
		International: 10%
		Alternative: 10%

(Note: To simplify this example, we have included alternative investments in our stock bucket.)

Ideally, the contents of the bond and stock buckets will increase in value over time. Periodically, we will dip into the bond or stock buckets to (1.) replenish the cash bucket and/or (2.) rebalance our holdings. In this way, there's a steady stream of funds to meet our spending needs.

It's important to note that we're taking *two* actions here: replenishing and rebalancing. While these two steps might look the same, there's a significant difference—one that involves timing.

Remember, the reason we have a cash reserve in the first place is to avoid having to sell long-term investments (like stocks) every month or two, especially when markets could be falling. We want to give our stocks and bonds time to increase in value for a better chance of maximizing the gains from bull markets and minimizing the losses from bear markets. So, every twelve months or so, we will bring our asset allocations back to their original levels within our bond and stock buckets. For example, after one year, the bond and stock buckets with which we began might look like this:

Cash bucket
Money-market: 17%

Bond bucket
Domestic: 17%
International: 6%

Stock bucket
Large-company: 28%
Mid/Small-company: 12%
International: 10%
Alternative: 10%

Note that our large-company holdings have increased in value—to 28 percent of our nest egg from 25 percent—while the small-company piece of the pie has shrunk slightly, to 12 percent from 15 percent. So, we *rebalance* to our original allocations.

But, at this point, we are not going to *replenish* our cash reserve because there's still about four years of living expenses in that bucket and we want to give our long-term investments as much time as possible to grow. For the time being, we'll accept a slightly fuller bond bucket. At some point—after, say, three years—we will start thinking about *replenishing* our cash reserve. The longer we can wait to do so, the better the chances that our stocks and bonds (our "investment" buckets as opposed to our "cash" bucket) will increase in value.

All of the above is simply a starting point to help you invest a good chunk of your portfolio in stocks for long-term appreciation and to maintain a reliable flow of income even if the stock market turns sour. You should adjust the number of buckets in your system to suit your own needs and preferences.

ACCOUNTING FOR TAXES

Of course, most nest eggs are more complicated. You might have stock funds in an IRA and stock funds in a taxable account. You might have two or three traditional IRAs and a

Roth. Which of these various buckets should be siphoned first—or last? Not only will you need to gauge market conditions in deciding which assets to sell and buy, you'll also need to pay attention to tax efficiency, meaning you should withdraw funds in such a way as to keep most of the money in *your* pocket as opposed to Uncle Sam's.

The traditional method for doing this makes sense for many families:

- First, draw down taxable accounts.

- Second, draw down tax-deferred accounts, like IRAs and 401(k)s.

- Finally, draw funds from a Roth IRA.

You want to tap taxable accounts first because, as the name implies, these investments already are generating gains, such as interest payments or capital gains distributions (if you're holding mutual funds), where taxes can't be avoided. This gives your tax-deferred and tax-free accounts more time to grow. (By definition, these investments should grow faster than taxable accounts because their growth isn't curbed by taxes.)

Next, you should move to tax-deferred accounts, including IRAs. (Of course, after age 70½, you must begin pulling funds from an IRA.) Yes, withdrawals from these accounts will be taxed at ordinary income-tax rates, but again, by turning to these accounts after drawing down taxable investments, you've given your nest egg its best shot at long-term growth. Finally, you can turn to your Roth IRA. Putting off Roth withdrawals for as long as possible gives you a hefty amount of tax-free funds that do not require minimum distributions and that you can pass to your heirs (who can also enjoy tax-free withdrawals).

Of course, there are always exceptions. Here's one example where the tax-deferred account could be tapped first: A man has $1.5 million in his individual retirement account and is turning 70½, the age at which withdrawals from an IRA become mandatory. His required distribution, as we write this, would be almost $55,000, leaving him in the 25 percent tax bracket, assuming a standard deduction.

If, however, the man had withdrawn funds annually from his IRA starting ten years earlier and reached age 70½ with $900,000 in his account, his required distribution would be about $33,000, leaving him in the 15 percent tax bracket. He could have invested the early withdrawals in tax-free municipal bonds or given the money as gifts to children or charity.

Again, this type of scenario argues for spending at least some time with a financial adviser.

CHAPTER 9

PENSIONS, 401(K)S AND IRAS

You gotta love Uncle Sam.

Here's a bit of advice from the federal government regarding withdrawals from your individual retirement account:

"You must receive at least a minimum amount for each year starting with the year you reach age 70½ (your 70½ year). If you do not (or did not) receive that minimum amount in your 70½ year, then you must receive distributions for your 70½ year by April 1 of the next year."

Got that?

The Internal Revenue Service, our employers and most financial institutions seem determined to make the process of getting our hands on our retirement funds as bewildering as possible. (If we had a nickel for every question we receive from *Journal* readers about the "70½ rule"—the age at which required distributions from IRAs kick in—we would be enjoying retirement instead of writing about it.)

In this chapter, we'll discuss the mechanics and the most common mistakes involved in applying for pension benefits and withdrawing funds from a 401(k) and an IRA.

PENSIONS

Although their numbers in the United States are dwindling, about 31,000 pension programs, or "defined-benefit" plans, remain in force. Such plans traditionally paid out a monthly check for life based on your years of service and your salary in the final years of employment. But starting in the early 1990s, growing numbers of companies began offering workers the option of taking their pension in a single, large payment. That decision—whether to "annuitize" a pension in the form of a monthly check or take a "lump sum"—is among the toughest that retirees face. Increasingly, people are opting to take the lump sum, which is a reflection, in part, of the precarious nature of some corporate pension plans.

This may not be a bad decision: Insured pension plans across the country are underfunded by a total of about $350 billion, according to the Pension Benefit Guaranty Corporation, a federal organization that guarantees the payment of basic pension benefits. (The size of the problem is probably worse than that; only those companies whose funding deficits exceed $50 million are required to file reports.)

The annuity versus lump sum debate comes down to a single question: If you take a lump sum, will you be able to convert that money into a steady stream of income that will last as long as you do? (Actually, a second question you might ask yourself is, "Will I have the self-discipline to convert *all* that money into a steady stream of income?" It's funny how pieces of lump sums can "disappear" into new cars, vacations, home improvements and what-not before they're actually put to work for your retirement.) Of course, you might do just fine with a lump sum. After all, millions of Americans already are receiving, in effect, lump sums from their 401(k)s and are starting the process of creating a monthly check in retirement. Still, consider the following before making a choice:

PENSION PLAN CHECKUP

Is your pension plan in good health? Or is it one of hundreds of defined-benefit plans nationwide that are underfunded? Here's how to check:

- To find out if your plan is insured by the Pension Benefit Guaranty Corporation, ask your employer or the plan administrator for a copy of the "Summary Plan Description," which states if your particular plan is covered.

- Most plans *are* insured, although plans offered by "professional service employers" (like doctors and lawyers) with fewer than twenty-six employees usually are not.

- The provider of your pension is required to give you written notice annually if the plan has been less than 80 percent funded for the past year or two and less than 90 percent funded for several years.

- You also have the right to request, in writing, information about your plan's funding from your plan administrator.

Source: Pension Benefit Guaranty Corp.

ANNUITY VS. LUMP SUM

The annuity crowd has two sizable advantages. First, assuming your pension plan is in good health, the income from an annuity is guaranteed for life; there's no risk of "outliving your savings." That sense of security—when the alternative means grappling with the stock and bond markets—is no small consideration, particularly if you have a spouse. You can choose a payment plan that provides a monthly check for as long as you live, and, after you're gone, for as long as your spouse lives.

The second big advantage is convenience. Someone else

is doing the work of calculating, funding and issuing your monthly check. Choosing an annuity also can be a wise move if you have other financial resources, like a taxable savings account or an existing IRA, that could provide the growth needed in your nest egg while the annuity delivers a steady stream of income. Finally, the lump sum is based on *average* life expectancy; if your family has a history of longevity, an annuity could reduce the risk of running out of cash.

When it comes to a lump sum, the primary advantages are control and flexibility. Most people transfer the money to an IRA, which means thousands of investment options and, ideally, an opportunity to earn a better return on your money than if you had opted for an annuity. Meanwhile, selecting well-diversified investments should help you keep pace with, or outpace, inflation—in contrast to annuity payments, which are fixed. (Consider that the purchasing power of a fixed monthly check would be cut roughly in half in just eighteen years at an inflation rate of 4 percent.)

Other advantages with a lump sum include the ability to invest part of the money and use the balance to buy an annuity from a commercial insurer, a possible best-of-both-worlds approach. In an emergency, a lump sum means you have quick access to a big chunk of money. And a lump sum, of course, can be included in your estate and left to beneficiaries, which you can't do with an annuity.

Running the Numbers

Let's say your company gives you a choice of collecting $1,600 a month starting at age sixty-five or a lump sum of $250,000. Which do you pick? The answer, in part, will depend on current interest rates and what might be available in the commercial market for annuities.

Start by visiting a Web site that prices annuities, such as www.immediateannuities.com. Here, you can evaluate a company's pension offer by calculating what your employer's lump sum might yield if you purchased an annuity on your own. For a sixty-five-year-old man, investing $250,000 in an annuity with a commercial insurer would generate a monthly check of almost $1,800; thus the employer's lump-sum offer appears to be the better deal than the $1,600 monthly check.

This is also where interest rates come in: Low rates at the time you retire mean that your company plan has to allot a large amount upfront to provide the needed return for your monthly check. And your retirement plan would have to pay you that larger amount as your lump sum, meaning there's a good chance the lump sum will be the more attractive offer.

The final decision, of course, would involve all the issues we raised above: security, control, flexibility, financial skills, inheritance plans, etc. Because this is one of the most important choices—not to mention one of the biggest piles of money you will see—in your financial life, we recommend consulting a financial adviser. Once you have picked an annuity or a lump sum, the decision is irrevocable, so you want to be sure of your choice.

ADVANTAGES:

Annuity Payment	Lump Sum
Guaranteed income for life	Chance for better returns
Simplicity	Access to cash
Protection for spouse	Money can be left to heirs
Hedge against longevity	Hedge against inflation

DISADVANTAGES:

Annuity Payment	Lump Sum
No inflation protection	Income tied to investing skills
No control over assets	Risk of running out of money

If you choose an annuity, you still have some additional decisions to make, primarily involving your spouse. If you choose a "life-only" annuity, payments end when you die. A "joint-and-survivor" annuity (or "joint-life" annuity) provides a monthly payment for you and for your spouse in the event of your death, but monthly payments are smaller. The list of annuity options involving spouses can be quite lengthy. Some examples include the following:

Annuity	Your monthly benefit	Surviving spouse's monthly benefit
Life only	$1,489	
Joint and 50%	$1,432	$716
Joint and 75%	$1,388	$1,041
Joint and 100%	$1,306	$1,306

Each of these options should be considered in the light of other assets and insurance policies that might be available to a surviving wife or husband. Not surprisingly, most couples with access to a pension take some form of joint-and-survivor annuity; indeed, your spouse is usually required to give his or her written consent if you choose a payout *other* than a joint-life plan.

401(k)s

A 401(k), which is named for the section of the Tax Code that describes it, is the single biggest piece of most workers' retirement savings plans. In 1997, assets held in 401(k)s, or "defined contribution" plans, first surpassed those held in traditional pensions; today, Americans have about $2.55 trillion invested in 401(k)s, compared with about $1.87 trillion in pensions, according to the Employee Benefit Research Institute. Building a 401(k) is relatively easy: Uncle Sam allows you to contribute a portion of your pre-tax salary, which is often augmented by contributions from your employer.

The trick comes in getting the money *out* of a 401(k). The Internal Revenue Service purposely makes it hard (or, at the very least, expensive) to do so before age 59½. And even after that age, mistakes or omissions in tapping a 401(k) can lead to some nasty tax bills. Let's look at the ways in which you can open these accounts.

BEFORE 59½ . . .

Before you retire, you can take a loan from your 401(k), though employers usually limit loans to those paying for medical or educational expenses or buying a house. Usually, you can borrow up to $50,000 or one-half of your vested account balance, whichever figure is smaller. Most loans must be paid back within five years, unless the loan is used to buy a house.

Still, a 401(k) should be one of the last sources, if not *the* last, from which to borrow money. There are three important reasons for this. First, you're costing yourself an enormous amount of interest. (When you borrow money from a 401(k), your nest egg is smaller and earns less money.) Second, you pay back the loan with *after*-tax money (in contrast to contributions to a 401(k), which are made with *pre*-tax dollars). Third, the loan isn't tax deductible. In short, if you need to borrow money, a home-equity loan (with which you can deduct the interest on your taxes) is often a better solution.

If taking a loan from a 401(k) is a bad idea, making a plain-vanilla withdrawal from your account before age 59½ is even worse. You immediately get hit with federal taxes on the withdrawal and with a 10 percent penalty called an "early-distribution tax." That said, there is one big exception to this rule that most people don't know: If you leave your employer (whether you jump or get pushed) after reaching age 55, but before 59½, you can make withdrawals of any size from your 401(k) without paying the 10 percent penalty. Note: You still owe taxes on the money withdrawn, and your 401(k) plan might restrict the frequency of withdrawals.

This exception is a major difference between a 401(k) and an individual retirement account. And while we don't recommend withdrawing money from any retirement savings account before you retire, if you're pushed out of a job after age fifty-five and if cash is tight, it's nice to know you can turn to your 401(k) without the threat of penalties and without having to calculate or withdraw specified amounts.

. . . And After 59½

Once you turn 59½ and decide to retire, most 401(k) plans offer the following options:

- Take a lump sum and
  - Keep the money and pay the taxes
  - Roll the funds over to an IRA
  - Roll part of the funds over to an IRA and keep the balance
- Convert your holdings to an annuity
- Keep your funds in the company plan

As with deciding between a lump sum or an annuity with a pension, this decision will rank among the most important in your financial life. Most people will roll over their 401(k) assets to an IRA, where they can continue to defer taxes or begin the process of creating a paycheck in retirement. But . . . Perhaps you have a large medical bill or other significant debt hanging over your head, and you wish to pay that off. Perhaps you prefer the comfort and security of an annuity. Perhaps you're content with the investment choices in your existing company plan and how your nest egg has grown. Any of these circumstances might argue against the "conventional" step of an IRA rollover. And each situation illustrates why you should sound out as many people as possible—a financial adviser, your retirement plan administrator at work, a tax attorney, etc.—before moving or tapping the assets in your 401(k). When it comes to retirement distributions, the more input, the better.

Let's quickly go over the pros and cons of each step, based on guidance from Marvin Rotenberg, director of individual retirement services for Bank of America's Retirement Solutions Group.

401(k) MANEUVERS

Cashing Out

ADVANTAGES

- Funds could be used to pay off large bills or credit-card debt
- People born before 1936 can qualify for tax breaks

DISADVANTAGES

- Savings can no longer grow tax deferred
- All money withdrawn is subject to federal income tax
- Withdrawal could be subject to state and local taxes

Converting to an Annuity

ADVANTAGES

- Guaranteed income for life
- Protection for spouse (if spousal benefit is selected)
- Hedge against longevity

DISADVANTAGES

- Little or no inflation protection
- No control over assets

Keeping Money in Company Plan

ADVANTAGES

- Familiarity with investment choices and management
- Assets are protected from creditors
- Mandatory withdrawals can be delayed beyond age 70½ if you're still working
- Opportunity to retain life insurance, if included in plan
- Ability to borrow from account

DISADVANTAGES

- Limited investment choices
- Limited access to funds
- Little control over investment fees

Rolling Over to an IRA

ADVANTAGES

- Assets continue to grow tax deferred
- Maximum flexibility in designing portfolio and choosing investments
- Hedge against inflation
- Maximum flexibility in naming beneficiaries
- Traditional IRA can be converted to a Roth IRA if income requirements are met

DISADVANTAGES

- Income tied to investing skills
- Required withdrawals begin at age 70½
- Creditor protection varies by state
- Life insurance can't be held in an IRA
- Loans are prohibited

Source: By Ed Slott, CPA, IRA Specialist, host of www.irahelp.com, and author of Your Complete Retirement Planning Roadmap *(Ballantine Books: 2007) and publisher of* "Ed Slott's IRA Advisor"

A partial rollover of your IRA funds would tend to have the same advantages and disadvantages of both a full rollover and of cashing out.

If you opt to roll over the assets in your 401(k) to an IRA, arrange for a direct transfer. Until 1992, the Internal Revenue Service allowed you to take rollover money in the form of a check made out to you, at which point you had sixty days to deposit the funds in your new account. Today, collecting a check will cost you dearly. First, your company will automatically withhold 20 percent of your check, which goes directly to the IRS. And if you fail to move the 401(k) funds to your new account within sixty days, you have to pay income tax on the entire amount. Suffice it to say, always—always—arrange for any rollover to be transferred directly from your retirement plan to your new IRA. (This is sometimes called a "trustee-to-trustee transfer," a "custodian-to-custodian transfer" or, simply, a "direct rollover.") As long as you don't handle the money, taxes won't be part of the equation.

Finally, if you have company stock in your 401(k) plan, take a big step back before you roll it into an IRA or before you make any withdrawal, at any age, of any assets from the plan. A little-known tax break for what's known as "net unrealized appreciation" allows you to pull out some or all of your shares in the company where you work at the same time that you roll the rest of your assets into an IRA. The big advantage is that any increase in the stock price after you originally acquired the shares would be subject only to long-term capital-gains tax, with a maximum 15 percent rate, rather than ordinary income tax, which can be as high as 35 percent. You still have to pay income tax on the original purchase amount, or "cost basis," but you wouldn't owe any capital-gains tax until you sell the stock.

Note: You have one chance to do this. You're no longer eligible once you take any distributions from your company retirement plan, including required distributions from your company plan after age 70½. Also make sure that both parts of the transaction—the withdrawal of the stock and the rollover of any remaining assets into an IRA—are completed in the same year. Otherwise, the IRS could deny the tax break.

INDIVIDUAL RETIREMENT ACCOUNTS

As IRAs have become increasingly important, Uncle Sam is watching more closely. They make up almost 26 percent of the $14.5 trillion U.S. retirement market, according to the Investment Company Institute. Assets held in IRAs are increasing on average 13 percent a year, a growth rate that's expected to continue accelerating. As of 2004, institutions holding IRAs are required to report annually to the IRS if you have to make a withdrawal from your account.

Withdrawing money from an IRA—initials that actually stand for "individual retirement arrangements," though "accounts" is the common usage—without running afoul of the Internal Revenue Service is no easy task. Rules vary for traditional accounts versus Roth IRAs and for distributions from your own IRA versus one you inherit. On top of that, the rules get tweaked from time to time, with some big revisions a few years ago still roiling many IRA owners and inheritors.

Here's what you need to know to help avoid IRA angst.

EARLY WITHDRAWALS

The lifespan of an IRA can be divided into three parts: from the time an account is first opened to the point when you reach age 59½; from 59½ to age 70½; and from 70½ and beyond. Withdrawals from an account before age 59½ normally result in a 10 percent penalty in addition to a tax bill. Withdrawals in the years between 59½ and 70½ are the easiest: There's no penalty, and the withdrawals may be as big or as small as you wish. (Of course, you still have to pay taxes.) After age 70½, you must begin taking specified withdrawals each year based on your life expectancy; these withdrawals are known (in IRS speak) as "required minimum distributions," or RMDs.

It is possible to take regular payments from your IRA before age 59½ and avoid paying the 10 percent penalty if you're willing to follow some strict guidelines. Section 72(t) in the federal Tax Code permits "substantially equal" withdrawals before age 59½ without penalty if you use one of three methods approved by the IRS to calculate the size of the withdrawals. Once you have determined (using one of the three methods) how much money you can pull from your account each year, withdrawals must continue for at least five years or until you turn 59½, whichever period is longer. So, if you start tapping your IRA at age fifty, you're on the hook for 9½ years; if you start at age fifty-seven, you would have to take withdrawals until you turned sixty-two.

So-called 72(t) payments can be risky. If you begin drawing down your retirement savings in, say, your early fifties, your nest egg might not last as long as you do. And the federal government doesn't look kindly upon mistakes made with 72(t) payments. If you take out too much money, or too little, in any given year, all your withdrawals up to that point will be hit with a 10 percent penalty—as well as interest on the penalty. In short, if you think you need or want to make early withdrawals from an IRA, you should work with a financial adviser, an accountant or an IRA custodian familiar with 72(t) payments to set up your plan.

REQUIRED MINIMUM DISTRIBUTIONS

While Uncle Sam tries hard to discourage you from taking any money out of an IRA before age 59½, he changes his tune after you hit 70½. At that point, assuming you haven't already started making withdrawals, the federal government requires that you start pulling out money and begin paying taxes.

Lots of people trip over the 70½ rule, primarily because they

If you turn 70½ on this date:	You have until this date to make your first withdrawal:
January 1, 2008	April 1, 2009
April 1, 2008	April 1, 2009
December 31, 2008	April 1, 2009

think withdrawals from an IRA must begin precisely on the day they turn 70½. In fact, you have until April 1 of the year *after* you turn 70½ to make your first withdrawal, a date known as your "required beginning date."

As you can see, a person could have as long as fifteen months, or as little as three months, before his or her first RMD. After the first withdrawal, the annual deadline for all future withdrawals is December 31.

Note: You don't have to wait until April 1 of the year after you turn 70½ to make that first required withdrawal; if you wish, you can take the RMD in the same year that you reach the magic number. If you *do* wait until the next calendar year to start pulling out money, you will have to make *two* withdrawals from your account that year: one for the year in which you turned 70½ and one for the current calendar year.

So, to use our example above:

- A person who turns 70½ on January 1, 2008, has until April 1, 2009, to make his or her first RMD.

- If he or she decides to wait until April 1, 2009, that first withdrawal—in the eyes of the IRS—will be for 2008.

- That person will then have until December 31, 2009, to make his or her RMD for 2009. The result is two required withdrawals in one calendar year.

There's one potential problem with taking two withdrawals in the same year: You will have to report both withdrawals on your tax return for that year. If you have a large IRA, two withdrawals in a single year could bump you into a higher tax bracket.

If you fail to take a required minimum distribution by the appropriate deadline, you'll wind up paying a penalty of 50 percent on the amount of money you should have withdrawn. So, if your required withdrawal for this year is $8,000 and you don't take the money by December 31, the penalty totals $4,000. You can, of course, withdraw more than the required minimum from your account each year, but the excess does *not* count toward the following year's required withdrawal. And if you're working at age 70½, you still must take an RMD from a traditional IRA, which differs from defined contribution programs, like a 401(k), which do not require a withdrawal as long as you're still working.

To calculate your RMD, simply take your account balance at the end of the previous year and divide it by the life-expectancy figure from this "Uniform Lifetime" table provided by the IRS:

Age	Life Expectancy	Age	Life Expectancy
70	27.4	93	9.6
71	26.5	94	9.1
72	25.6	95	8.6
73	24.7	96	8.1
74	23.8	97	7.6
75	22.9	98	7.1
76	22.0	99	6.7
77	21.2	100	6.3
78	20.3	101	5.9
79	19.5	102	5.5
80	18.7	103	5.2
81	17.9	104	4.9
82	17.1	105	4.5
83	16.3	106	4.2
84	15.5	107	3.9
85	14.8	108	3.7
86	14.1	109	3.4
87	13.4	110	3.1
88	12.7	111	2.9
89	12.0	112	2.6
90	11.4	113	2.4
91	10.8	114	2.1
92	10.2	115-plus	1.9

So, let's say you are turning 70½ on October 1, 2008, and you decide to take your first RMD before the end of that year. (You have decided that you don't want to be in a position where you have to take two withdrawals in 2009.) And let's say your IRA balance at the end of 2007 was $300,000. You take that figure and divide by 27.4—the life-expectancy factor from the IRS table. The result—$10,948.91—is what you must withdraw from your IRA by December 31. It's also the amount you include on your federal tax return for (in this case) 2008. If you have more than one IRA account, you simply add the balances of all the accounts and divide by the appropriate life-expectancy figure. You can then withdraw that amount from a single account or from several accounts.

Note: There is one exception to using the table: If you

have named your spouse as the sole beneficiary of your IRA and he or she is more than ten years younger than you, calculate your required minimum withdrawal using a second table provided by the IRS: a "Joint Life and Last Survivor Table." See the sources listed at the end of this chapter for a link to this table—and always double check for the latest IRS information.

Most IRA custodians will calculate the amount of a required minimum distribution for you. But, to be safe, you or your financial adviser should verify the math. If a custodian makes a mistake that results in too little money being withdrawn from an IRA (which could result in a penalty) or too much being withdrawn (which could push you into a higher tax bracket), you are the one who has to deal with the consequences.

Roth IRAs

Since their introduction in 1998, Roth IRAs have ranked among the best deals in retirement planning. As most people know, there are three big differences—and advantages—when it comes to comparing a traditional IRA and a Roth. First, once you reach age 59½ and once your Roth account is at least five years old, you will never pay taxes on your gains or withdrawals, as opposed to a traditional IRA, from which withdrawals are taxed. Second, you are not required to withdraw funds from a Roth after age 70½ (or at any age, for that matter) as you are with a traditional IRA. Third, a Roth makes a great present for your heirs because withdrawals are tax-free. If you inherit a traditional IRA, you pay taxes on withdrawals.

The tricky part of the Roth universe is the notion of "conversion." Uncle Sam allows you to convert a traditional IRA to a Roth, but your modified adjusted gross income in the year of conversion must be less than $100,000, and you have to pay taxes on the sum converted. Here's the question you have to ask yourself: Will I be better off converting to a Roth today—

and paying taxes *now*—in order to enjoy tax-free withdrawals down the road, or will I be better off leaving the money in my traditional IRA, where it can continue to grow tax-deferred, and pay taxes on withdrawals *later,* when I'm older and/or retired? The answer depends on your tax bracket in retirement relative to your current tax bracket. Let's look at the most frequent questions surrounding conversions and taxes and at some related issues:

WHAT IF I'M IN A HIGH TAX BRACKET TODAY AND EXPECT TO BE IN A LOWER TAX BRACKET IN RETIREMENT?

This situation might argue *against* a conversion. The conversion would cost you more in taxes today, because you're in that high tax bracket, than it would in, say, ten years, when withdrawals from your traditional IRA would be taxed at that lower rate.

WHAT IF THE SITUATION WERE REVERSED? WHAT IF I'M IN A RELATIVELY LOW TAX BRACKET TODAY AND EXPECT TO BE IN A HIGHER BRACKET IN RETIREMENT?

That might argue *in favor* of a conversion. You would be withdrawing money tax-free from your Roth IRA at a time—again, say, in ten years—when your tax rate is higher.

WHAT ABOUT MY PLANNED START DATE FOR TAPPING A ROTH IRA? HOW MIGHT THAT AFFECT MY DECISION TO CONVERT?

The more time your account has to grow, the bigger the advantage of tax-free withdrawals. A rule of thumb is that any conversion should be made at least five years before you plan to tap your IRA.

Where Will I Get the Money to Pay the Taxes on the Conversion?

If you can't pay the taxes from a source *other* than the IRA itself, you probably shouldn't convert. Doing so would put a large dent in your next egg, which defeats the purpose. Again, the larger your Roth and the longer it can grow, the bigger the advantage of tax-free withdrawals.

Let's take a look at the following conversion examples from T. Rowe Price:

Age	Amount transferred to new Roth IRA	Taxes due	Total after-tax withdrawals for a retirement starting at age 65 and lasting 30 years	
			Traditional IRA	Roth IRA
45	$25,000	$7,188	$219,348	$239,585
55	$50,000	$14,375	$208,415	$221,948

As you can see, each person benefits from converting to a Roth. The forty-five-year-old, after reaching age sixty-five, ends up withdrawing $239,585 during a thirty-year retirement—or $20,237 more in after-tax income than if he or she simply had stuck with a traditional IRA. The same is true for the fifty-five-year-old, but because he or she waited longer to convert, the total size of the withdrawals from the Roth IRA over a thirty-year period ($221,948) and the net gain when compared with the traditional IRA ($13,533) are smaller. This is the case despite the fact that our fifty-five-year-old converted a much larger sum of money ($50,000). Again, this illustrates the advantage you can gain by converting early.

Now, let's see how the results might differ if the tax brackets change. The figures above assume a 25 percent federal tax rate and a 5 percent state tax rate, both before and after retirement. The following chart looks at total withdrawals from a traditional IRA and a Roth IRA when federal tax rates in retirement are 15 percent, 25 percent and 35 percent:

45-YEAR-OLD	15%	25%	35%
Traditional IRA	**$242,416**	$219,348	**$196,282**
Roth IRA	$239,585	$239,585	$239,585
55-YEAR-OLD	15%	25%	35%
Traditional IRA	**$229,814**	$208,415	**$187,017**
Roth IRA	$221,948	$221,948	$221,948

Note that the total withdrawals in retirement from both Roth IRAs are unchanged from our first set of numbers because withdrawals from a Roth IRA are tax-free. But look at the numbers for the traditional IRAs at the extremes of our tax brackets. When taxes are low in retirement—15 percent, in the first case—our two individuals would have benefited from *not* converting to a Roth; the forty-five-year-old ended up with almost $3,000 more in withdrawals from a traditional IRA during a thirty-year retirement, and the fifty-five-year-old ended up with an additional $7,900. Again, that's because the big tax bite at the time of the conversion—when each person was hit with 25 percent in federal taxes and 5 percent in state taxes— did more damage to each person's nest egg in the long run than the 15 percent tax rate on withdrawals in retirement. Now, look at what happens when tax rates increase in retirement. At 35 percent (compared with 25 percent before retirement), converting to a Roth is clearly the better strategy for the long run. The forty-five-year-old ends up with an additional $43,300 in after-tax income, while the fifty-five-year-old ends up with almost $35,000.

One way to minimize the tax bite in conversions is to transfer small pieces of a traditional IRA to a Roth over a period of years. Let's say you're sixty-four years old and you have just retired. You have no earned income and you plan to delay filing for Social Security benefits until you're sixty-seven or older. At this point in your retirement, you likely will find yourself in a very low tax bracket for several years, so it is an ideal time to

CONVERSION TOOLS

The following online calculators can give you a rough idea about the wisdom of converting a traditional IRA to a Roth IRA:

www.dinkytown.net
KJE Computer Solutions—Financial Calculators
Click on "View all retirement calculators." Then, click on "Roth IRA Conversion."

www.fincalc.com
Financial Calculators Inc.
Click on "ConsumerCalcs." Under "Qualified Plans," click on "Should I convert to a Roth IRA?"

www.fool.com
The Motley Fool
Under "Personal Finance," click on "Calculators." Under "Roth IRA," click on "Should I convert my IRA to a Roth?"

www.moneycentral.msn.com
MSN Money
Under "Planning," click on "Retirement and Wills." Then, under "Retirement Tools," click on "Roth IRA Calculator."

www.morningstar.com
Morningstar Inc.
Click on "Tools." Under "Financial Calculators," click on "IRA Calculator."

www.principal.com
Principal Financial Group
Under "Tools," click on "Calculators." Under "Calculators," click on "Roth IRA." Under "Calculators," click on "Should I convert my IRA into a Roth IRA?"

www.smartmoney.com

SmartMoney magazine

Under "Personal Finance," click on "Retirement." Under "IRAs," click on "To Convert or Not."

www.tiaa-cref.org

TIAA-CREF Individual and Institutional Services

Click on "Planning Tools." Under "Select a Product," click on "Roth IRA Conversion Calculator."

www.irs.gov/publications/p590/index.html

IRS Publication 590, "Individual Retirement Arrangements"

This is the federal guide to IRAs and conversions. Another good resource is the book *Fairmark Guide to the Roth IRA,* by Kaye A. Thomas (Fairmark Press Inc.), which walks you through the process.

begin converting your traditional IRA, piece by piece, to a Roth. This assumes that you have other retirement savings (a taxable account, for instance) that will allow you to pay the rent in the interim. The downside is that the math involved in piece-meal conversions can be daunting.

You should also know that the rules will change again in 2010. At that point (under tax legislation passed in 2006), restrictions on income eligibility for Roth IRA conversions will be eliminated so that anyone with an IRA, including individuals whose modified adjusted gross income exceeds $100,000, will be able to convert to a Roth. What's more, you will be able to spread the taxes due on a conversion across your 2011 and 2012 tax bills.

In the long run, many investors will benefit from a conversion. But, as with most decisions involving the biggest chunks

DON'T PAY DOUBLE TAXES

If you're thinking about converting your traditional IRA to a Roth IRA, you'll want to avoid "double taxation."

With a traditional IRA, you can make contributions of as much as $4,000 a year (or $5,000 if you are age 50 or older) and deduct that figure from your taxes if (1.) you have no retirement plan at work or (2.) if you do have a retirement plan and (for tax year 2007) you make no more than $52,000 a year ($83,000 for married couples filing a joint return). If you don't fall into either category, you still can put money in a traditional IRA, but the contributions are nondeductible; you're making deposits with after-tax dollars.

That distinction—between deductible and non-deductible contributions—becomes important when you go to convert a traditional IRA to a Roth. The Internal Revenue Service tells us that we can convert all or part of a traditional IRA and that we have to pay income tax on any money that's converted. But let's say you have non-deductible, or after-tax, contributions in your traditional IRA. How can you convert these contributions to a Roth without being taxed a second time?

For example, a retiree has two IRAs, one that contains $200,000 rolled over from his or her employer's 401(k) and a second account, opened years earlier, with a balance of $50,000. The latter contains $40,000 in non-deductible contributions. As much as our retiree might wish, he or she can't convert the $40,000 alone—tax-free—to a Roth IRA.

Rather, he or she has to follow what's called the "pro-rata rule." This means a person must first add the balances in *all* of his or her IRAs—in this case, $250,000. Then, non-deductible contributions are divided by that total: $40,000 divided by $250,000. This gives the percentage—16%, in our example—of any conversion that's tax-free.

So, let's say our retiree wants to convert $30,000 of his or her two IRAs to a Roth. He or she multiples the $30,000 by 0.16 and comes up with $4,800, the amount of the conversion that would be tax-free.

of your nest egg, you would do well to spend some time with a financial adviser.

SELF-DIRECTED IRAS

We can't end our discussion of IRAs without taking note of one of the newest, most popular and riskiest strategies for increasing the value of your nest egg: so-called self-directed IRAs.

Unlike traditional IRAs, self-directed IRAs enable their owners to pursue a wide variety of investments well outside the scope of the usual holdings, including everything from putting IRA dollars into urban loft developments and mortgage notes to starting a small business. The problem is that many self-directed accounts are accidents waiting to happen. Perhaps the biggest risk is "self dealing." According to the federal government, an IRA is supposed to provide for your future retirement, meaning you shouldn't benefit from the investment before you start making withdrawals in retirement. So, if you use IRA money to buy an asset that you currently use (say, a vacation home or an apartment for a child in college), it could be in violation of tax law and the IRS could step in and simply disqualify the IRA, resulting in huge tax bills along with additional penalties for account holders who are younger than age 59½.

To set up a self-directed IRA, the holder of a traditional IRA simply opens an account with a custodian or an administrator specializing in self-directed IRAs and transfers the holdings. The IRA holder then seeks out investments himself or herself and directs the custodian to cut a check to buy them. A handful of custodial and administration firms specialize in handling self-directed IRAs, though most large investment companies don't handle the accounts. Some banks will also set them up for longtime customers. Annual costs, which can run $1,000 or more, typically include a custodial fee and transaction fees.

If you are considering opening a self-directed IRA—and again, the risks might far outweigh the value—first talk, at length, with a financial adviser, an accountant or a tax attorney. If, after listening to their advice, you *still* want to pursue this strategy, the following steps could help minimize any damage to your account and your sanity:

Split Your IRA

When opening a self-directed IRA, transfer only part of your existing retirement account into the new self-directed account. That way, if the investments in the self-directed IRA fail or if you run into regulatory problems, you haven't put your entire nest egg at risk.

Get Advance Approval

To determine *beforehand* whether your plans might be considered self-dealing, you can ask the Department of Labor for a "prohibited transaction" ruling. (In practice, you hire an attorney, who asks for a review of your plans from the Labor Department. The Labor Department has a role in this because of its oversight of pension plans.) In short, you might be able to obtain a seal of approval for your plans before you set up a self-directed IRA.

Bring in Outside Investors

If you use a self-directed IRA to start and operate a small business, bringing in independent investors with a big stake might make it possible for you to draw a salary—or at least cut down on possible self-dealing problems.

CHAPTER 10

Social Security and Medicare

ocial Security was never meant to be the primary source of income for people entering retirement. But today, for about 20 percent of Americans age sixty-five-plus, their monthly check from Uncle Sam is the only income they get. And fully two-thirds of beneficiaries rely on Social Security for more than half their income.

The situation is similar with Medicare, the federal insurance program for retiree medical care. In the past, Medicare worked hand-in-hand with the private health insurance that many retirees were lucky enough to get through their former employers. But that benefit is drying up—and even folks who still have such benefits are contributing ever larger parts of the premiums each year. Such employer cutbacks are leaving more retirees with Medicare as their sole source of health insurance in later life.

Government benefits are so important to retirees, thinking about them is a crucial part of retirement planning. Two reasons keep people from giving Social Security and Medicare the consideration they deserve. First, many people assume that

Social Security and Medicare are one-size-fits-all benefits, and that they don't have a say in how those benefits work. Second, there have been so many predictions about the programs' eventual collapse that people figure they should simply try to eek a few dollars out of Social Security before it falls apart. If you're thinking along these lines, it's time to think again. If you're already in your fifties, stop worrying about whether Social Security or Medicare will disappear, and focus instead on how to get the most out of the system for your own retirement.

SOCIAL SECURITY

Let's tackle Social Security first. To keep things simple, we're talking only about retirement benefits, not disability benefits, because disability benefits are not restricted by your age. Before we get into the ways to take your benefits, it's important to understand that most of the money in the Social Security system comes from you and your employer through payroll taxes. But there's no vault in Washington, D.C., holding a special account with your name on it. Your money already paid your Aunt Marge's benefits. Now, you're counting on younger workers to pay for yours. You're probably aware that great controversy surrounds the health of the Social Security system and whether private accounts are needed to save it, but for now, we'll leave that question to the inside-the-beltway think tanks and instead assume that, if you're already at least fifty years old, you'll be collecting benefits.

WHEN CAN YOU COLLECT?

Since Social Security plays such an important role in so many people's retirements, one of the most important financial decisions you can make is when to start collecting benefits. You have three choices: First, you can take early benefits any time between your sixty-second birthday and the date you reach what the Social Security Administration calls your normal, or full, retirement age. Doing so results in a *permanent* reduction in your monthly check. (See the chart on page 192.) Seventy-two percent of current beneficiaries receive reduced benefits because they started them before their full retirement age. Realistically, you may not have much choice. You could be pressured into early retirement by your employer or forced to quit working due to health reasons. But if you have more flexibility, the best financial deal for most retirees is to delay activating your regular Social Security payments as long as possible, according to growing numbers of accountants and financial planners.

Starting your payments at your full retirement age is another choice. Sixty-five used to be the age for collecting an unreduced benefit, but the government is gradually moving the benchmark to sixty-seven for people born in or after 1960. As the age at which you can collect full benefits is pushed later, the reduction for taking benefits early gets bigger. That's because you theoretically get the same amount of money from Social Security across your lifetime; depending on when you file for benefits, the government gives you smaller payments spread over a longer time—or larger payments spread over a shorter time.

Finally, you can wait beyond your full retirement age to file for benefits, postponing your check as late as your seventieth birthday and collecting *more* than 100 percent of your full retirement benefits each month as a result. (After age seventy, the monthly benefit no longer increases by postponing benefits.)

To compare the three scenarios, a person who would have received $2,000 a month by filing for benefits at the full retirement age of sixty-six would get $1,500 by starting payments at age sixty-two—or $2,640 by waiting until age seventy.

What if you like the idea of delaying Social Security, but you've already claimed benefits? There's a provision under the

YOUR AGE AND SOCIAL SECURITY

Your year of birth determines when you can start collecting full benefits—
and how much of a reduction you have to take to start collecting early.

Year of birth	Full retirement age	Age 62 reduction (in months)	Total percent reduction	A $1,000 benefit would shrink to . . .
1937 or earlier	65	36 months	20%	$800
1938	65 and 2 months	38	20.83	791
1939	65 and 4 months	40	21.67	783
1940	65 and 6 months	42	22.50	775
1941	65 and 8 months	44	23.33	766
1942	65 and 10 months	46	24.17	758
1943-1954	66	48	25.00	750
1955	66 and 2 months	50	25.83	741
1956	66 and 4 months	52	26.67	733
1957	66 and 6 months	54	27.50	725
1958	66 and 8 months	56	28.33	716
1959	66 and 10 months	58	29.17	708
1960 and later	67	60	30.00	700

Source: Social Security Administration

Senior Citizens' Freedom to Work Act of 2000 that lets you stop benefits, repay the money you have collected so far, and later restart Social Security. (Keep in mind, though, that if you have paid tax on the benefits you have received thus far, you would have to file amended tax returns to try to reclaim the taxes paid.)

There are all sorts of calculators at www.socialsecurity.gov to help you get started crunching the numbers. One important tool at that site is a "break-even" age calculator, which addresses one of the most common questions among retirees: If

I wait until my full retirement age to file for Social Security benefits, at what point in time will my *total* payments match—and begin to exceed—payments starting at age sixty-two? That calculator is at www.ssa.gov/OACT/quickcalc/when2retire. html.

DELAYING SOCIAL SECURITY

If you postpone your Social Security payments past your full retirement age, here are the increases you can expect:

YEAR OF BIRTH	ANNUAL RATE OF INCREASE
1933–34	5.5%
1935–36	6
1937–38	6.5
1939–40	7
1941–42	7.5
1943 or later	8

Note that the increases end when you reach age seventy; if you were born on January 1, you should refer to the rate of increase for the previous year.

Source: Social Security Administration

WHEN SHOULD YOU COLLECT?

There are four big factors involved in deciding when to start Social Security: your individual life expectancy, the way your benefit and other investment income will affect your taxes, the life expectancy and earnings history of your spouse and whether you plan to keep working—or start working again—in retirement.

Don't underestimate how long you might live. To be sure, you should take early benefits if your health is poor. But, increasingly, illnesses like heart disease, which claimed our parents and grandparents in their sixties and seventies, are becoming chronic conditions that the health-care system can help manage. In other words, you could be here—paying medical bills and other expenses—longer than you imagine. As such, it might be nice to hold out for a bigger check each month from Social Security. To get a better sense of overall life expectancy, first look at the Social Security Administration's "Period Life Table" at www.ssa.gov/OACT/STATS/table4c6.html. This shows the average life expectancies for all Americans from ages 0 to 119. At age sixty-two, for example, the average man can expect to live an additional eighteen years, and a woman an additional twenty-one. Then, to find out how you stack up, go to a site like www.livingto100.com and fill out a detailed questionnaire to estimate your individual life expectancy. Whatever number you settle on, keep in mind that it's an average, meaning you have a 50 percent chance of outliving that number.

Beware of the stealth tax. Generally speaking, Social Security payments are not taxed, but that changes when you reach certain income thresholds. Up to 85 percent of your Social Security benefit could be taxable if a combination of your other income plus 50 percent of your Social Security adds up to more than $25,000 if you're single or $32,000 if you're married and file a joint tax return. These numbers become important when you begin tapping other retirement accounts. For instance, taking Social Security early—and delaying withdrawals from tax-deferred retirement accounts (including IRAs and 401(k)s) until later in life—could bump you into a higher tax bracket when you start making those withdrawals after age seventy and a half, resulting in steep taxes. (For more on those withdrawals, see Chapter Nine.)

One way to minimize such taxes is to live off your retirement accounts in your sixties and put off collecting Social Security benefits until age seventy, according to James Mahaney, a certified pension consultant and chartered financial consultant with Prudential Financial, a Newark, New Jersey, insurer. Delaying Social Security would, of course, provide you with a larger benefit later in life. And, at most, 85 percent of Social Security income is taxable. In contrast, 100 percent of retirement-account income is typically taxable. So, in this strategy—with a greater percentage of your income in later life coming from Social Security and a smaller percentage coming from traditional retirement accounts—your total tax bill should be smaller than it would be if you started Social Security earlier and delayed your retirement-account withdrawals until later.

TAX IMPACT OF DELAYING SOCIAL SECURITY

Delaying Social Security payments until later and starting retirement-account withdrawals earlier may be a way to minimize taxes on your retirement income.

In this example, delaying Social Security and drawing income beforehand from an IRA results in $35,625 less in taxable income per year for a married couple filing jointly. That's because 85 percent of the couple's Social Security income is subject to tax under current law, compared with 100 percent of IRA income.

Approach A: Taking reduced Social Security early and supplementing with higher IRA withdrawals

Approach B: Delaying Social Security

	Approach A	Approach B
IRA income	$45,000	$20,000
Social Security	45,000	70,000
Total pre-tax income	90,000	90,000
Taxable income	70,975	35,350

Source: James Mahaney and Peter Carlson of Prudential Retirement

Think about Social Security for two. Another challenge involved in figuring out just how to start drawing Social Security is what to do as a married couple. A spouse who has not worked, or who has low earnings, may be entitled to as much as half of the higher-earning spouse's Social Security benefits. If your incomes are imbalanced, it may make sense to delay the higher earner's Social Security payments so that the lower earner winds up with the highest possible monthly payment as well. Keep this in mind: If you're married and you take early payments based on your spouse's work record, the benefit amount is reduced *permanently*. The amount of the reduction depends on when the spouse with the larger income would have reached full retirement age. For a worker with a full retirement age of sixty-six, the spouse could get 35 percent of the worker's full benefit at age sixty-two. Keep in mind that your spouse cannot receive spousal benefits until you file for your own retirement benefits.

For example, Martha Brooks qualifies for a $250 benefit at her full retirement age and a spousal benefit of $400. That means she would get her own $250 in Social Security, plus another $150, to bring her up to the level of her spousal benefit. (In other words, she would not get $650, the combined value of both benefits.) If she takes her retirement benefit before her full retirement age, both amounts would be reduced again—permanently. It's always worth double-checking with your local Social Security office to make sure you haven't missed a technicality. In this scenario, if Martha is taking care of a child under age sixteen or gets Social Security disability benefits, she would get full benefits regardless of her age.

(What if you're divorced? You can collect Social Security benefits based on your former spouse's work record if the two of you were married at least ten years and you are currently age sixty-two or older and unmarried. The amount you collect has no effect on what your former spouse collects.)

No small matter in all of this is the life-expectancy of the spouse who is expected to die second. Typically, it's the wife, who in many cases earned less on the job, is younger than the husband and is expected to live to an older age. In that case, it's probably worth delaying the husband's benefits to get the larger check, even if the husband's own health is middling, so the wife has the largest check possible once she's on her own. Unfortunately, there's a catch: While delaying until age seventy will enhance the husband's benefit and the widow's benefit, it could mean the wife would miss out on some spousal benefits in the meantime. Remember, a spouse with far lower lifetime earnings can receive a spousal benefit equal to as much as 50 percent of the main breadwinner's benefit.

But there's a way to have your cake and eat it too. James Mahaney at Prudential recommends having the higher-earning spouse—let's say it's the husband—file for his benefit at his full retirement age or later, so the wife can start her benefit. Then, the husband immediately turns around and suspends his benefit until age seventy so he can earn what are called delayed retirement credits. Those credits would boost his benefit and the survivor's benefit. If you decide to pursue this strategy and the workers at your local Social Security office say they haven't heard of it, explain that it's allowed under the Senior Citizens' Freedom to Work Act of 2000.

Finally, we don't like to think about it, but what happens to your family's Social Security benefits when your husband or wife dies? If you're a widow or widower, you have some flexibility in how you take benefits—namely, you can switch from your own benefit to your deceased spouse's benefit, known as your survivor's benefit, taking the one that provides you with the bigger check. For example, you could take reduced benefits based on your own work record at age sixty-two, and then claim your survivor's benefit at your full retirement age. Alternatively, you could take a reduced survivor's benefit at age sixty and then later switch to claim Social Security based on your own work record. The calculations are complicated, so you should consult a Social Security representative to make sure you are aware of all the options available.

HOW DELAYING SOCIAL SECURITY HELPS THE SURVIVING SPOUSE

Here's an example of benefit levels.

Couple A: Both start collecting at age 62, and he dies at 82

Couple B: She collects at 62, he delays until age 70, and he dies at 82

	Couple A	Couple B
Initial benefit for husband	$12,000	$26,172
Initial benefit for wife (on her own work record)	$12,000	$12,000
Benefit that will continue for surviving spouse	$20,700	$36,444

So, if the husband dies before his wife (after he's started collecting benefits), she steps up to $36,444. The calculations use the Social Security Administration's projected cost-of-living adjustments as of 2006.

Source: James Mahaney and Peter Carlson of Prudential Retirement

Consider how working in retirement affects you benefits. There are *two* downsides to collecting early benefits while working after age sixty-two: Your monthly Social Security check will be smaller *and* you will lose additional benefits if income from your job bumps you above a certain threshold. If you work and collect Social Security between age sixty-two and your full retirement age, you lose $1 of every $2 in benefits—in effect, a 50 percent marginal tax rate—if you make more than $12,480 a year (as of 2006), although in the year in which you reach your full retirement age, you can make up to $33,240 without losing any Social Security benefits.

Uncle Sam eliminates these penalties starting the month you reach your full retirement age. But even when you reach that milestone, your Social Security benefits could wind up getting taxed, depending on your "total income," which consists of three things:

- Your adjusted gross income, including earnings from work, retirement plans, interest, dividends and other taxable income

SOCIAL SECURITY ON THE JOB

If you're *already* collecting Social Security when you go back to work, your benefit actually might go up a bit. It depends on how your paycheck now compares to what you made way back when. Technically speaking, your benefits are based on your thirty-five highest-earning years, with re-ported earnings for past years indexed to reflect inflation. Each year, Social Security reviews the records for all recipients who work and automatically increases benefits as appropriate. By the fall of the year following the one in which you were working, the agency should have figured out whether your earnings were enough to increase your benefit, and any increase would be retroactive to that January. To try to speed things up, go to your local Social Security office in January or February with your W-2 wage statement.

So, let's say you spent twenty of your thirty-five highest-earning years as a newspaper reporter making $50,000 to $60,000 a year. Then, in retire-ment, you start consulting with big companies on how to handle media ques-tions during a crisis and you rack up $100,000 a year in consulting fees. Those bigger paychecks would replace the lower ones in the government's calculations of your monthly check, and your benefit would increase accord-ingly. Still, as we have pointed out already, much of that money could be gobbled up by increased taxes.

- Half of your Social Security benefits
- Any tax-exempt interest income

In 2006, for example, if your total income was between $25,000 and $34,000, half of your Social Security was taxed. If your income was higher than that, up to 85 percent could be taxed. (For married couples filing a joint tax return, the lim-its were $32,000 and $44,000.) To see the current limits, go to www.irs.gov. Again, it makes sense to figure out the impact of starting or delaying both Social Security payments and also retirement-account withdrawals.

As you can see, planning for Social Security is more complicated than you might have thought. Whenever you're making a retirement transition that could impact your Social Security benefit, we urge you to discuss the move—before you make it, if possible—with a Social Security representative. You can find your local office at www.ssa.gov—click "Find a Social Security office"—or call 800-772-1213. We realize that this is often not the most pleasant way to spend your day. But it beats trying to untangle any problems later.

NAVIGATING MEDICARE

No matter when you start collecting Social Security, don't forget to sign up for Medicare when you turn sixty-five. We repeat: Social Security's starting date and Medicare's starting date are not linked.

If you start collecting Social Security before you turn sixty-five, you won't get any government help with your health insurance until then, but you automatically will be enrolled in Medicare's basic hospitalization benefit once you hit that age. If you aren't yet collecting Social Security, plan to call or visit Social Security three months before your birthday to sign up for Medicare (Social Security's phone number, again, is 800-772-1213). Note that Medicare benefits are available before age sixty-five for people who have been collecting Social Security disability payments for two years, and also to those who have permanent kidney failure requiring dialysis or a transplant.

It's essential, if you plan to quit working before you turn sixty-five and your health insurance from work won't bridge you until then, that you make sure beforehand that you can get private health-insurance coverage to cover that gap. We frequently get letters from readers who are stuck with no coverage and left crossing their fingers that they won't have a heart attack or a stroke before Medicare kicks in.

There are tools out there to help you put it all into plain

FOR MEDICARE HELP

- Medicare's telephone hotline: 800-633-4227

- Medicare's Web site: www.medicare.gov. Includes comparison of drug plans (at plancompare.medicare.gov) that also estimates your costs

- Medicare's annual handbook, *Medicare & You,* which is posted every year at www.medicare.gov

- Medicare's beneficiary Web site: www.mymedicare.gov. Lets registered beneficiaries see information about their individual entitlement, enrollment and deductibles. The site also provides beneficiaries with preventive-services information

- Social Security Administration (for help with Medicare enrollment or questions about the drug plan's "Extra Help" program for low-income older people): 800-772-1213 or www.ssa.gov

- Your state health-insurance-counseling program (SHIP): Get local contact information at 800-677-1116, the Eldercare Locator, or www.shiptalk.org

- The Medicare Rights Center, an advocacy group for Medicare users: www.medicarerights.org

- AARP, which has information on Medicare's prescription drug coverage: 888-687-2277 or www.aarp.org/medicarerx

English. Start by reading the government's primer, *Medicare & You,* which is published every year by the Centers for Medicare and Medicaid Services, the federal agency that runs the government's health-insurance program for older people. It's available 24/7 at www.medicare.gov or by calling 800-633-4227. We'll also provide you with an overview.

Medicare Part A is basically hospital insurance, and most

people don't pay a premium for it because they or their spouse already contributed to Medicare through payroll taxes while working. Part A covers the most basic life-saving services: mainly inpatient care in hospitals, short-term coverage in a nursing home and hospice care at the end of life. However, contrary to what the majority of pre-retirees believe, it does *not* cover long-term care in nursing homes or assisted-living facilities.

Medicare Part B, or medical insurance, helps pay for doctors' services and other outpatient care. It also covers some medical services not paid for under Part A, such as some physical and occupational therapy. You have to pay a monthly premium to be covered by Part B, which was $93.50 a month in 2007. It's typically deducted from your Social Security check. You also have to pay a deductible each year ($131 in 2007) before Medicare starts paying its share. And if you don't sign up when you first become eligible, that premium could be higher. The cost of Part B goes up 10 percent for each full twelve-month period that you qualified for it but didn't sign up. You can sign up for Part B with no penalty while you are still covered through the employer's plan (and for up to eight months afterward).

Through the end of 2006, Part B premiums cost the same for everybody eligible, regardless of your wealth. But starting in 2007, Medicare charges folks with higher incomes more. The change, being phased in over three years, affects single beneficiaries with adjusted gross incomes greater than $80,000 a year and couples with incomes greater than $160,000. By 2009, when means-testing is fully phased in, beneficiaries with incomes above $200,000 are expected to pay more than $300 a month in premiums—triple what those with incomes under $80,000 would pay. (The income thresholds would be adjusted for inflation.) But if you have no supplemental coverage through a past or present job, it's still wise to make sure you sign up for Part B—even if you get slapped with the higher premiums.

MEDIGAP BENEFITS

Here are some of the services that you—not Medicare—might have to pay for in 2007, even if you're covered under Part A and Part B. A Medigap plan may help cover these costs:

Part A:

Hospital stays:
- $992 for the first 60 days of a benefit period
- $248 per day for days 61–90
- $496 per day for days 91–150

Nursing-home stays:
- $124 per day for days 21–100

Part B:

Blood:
- The first three pints
- $131 per year deductible
- 20% of the Medicare-approved amount for most covered services

Note: These services must be covered by Medicare Advantage plans, which typically combine Parts A and B and require patients to use a medical-provider network.

Source: *Centers for Medicare and Medicaid Services*

Another category of coverage—Medigap—is more debatable. Medigap is health insurance sold by private insurance companies to help cover the co-insurance, co-payments and deductibles not covered by Medicare A and B. (In other words, it fills the gaps.) Insurance companies can sell you only a "standardized" Medigap policy that must follow federal and state laws. Each type offers a different set of basic and extra benefits.

The basic benefits include co-insurance and hospital benefits for Medicare Part A, and co-insurance or co-payments for Medicare Part B. Extra benefits may include co-insurance for some nursing-home care, Part A and B deductibles, other Part B charges, foreign-travel emergencies, at-home recovery and preventive care. The good news is that Medigap policies are standard enough that comparison shopping is possible. Medicare has a 100-page guide, "Choosing a Medigap Policy," posted at www.medicare.gov.

It's hard to generalize about situations in which Medigap coverage does or does not make sense. The main reason to buy it is to help you lower your out-of-pocket costs, particularly if you anticipate dealing with a lot of health problems and you have no supplemental coverage through a current or former employer. Buying a Medigap policy also can help you budget for most of your medical costs; without it, your out-of-pocket costs could swing widely.

Another way to get more benefits at a set premium is through a Medicare Advantage plan, which wraps doctor and hospital services into one plan, sometimes with additional benefits. Instead of paying beneficiaries' claims directly, the federal government pays insurance companies to manage their care. And to entice people to sign up, costs for private plans are cheaper on average than for traditional Medicare coverage. This relatively new category of benefits includes health-maintenance organizations (HMOs), which generally require use of doctors and hospitals in a network; preferred-provider organizations (PPOs), which offer some out-of-network coverage; and other managed-care plans. Some Medicare Advantage plans include drug coverage, meaning you would not need to sign up separately for it; others don't. The main disadvantage can be a more limited choice of the doctors and hospitals to which you have access. And, as you might assume, there are typically more options in densely populated areas. Depending on your experience with a managed-care plan on the job, you may be more or less inclined to sign up.

One new type of Medicare Advantage plan, called "private fee-for-service," is gaining in popularity. There are no restrictions on the doctors or hospitals that participants can use, and there are often other benefits such as additional days in the hospital and drug coverage.

GETTING YOUR PRESCRIPTIONS

Medicare Part D, the prescription-drug plan, is the newest piece of the Medicare puzzle. The good news for people who haven't hit age sixty-five yet is that the kinks are starting to get worked out, and it's easier to comparison shop before signing up. The bad news is that plans come and go as private insurers figure out what works where. You'll have to stay on your toes because the plans that do stay in the market could add and drop drugs every year.

If you currently have low drug costs, it might be tempting not to sign up for Part D, but the idea is the same as with homeowner's insurance: You can't wait for a fire to buy coverage. And premiums automatically increase 1 percent for each month you delay, which means putting off enrollment for a single year would result in monthly premiums that are permanently 12 percent higher. The penalty doesn't apply if you have what the government calls "creditable" drug coverage, meaning that the drug coverage you're getting elsewhere is at least as good as the Medicare benefit. A letter from your current source of coverage, typically an employer or a former employer, should let you know whether its offering fits the bill before you have to sign up.

Though the government approves and subsidizes the drug plans, they are designed and sold by private companies, so the number and types of coverage choices vary depending on where you live. (Go to plancompare.medicare.gov to sort through current options using your ZIP code, the drugs you currently take and the pharmacy you prefer using.) Most drug plans have a monthly premium, on average $32.20 in 2006, plus a deductible and cost-sharing for prescriptions.

The specific drugs covered (listed in "formularies" at www. medicare.gov) vary from plan to plan, and they are covered at different "tiers." You typically pay lower co-payments for generic and older brand-name drugs in the lower tiers and higher co-payments for the newer, fancier drugs in higher tiers.

Then there's the "doughnut hole," the coverage gap in the middle of the drug benefit. Under the standard drug plans, beneficiaries as of 2007 generally paid a $265 deductible. Once total drug costs (including the deductible and co-payments along with what the plan has paid) exceeded $2,400, Medicare wouldn't pay any more benefits until out-of-pocket expenses reached $3,850. When they reached the upper limit, "catastrophic coverage" kicked in and beneficiaries were responsible for 5 percent of the costs.

GETTING HELP IN THE DRUG COVERAGE GAP

If the gap in Medicare drug coverage looms for you or a family member, make sure you're minimizing the bills with these measures:

- Switch to generic drugs or lower-cost drugs that treat the same condition, and ask your doctor if it's possible to split higher-dosage pills to save money.

- Apply for the U.S. government's "Extra Help" subsidy if your income is too high to qualify for Medicaid, but still small: about $1,225 a month for individuals as of 2006. The BenefitsCheckUp Web site (www.benefits checkup.org) can help you figure out if you qualify for that program— or if your state has a pharmaceutical assistance program. To get help with the BenefitsCheckUp tool, call 800-424-9046 or go to www.accesstobenefits.org to find a local group involved in the Access to Benefits Coalition, which provides help with the screening tool.

- Don't overlook state assistance. More than one-third of the states have offered help for older people and sometimes for younger, disabled people. Some states provide "wraparound" help and pay out-of-pocket expenses. Others help pay premiums or offer rebates.

- Figure out if there's a charity or drug-company program that would help pay your out-of-pocket costs. These are most common for expensive drugs used to treat cancer and AIDS.

- Even if your former employer hasn't offered equivalent, or "creditable," drug coverage, find out if it's offering wraparound coverage that might pick up costs Medicare won't.

- Try to keep paying your drug-plan premiums. The insurance will provide a lot of help if you're struck by a serious disease or condition treated with high-priced drugs. Plus, it's likely you're still getting better prices through a Medicare drug plan that has negotiated discounts than you could get on your own.

CHAPTER 11

LONG-TERM CARE STRATEGIES

Linda Blackwell, of Poway, California, and her sister began to worry that after four years, their mother's stay in a private long-term-care facility for Alzheimer's patients was leaving nothing to take care of their father if he became ill. So, they moved her to a nursing home that took patients on Medicaid, the government's medical program for the indigent, which also provides much of the country's long-term care for older people running out of money.

"It was dark and not as warm and inviting," Linda recalled. "The staff seemed a little more harried. . . . All you'd have to do is walk into [the two types of facilities] and see the difference."

No one wants to think they'll wind up in a nursing home, but if you reach age sixty-five, you have a two-in-five chance of spending some time in one, according to federal statistics. Add in home care and assisted living, and almost 70 percent of sixty-five-year-olds are projected to need some type of long-term care, according to predictions by health-care researchers.

Study after study has found that Americans mistakenly believe they have a low risk of needing long-term care, underestimate the costs involved and think Medicare and Medicaid,

A WOMEN'S ISSUE

As an adult daughter or daughter-in-law, wife, sibling or mother, it is highly likely that you are a caregiver. And it's also likely that you could outlive your own support: Statistically speaking, you are expected to outlive your husband and, possibly, other family members. Consider the fact that in 2004 there were roughly four times as many widows (8.2 million) as widowers (2 million), according to the U.S. Administration on Aging. When you're the one in need of care, professional aid may be your only option.

the government's health-insurance programs for the elderly and poor, respectively, will pay for it. Even if you're a short-timer in long-term care, you could be facing some hefty bills. The going rate for a shared nursing-home room in early 2006 averaged $62,532 a year. Then there's any home health care—at an average cost of $25.32 an hour—that you might need leading up to a nursing-home stay. Medicare covers only a brief period of long-term-care bills during rehabilitation, and it's getting tougher to qualify for Medicaid help.

TYPES OF CARE

There are growing numbers of alternatives to nursing homes for people who need long-term care:

FAMILY CAREGIVERS

Two-thirds of older people with disabilities relied solely on family caregivers as of 1999, up from 57 percent in 1994, and the numbers continue to rise. Many caregivers spend more than twenty hours a week caring for their charges. To help relieve some of the burden, nonprofit groups and government agencies are adding programs such as adult day services (many of which provide transportation) and other respite services that send a substitute caregiver into the home or provide a weekend stay at an assisted-living facility for the care recipient. Organizations such as the Alzheimer's Association provide grants for some respite care at no charge. The biggest problem with respite care, at the moment, is that the supply cannot keep up with the demand.

GERIATRIC CARE MANAGERS

This relatively new type of professional is helping family members assess their loved ones' needs and hire help—especially in long-distance situations. Services include identifying and explaining options for home care, retirement communities, assisted-living facilities or nursing homes. They also guide families through Medicare, long-term care insurance and locating community resources such as Meals on Wheels and other free caregiving services. There's a directory of such managers and a list of questions to ask when hiring someone at www.care manager.org, the Web site for the National Association of Professional Geriatric Care Managers. Costs typically run $85 to $200 an hour, and long-term care insurance sometimes pays for a portion. (When interviewing care managers, families should ask about any potential relationships with assisted-living centers or nursing homes to make sure they are getting unbiased advice.)

HOME-HEALTH SERVICES

This includes assistance from simple house-cleaning and errand running to various types of medical treatment. Registered nurses can provide hands-on medical care. Certified nursing assistants and home health aides, who get several months of training and are licensed by many states, can help with bathing and dressing. If you just need someone to help run errands,

A BREAK FOR CAREGIVERS

Sharon Cox and her husband took her mother, who was developing Alzheimer's disease, into their Atlanta home three decades ago. At first, her mother became her sidekick during errands and carpool duty. But things got tougher. In her 90s, Sharon's mother hasn't recognized any family members for several years and also has gone blind, making it difficult for her to go out anymore.

Sharon finally hired a caregiver when she went back to work full-time, but recently, the caregiver needed an extended medical leave. Sharon turned to the Alzheimer's Association, a nonprofit research and support group based in Chicago, for help finding a new caregiver. She got more than she expected: She learned that she qualified for a grant of $1,200 a year from the association toward "respite care"—money she can use to buy additional time with a caregiver so that she can better attend to her own needs and those of the rest of her family.

Respite programs are available nationwide through various social agencies and nonprofit organizations. Sometimes they provide grants like Sharon's, or free services; other times, they connect caregivers to services they must pay for themselves. Typically, respite services fall into these broad categories: programs that provide the patient with social stimulation outside the home—mainly other people to talk to—on a day-to-day basis; short-term stays ranging in length from a weekend to a few weeks at an assisted-living facility or nursing home and one-on-one care within the patient's home; provided either by a professional or by another family member who is sometimes paid, especially if travel expenses or time lost at work are costly for that person. For example, a nonprofit might pay your sister from another state to come and stay with your father for a week so that you can take a break.

"Respite is needed because you get physically tired, and also emotionally tired," said Donna Schempp, program director for the Family Caregiver Alliance in San Francisco. "When you get burned out, there's a possibility that you're going to become abusive toward the person you're caring for or that the likelihood is higher that you're going to put them in an institution."

Caregivers often "are afraid to leave their people because it feels selfish, and things do happen when the caregiver is away," Donna told us. "But things can happen when you're there, also. We forget that piece of it."

To find a respite program near you, start with the Eldercare Locator, a federal-government service you can access online at www.eldercare.gov or by calling 800-677-1116. Another good resource is your state or local area agency on aging. If your loved one suffers from a widely researched disease that has a strong advocacy group, you may be able to get some help from a disease-specific organization, as Sharon did from the Alzheimer's Association.

cook or remind you to take a medication, a "companion" provider might do. Make sure a potential caregiver has undergone a criminal background check and that his or her agency pays worker's compensation and Social Security taxes. The American Association for Homecare has a Web site where users can search for local agencies (www.aahomecare.org). Generally, the hourly cost rises with the level of training, from an average $17.09 for homemaker services to $36.22 for Medicare-certified home-care providers, according to a 2006 survey by insurer Genworth Financial Inc. Long-term care insurance typically will pay for in-home services, though policies differ as to whether they will pay the same amount for in-home and institutional care. That's an important point because the gizmos and hands-on care you need can make home care cost as much as an assisted-living facility or nursing home.

Assisted-Living Facilities

Designed for people who need a minimal level of care, such as help with medications and an escort to meals, this option appeals to many because residents typically have their own apartments and more privacy. Depending on where you live, facilities offer varying degrees of nursing care, and some will ask late-stage dementia patients to leave unless the family or patient can pay for additional care. In most states, Medicaid won't pick up the tab for assisted living. You have to pay for it yourself, either out of your own pocket or with insurance. The average annual cost for a private one-bedroom unit in an assisted living facility was $32,294 in 2006, according to Genworth. If you're interested in assisted living, you might also consider a continuing-care retirement community (CCRC), which typically offers escalating levels of care. (See Chapter Four and p. 222 for more information on CCRCs.)

Nursing Homes

Here people who need help with multiple daily-living activities will find the most highly skilled, around-the-clock care available. Costs can vary wildly in different parts of the country, as well as between urban and rural areas, but on average a private nursing-home room cost $70,912 in 2006, or $62,532 for a shared room, according to Genworth. Medicaid pays for a great deal of nursing-home care, spending about $53.5 billion in 2005 (almost half of the country's nursing-home tab). Though many people feel that it's their right to leave their home to their children and have the government pay their nursing-home bills (since they have dutifully paid their taxes), there are significant drawbacks involved in relying on the government at the time in your life when you are the most vulnerable. (More on that in a moment.)

WHAT ABOUT MEDICAID?

For decades, retirees whose main source of income is Social Security have relied on Medicaid to pay their nursing-home bills, and the wealthiest individuals have paid their own way (though some people who can pay out of pocket are starting to buy long-term care insurance for peace of mind). The middle class has been left to agonize over three tough choices:

- Spending thousands of dollars a year on a long-term care insurance policy you may never use

- Trying to self-insure and potentially winding up spending everything you have on your care

- Transferring your house or other assets to your children before spending everything else on your care

Most people have chosen one of the latter two approaches, explaining the large proportion of long-term care paid for by Medicaid. But the government is trying to tighten access to Medicaid for long-term care. A federal law enacted in 2006 has made it more difficult to give away assets and then qualify for Medicaid-paid nursing-home care. Your eligibility could be limited by gifts you have made in the five previous years, up from three years under the old rules. And you may not qualify at all if you have home equity of more than $500,000.

Even if you do meet Medicaid requirements, it's important to point out that we have talked to some adult children, like Linda Blackwell, who regretted using it to pay for their parents' nursing-home stays. Nursing homes generally get paid less by Medicaid than by people paying their own bills or using private insurance. One adult daughter we interviewed blamed her mother's death, after breaking her hip, on a tough transition from an assisted-living facility to a Medicaid-paid nursing home. Many facilities try to limit the number of Medicaid patients they take, meaning you could wind up on a waiting list for the placement you want or find yourself in a facility that's much farther from your family than you would like. Another minus is that long-term care offerings through Medicaid vary from state to state, each of which designs its own program, and home care or assisted living are not options in many places. There's no way to be sure, in advance, that the Medicaid program in your state will be offering any alternatives to nursing homes when you need care.

A POLICY FOR PEACE OF MIND

Milo Tedstrom, the first certified cardiologist in Orange County, California, died in 2005 at age 104. His long life taught his family, including grandson Peter Tedstrom, a certified financial planner in Denver, a lot of lessons, including the emotional value of long-term care insurance even in a case in which the amount paid in essentially equals the benefits paid out.

Milo lived independently until the last few years of his life, when, weakened by pneumonia, he was tended by round-the-clock caregivers costing $12,000 a month. "There was a concern that he might ultimately run out of money if he might live too long," Peter said. "That's sort of an awkward statement to make. It brought into question what we would do if he does run out of money."

But the family did have one backup: long-term care insurance. Peter had persuaded his grandfather to buy a policy at age ninety-two. The premiums cost $7,000 a year and provided a benefit of $100 a day for two years. "Six or seven years into it, we really thought about canceling. But already a $40,000 investment had been made. Then we talked about it again when Grandy [as Milo's grandchildren called him] turned 100," and again they decided to keep the policy, Peter said.

At age 102, Milo started tapping his long-term care benefits and used them up at age 104. In the end, the cost of the premiums and the benefits paid out—each about $70,000—were basically a wash. But the policy had an intangible value that Peter hadn't expected: "My grandfather really anticipated that check every month. Every month when it was expected, he would say to me or my dad, 'I haven't received my check yet.' It was an interesting emotional benefit to have that check waiting for him each month."

There are certainly times when using a nursing home makes sense, particularly when a loved one's custodial needs have outstripped a family's physical and emotional capabilities. But we cannot stress strongly enough that using Medicaid to pay for it means that you lose a lot of control over the circumstances in which such care will be provided. Marilee Driscoll, an author and a consultant on long-term care planning, told us that even if your parents and grandparents "had wonderful experiences receiving their care under Medicaid, it may not necessarily be relevant today." That's because assisted-living facilities and continuing-care retirement communities "have really skimmed the cream from nursing homes. Now, the population in nursing homes is older and sicker than ever before." As a result, staffs are stretched to provide time-consuming care to increasingly frail patients.

THE LTC NEST EGG

Before you consider buying an insurance policy, you may want to consider a few tools that could help you pay for long-term care yourself: reverse mortgages, health savings accounts, individual retirement accounts or your own savings. (Of course, you could use any of these to help pay insurance premiums, too.)

Reverse mortgages increasingly are being viewed as an untapped piggybank for medical expenses, including long-term care in the home (see Chapter Seven). More than 13 million households could qualify for an average of at least $72,000 apiece in reverse-mortgage loans, for a total of nearly $1 trillion, based on 2000 data, according to a study by the National Council on Aging, a Washington, D.C., advocacy group. Here's what $72,000 could buy as of 2005, according to the council's research: a home health aide, working four hours a day, for three years; adult day care for an Alzheimer's patient for six years; or $500 a month for a family caregiver, including one day of respite each week for fourteen years.

If you have a high-deductible health plan, you can sock away pretax dollars in a health savings account, or HSA, to pay for out-of-pocket medical expenses, including long-term care costs. The two big advantages with HSAs are that you don't pay tax on money spent for medical costs and you don't forfeit any funds that remain in the account at year end (as you do with traditional medical savings accounts). Rather, the funds can keep growing year after year and eventually can be used for health-care costs in later life. Here are the basics: As of 2007, the Internal Revenue Service defines a high-deductible health plan as having a minimum annual deductible of $1,100 for individuals and $2,200 for families. (There are directories of companies that will open HSAs at www.hsainsider.com and www.hsadecisions.org.) The maximum you can contribute each year to an HSA as an individual is $2,850. For families, the maximum is $5,650. People age fifty-five and older can make an additional $800 catch-up contribution.

In some states, your individual retirement account can work as a long-term-care piggybank, too. If you have started taking withdrawals from your IRA, some states won't count it toward Medicaid-qualifying requirements, according to Vincent Russo, an attorney specializing in elder-law issues in Westbury, New York. Instead, you could use that regular source of income to pay your rent in an assisted-living facility, a service rarely covered by Medicaid, or for other care needs. Whatever strategy you use, don't forget to look for tax deductions for any long-term care bills you pay.

Some of our readers have socked away their own long-term-care nest eggs that they're investing themselves. Robert Prechter Sr. of Atlanta decided to take his chances paying for care himself "due to the low probabilities of ever having to spend an extended time in a nursing home." Among his assumptions was that he would use a nursing home, at most, for two years, and his investment would earn a 6 percent return. He also pointed out that by paying the costs himself, he would be able to take a deduction on his income taxes for medical costs exceeding 7.5 percent of his adjusted gross income.

The risks, of course, are that your investment strategy might not pan out the way you planned or that one spouse could use up those savings. If you go this route, be mindful that long-term care costs often increase more quickly than the common benchmark for inflation, the consumer price index.

CAN YOU DEDUCT THOSE LONG-TERM CARE COSTS?

Medical expenses that exceed 7.5 percent of your adjusted gross income are tax deductible.

First, here is a note to caregivers: To deduct any medical expenses for the care recipient, you also must be providing more than half of the person's financial support, the person must be a relative or have lived with you for the entire year, and he or she must be a U.S. citizen or resident. All sorts of things qualify: hospital bills, doctor visits and prescription drugs, transportation costs, insurance premiums and equipment. When it comes to long-term care, a percentage of both the entry fee and monthly fee for nursing homes and other long-term care facilities typically are identified by the facilities' administrators as medical expenses. For example, a caregiver pays $150,000 for a room in a nursing home for an elderly patient. If one-third of that entry cost is allocated for medical fees, then $50,000 could go toward the caregiver's total medical expenses when calculating his or her tax return. And if the care recipient reaches the point where he or she needs help with two or more "activities of daily living" or becomes bed-ridden, the entire monthly bill could become a medical expense.

Keep in mind that the caregiver has to pay the medical providers directly. And if you have to pay the alternative minimum tax, medical expenses must exceed 10 percent of your adjusted gross income, not 7.5 percent, before you can take the deductions.

And, as more baby boomers need care, inflationary pressures are expected to increase.

TO BUY OR NOT TO BUY

Now, let's say you *like* the idea of owning long-term care insurance, at least to insure a portion of the care you might need, but you have no idea if you can afford it. To figure it out first-hand, Kelly and her husband "secret shopped" for long-term care insurance themselves, hoping to answer these three questions: Do we need this product? How complicated is it? What kind of bang could we get for our buck?

We quickly discovered that comparison shopping is all but impossible. Policies from different carriers are packaged with different bells and whistles. The four insurance agents we spoke with gave conflicting advice. (One warned us against "underinsuring" and another against "overinsuring.") And though Kelly and her husband are in their thirties, which should be an advantage in buying a policy (the younger you are, the lower the cost), the annual premiums we were quoted were all over the map. The low was $1,334.33 and the high was $5,723.55. It's easy to walk away. That's because the variables, no matter what your age, can drive you crazy. Should I plan for six months of care or six years? Will home care suffice or will I need to move to an assisted-living facility? And how much will long-term care actually cost? Depending on where you live and when you might need care, that figure could vary significantly. It also depends on your age and health and the terms of your policy. On average, it would cost $772 for a fifty-five-year-old to buy a three-year policy providing $110,000 in coverage in 2006, and it would cost $1,456 for a sixty-five-year-old, according to the American Association for Long-Term Care Insurance. Such policies include a feature called "compound inflation protection," the most conservative way to try to make sure that your policy maintains its value over time.

For the question of whether to buy coverage or not, we turned to the National Council on Aging, which has spent years researching the issue. It offers these guidelines for considering buying a policy. To put yourself in the ballpark for buying a policy, you should meet the following criteria:

- Own assets of at least $75,000 (excluding your home and car)
- Have annual retirement income of $25,000 to

$35,000 if you live alone or $35,000 to $50,000 for couples. (This is a national average and may be high or low depending on where you plan to live in retirement.)

- Be able to pay premiums without adversely affecting your lifestyle

- Be able to absorb possible premium increases without financial difficulty

We'd like to stress that last point: If your personal finances go south and you quit paying the premiums or if you lose track of your bill and miss a payment, you lose the policy. Period. You might get a check for some sort of residual value, depending on the state law where you live, but there's no way you'll ever get anything close to a full refund. And if the insurer goes belly up, you could be left with little or no coverage. Whether you can swing the premiums is ultimately your call, though some states require insurance agents to go through a worksheet with you to decide if long-term care insurance is right for you. If you expect Social Security to be your only source of retirement income, then you can't afford the premiums. But that's about the only consistent rule.

Some good ideas for starting to think about the sort of coverage you actually need come from the Kaiser Family Foundation: For working-age adults in their fifties or younger, stand-alone policies might not be a good investment because the amount of time likely to pass before you would tap your benefits, and the evolving nature of the product itself, could quickly make a policy bought today obsolete. Older purchasers probably will want to pass on comprehensive policies that cover nursing home stays of five years or longer and provide daily benefits of as much as $200; those plans are simply too expensive for most people. Instead, identify the reasons you're seeking coverage, and then begin to build a plan to best meet those needs. Let's say you want help paying for home care down the

CCRCS AND LONG-TERM CARE INSURANCE

Do you need long-term care insurance if you move to a continuing-care retirement community? Because various forms of long-term care already are part of a CCRC package, living in such a setting would seem to preclude the need for a separate long-term care insurance policy. But that's not necessarily the case. Some continuing-care communities offer nursing care at the same price as your usual monthly payment, but others have a cap for such services or require you to pay full daily rates as your level of care increases. So, whether it makes sense for you to have long-term care insurance depends on your specific contract and the way the individual community is licensed in your state. Some CCRCs do their own health screening, after which they may exclude any coverage for care you get for a pre-existing condition.

Even if you enter an all-inclusive arrangement and you already have long-term care insurance, consider holding onto your policy for a year so you're certain you're going to stay at the CCRC. If you leave, you would have to start all over with the insurance application process—at an older age.

road and a nursing-home benefit that's large enough that you won't have to sell your house to pay the bill. In that case, you might want to shop for a policy that covers a year or two of nursing-home care, along with home care, with no waiting period for your benefits. That thinking flies in the face of conventional wisdom about long-term care insurance: that you should get a policy that covers at least three to five years of care and has a long waiting period before benefits start (typically ninety days) to help lower premiums. (You can read the complete Kaiser Family Foundation report at www.kff.org/insurance/6072-index.cfm.)

HOW TO SHOP

Okay, so you have decided to purchase a policy, but you don't feel like you have thousands of dollars sitting around to pay for the most expensive premiums. Here are some things to keep in mind based on our own experiences.

AGENTS

Before you shop for a policy, shop for an agent. We started by calling three agents from some of the largest long-term care insurers: John Hancock, a Boston-based unit of Manulife Financial Corp.; Prudential Financial Inc., Newark, New Jersey; and Genworth Financial. We also found an independent agent by filling out an online questionnaire. Expect to spend an hour with each agent at your initial meeting (maybe more if he or she wants to walk you through many details in the policies). The downside is that you'll probably get conflicting advice, as we did.

Unfortunately, there aren't really any shortcuts. The best strategy is to keep interviewing agents until you find an independent one—meaning he or she is not beholden to one big insurance company—with whom you're comfortable and who knows long-term care planning and insurance inside out. So, how do you find someone like that? The basics are word-of-mouth, recommendations from friends and phone conversations with agents in which you grill them about their education and background. You still may have to meet with several people, but the goal of those first meetings is to find someone who seems knowledgeable and understanding of your situation rather than someone who delves into policy features and quotes right away. You can get started finding agents using the directory at www.ahia.net, the Web site for the Association of Health Insurance Advisors, a trade group in Falls Church, Virginia, for agents selling health-oriented insurance products.

UNDERSTANDING YOUR AGENT'S CREDENTIALS

The designations after your insurance agent's name refer to these various training programs:

CASL: Chartered Advisor for Senior Living
Awarded by the American College
Average completion time: over forty-five hours

CECA: Certified Elder Caregiver Advisor
Awarded by American Society of Specialty Counselors
Average completion time: thirty-five to forty-five hours

CLTC: Certified in Long Term Care Advisor
Awarded by Corp. on Long-Term Care
Average completion time: two classroom days

CLTCA: Certified Long Term Care Advisor
Awarded by Society of Long Term Care Advisors
Average completion time: two classroom days or fifteen hours
correspondence

CSA: Certified Senior Advisor
Awarded by Society of Certified Senior Advisors
Average completion time: 3.5 classroom days or 8–12 weeks
correspondence

CSS: Certified Senior Specialist
Awarded by Center for Senior Studies
Average completion time: two weeks to one month

LTCGS: Long Term Care Group Specialist
Awarded by Carequest University
Average completion time: over forty-five hours

LTCIS: Long Term Care Insurance Specialist
Awarded by Center for Senior Studies
Average completion time: two to four classroom days

LTCP: Long-Term Care Professional
Awarded by America's Health Insurance Plans
Average completion time: 2.5 classroom days

Source: Association of Health Insurance Advisors, www.ahia.net

Sadly, most agents "don't really know what they're selling," according to Phillip Sullivan, an insurance consultant in Rabun Gap, Georgia. That's why it's so important to ask the right questions. (See worksheet on page 232.) Often, an agent's name will be followed by a series of letters—designations that signify completion of one of at least eight nationally recognized training programs, which can help you gauge an agent's expertise. We like this informal way to measure your agent's interest in making sure you know what's what: The National Association of Insurance Commissioners publishes "A Shopper's Guide to Long-Term Care Insurance," a sixty-eight-page booklet with all sorts of handy information. Page two reads, "In most states, state law requires insurance companies or agents to give you this guide to help you better understand long-term care insurance and decide which, if any, policy to buy." Only one of the four agents we met with provided us with the book at our initial meeting. So, were the others breaking the law? A spokeswoman for the association said no—agents must simply pass it along at some point before you sign a contract. But why wouldn't every agent want you to have that information from the start, when you have the most questions?

AMOUNT OF COVERAGE

Everyone we talked with agreed that the most important thing you're purchasing is the dollars-per-day that will go toward your eventual care. All the agents advised using the "average" $140 cost of care per day in Atlanta, where we live, as our goal. But the National Association of Insurance Commissioners recommends that you do your *own* research, calling two home-health agencies, two nursing homes and two other facilities in your area—and, we would add, the area where you plan to retire—to find out what they charge. Our conclusion is that we would need at least $140 a day, if not more. It seems the decision you make depends on whether you feel comfortable with "average" care and with knowing you still might need to dip into your own savings to make up for any shortfall.

YEARS OF CARE

Deciding how many years of care to insure is a tough call, too. Choices usually range from two years to a lifetime, and agents generally recommend going for the most time you can afford. Many agents recommend purchasing lifetime coverage if you can swing it, particularly if you haven't hit your mid-fifties. That's because long-term care insurance isn't just for the elderly; an auto accident at age forty could lay you up for months, too. Indeed, nearly 58 percent of the people receiving long-term care with long-term care insurance through group policies today are younger than sixty-five, according to UnumProvident Corporation. Still, because of its high cost, lifetime coverage could cancel out any savings you achieve by buying a policy at a younger age. David Glass, an Atlanta agent selling Hancock policies, told us many of his clients split the difference, going for coverage of six or ten years.

You can also buy a "shared-care" benefit that would let you share care with your spouse or sometimes even pool benefits among family members. (Of course, any additional feature like this would raise your premiums.) There are three options: You and your spouse share a benefit period; you have separate benefit periods, but can tap into your spouse's benefit if he or she hasn't used it and you need it; or you each have your own benefit period, plus a third period that either of you can tap into if you use up your own.

It's worth asking your agent to calculate how an extra year or two of coverage might affect your premium. If you're in your fifties, you might be able to swing lifetime coverage. In your seventies, however, you might be better off going for a shorter plan and larger benefit.

INFLATION PROTECTION

This option, though costly, is a must-have: automatic inflation protection, which generally compounds at 5 percent a year. The only situation in which you might not buy it is if you're over seventy-five years old. In that case, you should either pad your daily benefit or buy simple inflation protection, which increases your benefit by 5 percent of the original benefit level every year (in contrast to compound inflation protection, which increases your benefit by 5 percent of your new benefit level each year). Take a look at the math: With the compound option, a $140 daily benefit would be worth $371.46 a day in twenty years. With the simple inflation option, it would be worth only $280.

ELIMINATION PERIOD

If you need to find a way to lower premiums, consider increasing the elimination, or waiting, period, which most agents liken to the deductible on your car or house insurance. Basically, once you qualify for benefits, the longer you wait to start tapping them (with choices typically including 0, 7, 30, 60 or 90 days), the better the break you'll get on your premium. Of course, you would have to pay any bills in that gap yourself, right? Maybe, but maybe not. Many health-insurance plans have short-term rehabilitation benefits, one agent pointed out as she encouraged us not to "over-insure." Medicare, the government health program for people sixty-five and older, provides a brief period of skilled nursing care in some situations after a hospital discharge.

You should be particularly careful about understanding the language in your policy regarding the elimination period. With home-health benefits, for example, some insurers include every calendar day in the countdown; others count only days when you get a visit from a care provider. So, for example, if a nurse called on you once a week and you had a thirty-day deductible, it could take thirty weeks for your coverage to kick in. And make sure you understand the laws that regulate long-term care insurance in your state. Two agents told us that the law in Georgia, where we live, would not allow a waiting period of more than ninety days for nursing-home care or sixty days for home-health care. But when we called the state insurance department, we were told that the maximum wait allowed was 150 days for nursing-home care or sixty visits, not days, for home-health care. That's a big difference.

RIDERS

Insurance companies offer all sorts of riders to these plans, most of which would be nice perks but may not be worth the money. Again, if you work with more than one agent, you'll get varying opinions on the subject. We decided that the next time around, we would ask for a basic quote and then ask for a second quote with the add-ons that we consider necessary (along with the exact wording in the policy that describes each rider). For us, only two riders seemed crucial: the compound-inflation option, which we've already described, and a rider that doles out your benefits on a weekly or monthly basis rather than daily. That way, if you're receiving home health care two or three times a week and the bill each time exceeds your daily allotment, the total might still come to less than your weekly or monthly benefit. And you're not losing out on a potential payment for the days when you get no outside care.

TAX-QUALIFIED

All of our agents talked up "tax-qualified" policies, but when we pressed them on what that means, the deduction involved turned out to be less than advertised. On your tax return, you can deduct a small portion of the premiums for a tax-qualified policy, with the amount rising as you get older, but only if you itemize your deductions and spend more than 7.5 percent of

"ACTIVITIES OF DAILY LIVING"

Many long-term care insurers start coverage when you can no longer independently perform two "activities of daily living," or ADLs. Here are the basic categories, which may vary somewhat from policy to policy:

- Bathing or showering

- Dressing yourself

- Moving your body, as from bed to a chair

- Getting to, and using, the toilet

- Eating

- Taking medication

your adjusted gross income on medical expenses. The more meaningful benefit comes down the road: You won't be taxed on your policy's payout when you use it.

Before you sign up for a tax-qualified policy, talk with your agent in detail about your individual situation. It's important to be aware that such policies occasionally backfire because they usually have higher thresholds that you have to meet before you qualify to get reimbursed for care. With tax-qualified policies, for example, federal law requires that you must need "substantial assistance" to do two "activities of daily living" before you can qualify for your policy's benefits. Policies that don't qualify for tax breaks may be more lenient. Likewise, tax-qualified policies require that a disability be expected to last at least ninety days, but nonqualified policies don't have to. And for cognitive impairment to be covered by a tax-qualified policy, you would have to need "substantial supervision," which would not be necessary with a policy that's not tax-qualified.

CHECKING UP

These Web sites offer rating services where you can check on the financial strength of insurance companies.*

- A.M. Best Co. (www.ambest.com)

- Fitch Inc. (www.fitchibca.com)

- Moody's Investors Service Inc. (www.moodys.com)

- Standard & Poor's (www.standardandpoors.com)

*Most rating services provide some basic information at no charge on the Internet and charge a fee for longer analyses. Different services use different rating scales.

THE INSURER'S HEALTH

As we noted earlier, if your insurance company goes belly up, you lose your policy. What's more likely to happen, however, is that an insurer miscalculates its future financial needs and raises premiums. Long-term care insurers are barred by law from raising rates for individual customers, but if they run into financial trouble, they can ask state regulators to raise the premiums for an entire group of policyholders.

Several rating services analyze the financial strength of long-term care insurers, though each one uses a different scale. You can get the ratings from most of the services free online. One financial adviser, Jeff Schaffer in Forth Worth, Texas, has compiled a list of insurance ratings on his Web site, www.ask yourbroker.com. The list is made up of what he considers to be the most conservative rankings, moderately conservative and least conservative. (He recommends buying policies only from the first two categories.)

To screen for troubled insurers that are most likely to increase their rates, ask your agent

- whether the companies you're considering have had to raise premiums on existing policies in your state.

- for information about the claims-paying histories of the companies in which you are interested.

- the length of time that the insurer has underwritten long-term care policies. (Look for at least ten years. Newer players may not have enough experience to peg rates well.)

Your Own Health

If you're in good physical shape, you also should look for companies that go to great lengths to evaluate your health status. "The more careful the insuring company is about estimating the risk and determining who to accept, the more likely the premium rate will be lower and more stable," explained Joan Ogden, a consulting actuary in Salt Lake City. Some companies offer so-called "super-marathoner" discounts ranging from 10 percent to 50 percent. To qualify for such a rate, you typically have to supply the last two years of your medical records. Some insurers conduct mini-exams, including mental-status checks. Even if you've done well already on a life-insurance exam, it doesn't necessarily mean your long-term care insurance checkup would turn out the same. Arthritis, for example, doesn't mean much to life insurers, but it does to long-term care insurers. They also watch for cognitive impairment, drugs used to control hypertension, osteoporosis and, for diabetics, a hemoglobin A1c reading, which is a measure of a diabetic's control of diabetes over a long time period. So, if you expect to go through such scrutiny, be careful what you complain about to your doctor, who is likely to take notes. And if you think such exams could work against you, you may be better off with group coverage.

Paying It Off

In a few situations, it may be possible to pay off your premiums while you're still working. A few long-term care insurers offer "limited pay" options that allow you to pay off a policy over ten or fifteen years or finish paying when you turn sixty-five. After that, you never again have to worry about a possible premium increase, particularly when the first wave of baby boomers starts to rack up long-term care bills. You can expect premiums to be two to three times what they would be for a regular policy, but sometimes you hit on a deal. My husband and I, in our 30s and in good health, received a quote of less than $3,000 a year in premiums for a policy we could pay off in fifteen years. And if you or your spouse owns a standard business or "C" corporation, you can buy a long-term care policy, including a limited-pay policy, through the company and write off the premiums as a business expense.

Feeling intimidated? The following worksheet can help you keep track of all the variables as you shop. We also suggest that you share it with your agent (or agents) so that he or she knows how serious you are about being financially prudent.

	Policy A	Policy B	Policy C
1. Company name/policy	_____	_____	_____
2. Deductible	_____	_____	_____
3. Elimination period	_____	_____	_____
4. Benefit amount			
a. Respite care	_____	_____	_____
b. Adult day care	_____	_____	_____
c. Home care	_____	_____	_____
d. Assisted living	_____	_____	_____
e. Nursing home	_____	_____	_____
5. Inflation adjustment			
a. Inflation rate	_____	_____	_____

	Policy A	Policy B	Policy C
b. Simple or compounded	_____	_____	_____
6. Maximum amount of benefit (indicate in days or dollar amount)	_____	_____	_____
7. Requirements for coverage			
a. Prior hospitalization (yes/no)	_____	_____	_____
b. Medically necessary/ illness, injury (yes/no)	_____	_____	_____
c. Activities of daily living (How many?)	_____	_____	_____
d. Which ADLs? How defined?	_____	_____	_____
e. Cognitive impairment (yes/no)	_____	_____	_____
f. Linked to ADLs or medical necessity? (yes/no)	_____	_____	_____
8. Alzheimer's coverage? (yes/no)	_____	_____	_____
9. Is coverage linked to ADLs or medical necessity? (yes/no)	_____	_____	_____
10. Pre-existing condition immediately covered if disclosed? (yes/no)	_____	_____	_____
a. If not, definition	_____	_____	_____
b. Waiting period	_____	_____	_____
11. Level of care (yes/no)			
a. Skilled	_____	_____	_____
b. Intermediate	_____	_____	_____
c. Custodial	_____	_____	_____
d. Home care aides	_____	_____	_____
e. Assisted living	_____	_____	_____
f. Adult day care	_____	_____	_____
g. Respite care	_____	_____	_____

	Policy A	Policy B	Policy C
12. What is not covered	_____	_____	_____
13. Guarantee renewable (yes/no)	_____	_____	_____
a. Unconditional guarantee (yes/no)	_____	_____	_____
14. Premiums level (yes/no)	_____	_____	_____
15. Premiums waived for:			
a. Nursing home care (yes/no)	_____	_____	_____
b. Home health care (yes/no)	_____	_____	_____
c. Time period for waiver	_____	_____	_____
16. Company rating			
a. A.M. Best Co. (www.ambest.com)	_____	_____	_____
b. Fitch Inc. (www.fitchibca.com)	_____	_____	_____
c. Moody's Investors Service Inc. (www.moodys.com)	_____	_____	_____
d. Standard & Poor's (www.standardandpoors.com)	_____	_____	_____
17. Total benefit amount	_____	_____	_____
18. Total benefit period	_____	_____	_____
19. Premium—monthly	_____	_____	_____
20. Premium—annual	_____	_____	_____

Source: Used with permission of The National Council on Aging

ALTERNATIVE POLICIES

Some new kinds of policies are starting to develop—along with new ways to buy traditional long-term care insurance. If you work for a big company, see if it offers group coverage as an employee benefit. The advantages include a better chance of securing coverage if you have a health problem already. And if you're single, buying a policy through a group is probably the only way you can get a discount. You may find the shopping experience smoother as well. Some employers, such as the federal government's joint venture, have put together plain-vanilla package policies to simplify the process.

The disadvantages are that most workers are buying policies without adequate inflation protection. A bed in a nursing home that currently costs $150 a day would cost almost $400 a day in twenty years if health-care costs continue to rise about 5 percent a year. In general, group plans offer two types of protection: an automatic benefit increase, or ABI, and a future purchase option, or FPO. The former guarantees that a person's benefits will grow automatically each year; buying the feature, at a policy's outset, is a one-time decision. The latter gives policyholders an option to buy extra coverage at selected intervals, usually every two or three years. Policies with an ABI cost more to start, but the monthly premiums typically remain fixed. Policies with an FPO start with lower premiums, but those premiums can rise sharply if policyholders periodically buy additional protection. The reason is that premiums for the added coverage are based on a policyholder's age at the time the increase takes effect. So, in the first year of coverage, a fifty-five-year-old man might pay $140 a month for a policy providing a $150-a-day benefit with an ABI, or only $50 a month for the same policy with an FPO. But in twenty years, the first policy still costs $140 a month, and the second costs $300 a month.

Another drawback to group coverage is that if you're married, you could lose out on a spousal discount, sometimes as much as 20 percent. And a group deal could limit your options, too. Some group policies, for example, reimburse home health care at 75 percent of the daily maximum benefit for nursing-home care. Whether you're comfortable with a smaller benefit for home care than for nursing-home care probably depends on your age. We decided we wouldn't be comfortable with a policy that didn't have equivalent payments for home care and facility care. After all, we'd rather stay home if we could.

Another way to buy long-term care insurance is through the Partnership for Long-Term Care. This is a public-private long-term care insurance program that has been available in four states—California, Connecticut, Indiana and New York— but is being expanded elsewhere through a 2006 law allowing the program in any state that opts to add it. (Your state Medicaid department or insurance commissioner's office can tell you if the program is available where you live or if it's being added soon.) Under the partnership program, a person buys a private long-term care policy that has received a stamp of approval from state officials in exchange for some relief from Medicaid restrictions if those insurance benefits run out. In most states, the policyholder still could apply for Medicaid to help cover any additional costs and keep assets worth up to the value of the insurance payments already received. For example, if you bought a policy with $50,000 in benefits and then used those up, you could keep $50,000 in personal assets (plus your house and car) and still qualify for Medicaid coverage. A big advantage to a partnership policy could be peace of mind and lower premiums. Partnership policies let you know upfront how much of your own savings you would get to keep, making it less risky to buy a shorter-term, and cheaper, policy. A 2005 study found that only 8 percent of claimants with a three-year benefit period had exhausted their policies since the partnership program started in 1993.

Finally, to try to make long-term care insurance more palatable to boomers, insurers are linking it to other products so that purchasers feel like they're still getting something for their money, even if they never need long-term care. The first "linked" policies (also called "combination" or "hybrid" policies) that emerged were those pairing long-term care insurance with life insurance. If the buyer at some point needs care, the policy pays a benefit. But if the buyer never requires long-term care, the policy pays a death benefit. Now, new hybrids are emerging: Genworth, for example, is working on a policy that marries long-term care coverage with an annuity. The main drawback is that most are purchased by means of a single, sizable premium. And such coverage tends to have fewer options than traditional long-term care insurance. While that simplicity appeals to some, it might also make it tougher to tailor a linked policy to your personal needs.

Then there's "longevity insurance," a product that MetLife Inc. and a few other insurers rolled out starting in 2005. It generally lets people who are fifty-five or older invest a lump sum, from which they start getting an income stream at age eighty-five. For example, a sixty-year-old woman who invested $25,000 would get $17,000 a year for life starting at age eighty-five—money that could be used to pay for long-term care, if she needed it. But she would still get the money if she were healthy. What if she gets sick before age eighty-five? In that case, she would need to make sure she had enough savings to pay for any long-term care expenses in the intervening years.

CHAPTER 12

ESTATE
PLANNING

state planning isn't just for multi-millionaires with fancy trusts. You should figure out how to best pass along your legacy whether or not you've accumulated enough assets for Uncle Sam to take a chunk. That includes talking with spouses, parents, siblings and children about who's going to get what. You also should be figuring out what you need to get in writing to make sure your wishes are met, including various powers of attorney and directives. And if you're lucky enough to have amassed a large estate, there are (legal) ways to save assets for heirs that might otherwise wind up being paid in taxes—but only if you plan in advance. In this chapter, we offer a primer in the four most crucial estate-planning areas:

- The emotional side of estate planning

- The documents that speak for you during illness or after death

- The separate planning you should do for IRAs

- Some basic thoughts about your overall tax strategy

We'll give you a framework, but we also suggest getting professional advice to help keep track of all the moving parts, particularly if you'll be planning for a sizeable estate.

THE SOFTER SIDE

One of the hardest parts of passing on your wealth, whether it's $10,000 or $10 million, is the emotional stuff—figuring out how to divide your assets so that your family isn't hurt, angry or fighting once you're gone. We asked lawyers, financial planners and therapists to help us identify the most important questions we should all ask ourselves about estate planning—questions designed to head-off future feuding. Here are our top picks, which are mostly for parents, but there is one at the end for children.

Q: Should I Talk with My Children About Their Inheritance?

A: Yes! That said, parents often have legitimate reasons for not doing so. Some worry, for instance, that if their children learn what they're going to inherit too early, they could get lazy or, worse, gripe about how things are being carved up. Still, discussing your plans in advance can yield one big benefit: the chance to gauge your children's reactions. And even if you don't change your plan based on their concerns, your children should have a chance to work through their frustrations while you're alive, meaning there's less chance they'll be bitter once you're gone.

First, tell each child separately that you're trying to decide what to do and that you want to find out what he or she expects and wants. Once you have collected that information, you can figure out where the conflicts are. (Both daughters want the silver, both sons want the antique canoe, etc.) A discussion that turns up differing expectations about the future could give you the chance to go back to the drawing board now, rather than having your children fight over your plans in the future. And however much or little you feel comfortable divulging to your children, don't mislead them, we were advised by Susan

Bradley, a financial planner in Palm Beach Gardens, Florida. Even adult children who get more than they expected sometimes get angry. That's because they remember times in their lives when they really could have used a helping hand from their parents, and now they know their parents had the ability to help them and chose not to. It's even worse when parents assure children they will be "taken care of" and then give much less than their children anticipated.

Q: SHOULD I GIVE EACH CHILD AN EQUAL PIECE OF THE PIE? WHAT IF I WANT TO CUT ONE OUT?

A: It seems perfectly fair to divide up everything based on the number of children in the family, right? Not necessarily. Have you factored in the tuition that you provided for the child who became a lawyer or a doctor? Have you considered the $20,000 loan to buy a house that another child never paid back? You may not be keeping score, but at least one of your children— or his or her spouse—probably is. Things could get even stickier if there's a family business involved, especially if only one of your children works there or if the business makes up the bulk of your estate. To balance things out, some parents buy extra life insurance that is payable to the children outside the business or they ask the child involved to buy them out.

Another common pitfall is penalizing one child for being more successful than the other siblings by leaving him or her less. The brain surgeon in the family could wind up feeling unloved and resenting his or her brothers and sisters. One way to treat everyone the same, but still provide a cushion for the children who need it, is to divide 80 percent of your assets among all your children and place the remaining 20 percent in a trust for emergency needs.

What if you have a child who hasn't talked to the family for twenty years or who has a terrible drug problem? No matter how tempting, you shouldn't write anyone completely out of a will. That child may try to reconcile when you're on your deathbed. More likely, the child you cut out could make things miserable for your other kids by contesting the will or hitting them up for money. To prevent such problems, consider leaving the child in question a large enough amount so that he or she wouldn't want to risk putting it in jeopardy. Then, add a clause that essentially says, "If you contest this will, you lose your bequest."

Q: What's the Best Way to Handle Estate Planning for a "Blended" Family?

A: As Jeffrey Condon, an estate-planning attorney in Santa Monica, California, put it, "Men, if you hate your second wife and you want to punish her, leave her in a situation where your children have to wait for her to die for them to inherit."

One alternative is to give your children their inheritance—or at least a nice chunk of it—now. When Stephan Leimberg, an estate-planning consultant in Havertown, Pennsylvania, remarried, he decided to give each of his two adult daughters from his previous marriage a sizable chunk of mutual funds. "I told them, 'You may get more, but think of this as your inheritance.' It took a lot of the pressure off." His older daughter used the money to help buy her first house; his younger daughter, a social psychologist, "is doing wonderful things with wonderful children and living a dignified life economically that she might not otherwise be able to." If you can't afford to give away money now, or you don't feel comfortable jumping the gun, you might want to consider setting up an "irrevocable life-insurance trust" with your children named as the beneficiaries. The trust would own the life-insurance policy, and when you die the benefits would go to your children free of estate taxes. That way, your children would receive an inheritance, and you could leave the rest of your assets to your spouse. Still, before you do something that cannot be reversed, you need to reflect on your own values. How much do you feel that you owe your children? How much do you feel that you owe your spouse?

Things get more complicated, of course, if you have children from more than one marriage or if your spouse has his or her own children. When the children range in age from three to thirty, you may want to allot an equal share for each child, but also hold 25 percent in trust for tuition and weddings for the younger crew. At times, the simplest solutions are the best. Don and Jackie Reed of Hilton Head Island, South Carolina, struggled for months over plans for splitting their combined estate. Don had two children from an earlier marriage; Jackie had no children of her own, but did have a niece and nephew. "Don finally said, 'For purposes of planning, we've got four kids and should divide it up equally,' "Jackie recalled. "We had an unusual situation, and we talked for a long time about how to make it fair."

Q: If I Make My Heirs Meet a Lot of Requirements for Getting the Money, Am I Pulling the Reins Too Tight?

A: Lawyers and financial planners are divided on the merits of so-called "family-incentive trusts," in which parents create hoops their children must jump through before they get their inheritance (such as attending a certain college or marrying within a religion). Myra Salzer, who heads the Wealth Conservancy Inc., a financial-services firm in Boulder, Colorado, favors the approach because it can encourage children to earn their inheritance "as the result of action" and thus "own that money in a much more healthy way" than if it were simply handed to them.

But many planners worry that incentives could backfire. What if you set up a trust to give a child money for reaching milestones in a business career, but the child wants to be a teacher? Or, what if the child gets cancer at age twenty? Some lawyers refuse to set up restrictive incentive trusts, noting that the requirements typically don't kick in for decades. "You might have a son who's a brilliant piano player, but his doctor father only leaves money if he goes to medical school. You're ruining your kid's life," said Charles Plotnick, an estate-planning lawyer in Jenkintown, Pennsylvania. "Children for the most part resent it, and those are things that lead to lawsuits." Instead, he tries to set up more general trusts to be used for children's "health maintenance, education and support, and for that of their children."

Q: Should I Include My Grandchildren in My Inheritance Plan?

A: Grandparents these days are typically more involved in their grandchildren's lives, often because they have so many more years to spend with them. But there is one possible downside to being a generous grandparent: Your children may view large bequests to your grandchildren, particularly if they can spend the money before they finish college, as usurping their authority. And grandchildren receiving a fat inheritance at an early age could wind up rudderless. "When your goal in life is to not screw up what you have, as opposed to seeing what you can build and create yourself, it doesn't promote high self-esteem," said Myra Salzer, who favors the family-incentive trust. To keep your benevolence from backfiring, be sure to tell your children what their children could be getting, and ask how they feel about it. One possible strategy is to pass money to a grandchild through a trust fund for which the child's parent is one of the trustees.

And put some thought into the *age* at which your grandchildren would get control of the money. You may want to wait to hand over the money at least until they are in their early twenties or parse it out gradually, letting them use part of it to pay college bills. Christine Fahlund, senior financial planner at T. Rowe Price Associates in Baltimore, recalled being told at a family get-together about an estate plan that would give grandchildren their whole inheritance as teenagers. "Do you really want Joey to inherit something like $800,000 when he's eighteen?" she asked. "I don't think so."

Q: Should I Give My Heirs Part of Their Inheritance Before I Die?

A: Before the estate-tax exemption started to rise in 2002, many people gave large sums of money to family members each year as a way to avoid future taxes. Should you still give money away while you're alive? It depends. First, you need to make sure you won't need any of that money to take care of yourself, keeping in mind the six-figure amounts a few folks wind up spending on long-term care or simply on basic health-care needs, as we discussed in earlier chapters. If you still expect to have money left over, you might want to consider doing something more meaningful than writing a check: funding family vacations, college tuition, medical bills, house down payments or start-up capital for a small business—contributions that could have a major impact on your children's or grandchildren's lives in your lifetime.

Olen and Eloise Douglas, who owned a drugstore in Clarksville, Texas, bought a travel trailer after retiring with part of their savings. They used their home on wheels to introduce their five grandchildren to large swaths of the country, including New York, the Grand Canyon and California, on *month-long* trips. Think of the memories that the grandparents and grandchildren all have as a result. "I think you need to share it as you go, not just stick it all in the bank and not ever use it," Eloise said.

Q: Who's Going to Dole Out My Estate When I'm Gone?

A: You're going to have to designate someone as executor of your estate. If you have trusts, you'll need to designate the trustee who manages them. Some attorneys and financial planners suggest naming a lawyer or trust officer along with a family member; others advise choosing only a professional or only a family member. Most say you should think twice about naming children who live far away as co-executors because they can slow down the process. Jeffrey Condon cautions that "making one child the boss is the quickest way to develop a breeding ground for conflict and jealousy among all the children."

On this much everybody agrees: Include a provision in your will to let your family switch professional trustees if need be. After all, the bank where your trust officer works may be acquired or the lawyer you work with may retire. And take time now to make sure your family, particularly your spouse, is comfortable with your executor or trustee. Consultant Stephan Leimberg said he persuaded his wife to start working with his own lawyer now. "She has to do it anyway. Why not do it while it's safe and find out if they get along? Do I need to make a change? Once I'm dead, it's too late."

Q: Should I Make Provisions in My Will for Anything Other Than Money?

A: Maybe you have boxes of work papers, historical records, paintings or some other collection that might be valuable to a museum or library. For example, financial planner Christine Fahlund's father, Richard Stoiber, was a geologist who taught at Dartmouth College for many years and who took 20,000 photos of volcanoes around the world. When he was diagnosed with leukemia, she persuaded him to use a dictation machine to document as much information about them as he could and to leave some money to have his notes transcribed and archived as part of the university's collection.

Q: What Are Other Estate-Planning Ideas for Bringing My Family Together?

A: Regardless of the size of your estate, if there's a cause that's close to your heart, you might want to consider setting up a family foundation to support it. The goal can be as modest as turning a small plot into a park, a cause that brought together a California family that Susan Bradley knows. "It's probably less than ten acres, but they feel very invested in this," she told us. "It's sort of like a family statement." Other grandparents have created private charitable foundations with themselves and their children as the trustees. That way, the foundation can hold its annual meeting on a holiday, such as July 4, and the family can have a reunion at the same time.

Q: If My Parents Don't Bring Up Their Plans About Inheritance, Should I Ask Them About It?

A: It's tougher to get this conversation going, but it's often worth it. Here's one approach: Try telling your parents that you'd like to talk to them about their inheritance plan not because you're after their money, but because you want to make sure the transfer of money goes as smoothly as possible after they die. After all, you, as their child, ultimately would be responsible for carrying out their wishes. But if you're like us, and you wouldn't feel comfortable with such a blunt approach, here's another way into the conversation: Try telling your parents that you're doing your own estate planning, and the more you know, the better job you can do. It's an argument that any curmudgeon who resents paying taxes could appreciate. Finally, if you really care about a particular heirloom, talking with your parents is even more important.

Having suggested these approaches, we realize that our parents are called the "Silent Generation" for a reason. Still, your effort may prod them into making an appointment with their lawyer to spell out their wishes more clearly. Knowing

WHO GETS THE PIE PLATE?

Some of the biggest family feuds can erupt over the eventual division of day-to-day objects because of their sentimental value. To get people talking about this often-overlooked part of inheritance planning, the University of Minnesota Extension Service put together a guide called "Who Gets Grandma's Yellow Pie Plate?" The service's Web site has free content at www.yellowpieplate.umn.edu, or you can call 800-876-8636 to order a workbook or video. "We all have something like that pie plate in our families," said Marlene Stum, an associate professor of family social science at the university in St. Paul, who led the development of the guide.

It can be hard to determine what's fair when dividing personal items, but there are steps that the researchers have seen families take to work through such situations. "Ask your children what they want, and why, or what they think someone else should have, and why," Marlene Stum advised. Parents often are surprised to find out how important seemingly mundane stuff is to their grown children or how uninterested the kids are in something the parents hold dear, such as a stamp collection. "I hear children say, 'My parents won't talk about it,' and parents say, 'My kids won't talk about it.' One generation blames the other," she said. You have to be willing to open the conversation with your kids and to have the conversation with your own parents when they bring it up.

It's best to make decisions about your personal possessions while you're still alive and in good health. That way, you "get to tell the stories that go with those items," Marlene Stum said. "Whatever the object is (the christening gown or the pie plate), really sharing and knowing the story behind the possession probably has the biggest value." If you aren't comfortable parting with some of your things now, make sure to put your wishes in writing, typically in a separate listing in your will.

Jacquelyn Cotter, of Sacramento, California, said her family found a good strategy for dividing things fairly. For starters, gifts given by an heir to the person who died went back to the heir. So, for example, her brother got back the string of pearls that he had bought for their mother in Japan while he served there in the Navy. Next, the family had an appraiser value every item in the home. "When that was done, the heirs gathered on a weekend, and we went through the house item by item. If two or more people wanted the same item, a coin was flipped until there was a final winner." Anything that went unclaimed was sold. "In the end, every person's items were added for an individual final value number, and since naturally some people had taken more than others, the dollar amount was evened up in the final distribution of cash" after the estate was settled. "That way everyone felt that they were treated fairly, although they may have regretted losing a coin toss or two. And best of all, there were no hard feelings!"

that your parents have a will in place, at the very least, and that they have met with their lawyer in the past five years can give you some peace of mind.

THE PAPERCHASE

The road map for your estate planning is, of course, your will. It spells out who gets your assets, and, if you have children who are not adults, it spells out their future without you. There's no question that you need one. The following guidelines apply for all wills:

- The document should be typed.

- The person making the will should be clearly identified.

- The will should clearly say that this *is* your will and that it supersedes any previous wills.

- You need to sign and date it.

- You need to get at least two people to witness it. (Choose witnesses who are not going to receive anything under the will and who would be easy to locate if they needed to appear in court; your lawyer typically would handle getting the will notarized.)

The most important reason to have a will is that it helps get your assets distributed in the way you intended and should help your heirs through probate, the legal process of administering an estate after someone dies.

We hear from readers all the time who get sales pitches for so-called "living trusts," which are designed to avoid probate. In fact, about two-thirds of all personal trusts are revocable living trusts (the word "revocable" here means you can change its provisions), according to Tiburon Strategic Advisors, a financial-services consulting firm. Living trusts, in addition to helping you avoid probate, are useful for designating someone else to manage your property if you become incapacitated. But before setting one up, check with a probate lawyer in your state to make sure the cost to set up such a trust doesn't exceed likely probate fees.

When you hire a lawyer to do your will, should you seek out an estate attorney or an elder-law attorney? Generally, estate-planning attorneys focus on planning that anticipates a client's death (distributing assets to heirs, for example) and elder-law attorneys do the same but also specialize in addressing needs that can arise before that event, placing special emphasis on preparing for a period of illness, a disability or an incapacity.

Another important legal document is a durable power of attorney, also known as a financial power of attorney, because it allows a loved one to take care of your finances when you no longer can. This, too, should be set up carefully to avoid family strife. Vivian Hartin's children, for example, spent more than a year wrangling in the Charleston, South Carolina, courts after Vivian's older daughter accused her younger sister of misusing the power of attorney that the younger sister held in Vivian's name. Vivian suffered from dementia and lived in an assisted-living facility. Before her husband died, he had written a will leaving a piece of real estate to each of three heirs and about $300,000 in certificates of deposit to his wife, according to court records. When it came time to settle his estate, his

ONLINE WILLS

After the terrorist attacks on September 11, 2001, online wills surged in popularity. The Internet services will tell you that their online forms work just fine; lawyers will tell you that writing a will contains too many pitfalls for most people to do it on their own. But a lawyer isn't needed for a will to be valid. Generally, all that is needed is that the person making the will to be of sound mind and that the document be uniform in appearance and signed in front of two or three witnesses who are not family or heirs. Certainly, the do-it-yourself Web sites at least help the reluctant get started by providing them with necessary legal forms. But keep this in mind: A lawyer who makes a mistake can be sued for damages; no such recourse is available if you use an Internet service because it isn't practicing law. Whether you decide to use the Internet or consult a lawyer is ultimately up to you.

Here are some Web sites for do-it-yourself-wills:

LegalZoom: www.legalzoom.com; $69 to $119 per will; includes a questionnaire, review by "document specialists" and printed will within forty-eight hours

The Will Expert: www.thewillexpert.com; $18.95 and up; a questionnaire asks for information, including marital status and burial instructions. Checklists include legal definitions

Wills for America: www.willsforamerica.com; $20 to $40 per will; links connect users to information about legal requirements in various states and to a glossary of legal terms

older daughter alleged that his younger daughter—using her power of attorney—had converted the CDs to her own name and that of her father, leaving their mother with less than $20,000. After fifteen months of legal wrangling, the case was settled—without the mother getting the money back.

So how do you avoid such strife? If you have two children, it works best to require both of them to sign off on transactions

HOW DO YOU FIND AN "ELDER-LAW ATTORNEY"?

Attorneys who specialize in later-life planning are listed in these four Web directories:

- The National Academy of Elder Law Attorneys' membership list (www.naela.org)

- The National Elder Law Foundation's list of lawyers who have passed its certification test (www.nelf.org)

- The American Bar Association's state-by-state directory of local bar associations (www.findlegalhelp.org), many of which can make referrals to attorneys practicing elder law

- Elder Law Answers' database of elder-law attorneys, searchable by area code, state or city, and referral service (www.elderlawanswers.com)

dealing with large dollars or titled real estate and to allow them to act by themselves on little things. If it's not logistically possible to involve all your children, you could assign a single family member to act as your "attorney-in-fact," but make sure all of the children would get copies of your financial statements for as long as the power of attorney is in effect. What if there's no one in your family whom you feel comfortable burdening—or entrusting—with your finances? Spread the responsibility around: You could have a financial planner handle your investments and then have a family member keep your household running.

A few technical points: A plain-vanilla durable power of attorney goes into effect as soon as you set it up, which theoretically means your attorney-in-fact could start diving into your finances even though you're still competent. But a "springing" durable power of attorney doesn't go into effect until you're judged incompetent, which means you don't have to worry about anyone meddling in your finances as long as you can still handle them. Edward Carnot, an estate-planning attorney in La Jolla, California, suggested preparing a power of attorney subject to a disability, which means the power-holder gets control only if "a doctor is willing to certify, under penalty of perjury, that the person is incapable of handling his affairs. It becomes effective when the doctor's certification is attached." Sometimes, banks, brokerage houses and even the IRS prefer that you fill out their own durable power of attorney forms; they may be reluctant to accept yours. Also, read the fine print closely so you avoid wording in one power of attorney document that revokes another one.

Then there are the health-care documents. Living wills gained attention with the death of Terri Schiavo in March 2005. You may recall that a feeding tube kept her alive for more than a decade. She was forty-one years old when she died, following a nasty court battle in which her husband argued that she wouldn't have wanted to live in a vegetative state. Her parents fought unsuccessfully to keep her alive, contending that she tried to interact with them and might have improved with therapy. As the debate became a national obsession, many people scrambled to write down their own end-of-life wishes, most frequently with living wills. But these documents could turn out to be inadequate, depending on where you live. There are actually three related documents that make up the most comprehensive set of "advance directives," and many states have specific requirements that could undo your best intentions.

The three documents are as follows:

- A living will, which says how you want to be treated if you aren't able to make your own decisions about using life-sustaining medical treatment. (This is entirely different from a living trust, which is simply designed to keep your heirs from having to go through probate.) It can ask for specifics, such as continuous medical treatment regardless of your

STATE OF THE STATES

The best-laid plans for living wills and related documents can go haywire if you move to another state or if you split your time between two states.

Certainly, what you did in one state is supposed to be honored by another one. "However, that's when you get to court," said Lawrence Davidow, an attorney in Suffolk County, New York. "When you're sitting there in a hospital talking to social workers in one state who are not familiar with the forms from another state, they don't know what to do. It delays things and creates controversy." He recommended talking with lots of people in your family about your wishes and carrying condensed versions of your health-care proxy and living will in a plastic sleeve in your wallet.

Here's a list of the states with specific requirements from www.naela.com, the Web site for the National Association of Elder Law Attorneys. There's a list of forms that you can print out from all fifty states at www.uslivingwill-registry.com/forms.shtm.

Mandatory Forms

Seven states require the use of a mandatory form for health-care powers of attorney, health-care proxies and living wills: Alabama, Kansas, Kentucky, Oklahoma, Oregon, South Carolina and Utah.

Four states apply a mandatory form only to health-care powers of attorney: Nevada, New Hampshire, Ohio and Texas.

Three more jurisdictions apply a mandatory form only to a living will: Indiana, Minnesota and Washington, D.C.

Witnessing Requirements

Seven states impose special witnessing requirements for the advance directive documents where the maker of the advance directive is in an institutional setting: California, Connecticut, Delaware, Georgia, New York, North Dakota and Vermont.

Two jurisdictions—Washington, D.C., and South Carolina—apply a witnessing requirement only for a living will signed in an institution.

Eight states—Nevada, New Hampshire, Ohio, Oregon, South Carolina,

Texas, Vermont and Wisconsin—require specific disclosures or notices to warn people who are completing documents to appoint a health-care agent in case they become incapacitated (health care powers of attorney).

Wording for Specific Instructions Differ

Two states prescribe specific phraseology for certain instructions: Indiana and Ohio.

medical condition, or request that feeding tubes be withdrawn or withheld under certain conditions.

- A health-care proxy, which authorizes one or more people to communicate your wishes regarding end-of-life treatment.

- A health-care power of attorney, which authorizes an individual to communicate your medical instructions, hire and fire medical providers, access and provide your medical history and consent to a "do-not-resuscitate" order.

Some states require specific forms. So, if you have all these documents, then move to another state, you need to make sure you update your paperwork accordingly.

You might also consider an "ethical will." It's not a substitute for a legal will; instead, it's more of a narrative supplement or memoir intended to include personal reflections and stories you wish to pass along—usually in your own words instead of legalese. Most are handwritten or typed and are one to five pages long, though some are longer and involve scrapbooks, photos, letters or DVDs. Some people read them to their children during their lifetimes; others choose to include them with other documents in their estate plans.

"The lawyers try to get rid of all the adjectives and adverbs in your life," said Gary Hirshberg, the chief executive of Stony-field Farm, an organic dairy-products maker in Londonderry, New Hampshire. He wrote an ethical will after deciding that, in a legal will, "there was no room for me to explain what we did and why we did it." He wanted to make sure that his three children and unborn grandchildren understood that he wanted to prove it was possible to make money with an environmentally friendly business and that they hear the stories of its early days. "Without this, our kids would never know about milking the cows with our feet blistering because of the chlorine rinse in the boot wash."

Ethical wills drew increased attention after the terrorist attacks on September 11, 2001, and Hurricane Katrina in 2005, according to Barry Baines, a doctor and associate medical director of a hospice program in Plymouth, Minnesota, who started a Web site focused on these documents (www.ethical-will.com).

THE BIG GOTCHA: INHERITED IRAS

Your will determines how just about everything is handed down *except* your individual retirement account—no small matter at a time when more and more retirement savings are shifting from traditional pensions into such accounts. The way an IRA gets passed along to your heirs is governed by the beneficiary form you are supposed to fill out when you open the account. You should review those forms regularly and keep your own copy in an easy-access spot because banks and brokerage firms that hold your IRAs can lose track of the paperwork over time. And make sure you fill out a beneficiary form when you inherit an IRA. You may see a box on the forms to check for a "per stirpes" designation. That means the assets would go to your beneficiary's children if he or she dies before inheriting the IRA. If you name no beneficiary or you name your estate, your heirs lose the ability to stretch withdrawals from the account over their life expectancies, which means they also would lose out on the potential for decades of tax-free growth of your assets. In some cases, naming the estate as the beneficiary might even prevent your spouse from being able to roll the plan into his or her own IRA.

Naming a trust as an IRA beneficiary can create a lot of problems as well, even though many people are advised by estate planners to do so, contends Ed Slott, an IRA consultant in Rockville Centre, New York. It can make sense if your heir is a minor (because minors can't make tax elections), has a disability or needs help managing IRA distributions, or if you're trying to shelter assets in a divorce. Otherwise, using a trust to inherit an IRA poses two big risks. First, the trust could wind up owing more in taxes than your heirs would because trust tax rates are higher than most individuals' rates. (If you must use a trust to hold an IRA, try to make that IRA a Roth because in that case, no tax would be owed on distributions.) Second, the IRS could decide that the trust doesn't qualify as a "look-through" or "see-through" trust, meaning your heirs wouldn't qualify to stretch withdrawals across their life expectancies even though you may have set up the trust in the first place to make sure they did just that. Trusts that fail to qualify to let your beneficiaries take stretched-out withdrawals typically include beneficiaries without a life expectancy: the estate, a charity or another trust. A few recent court rulings indicate that the IRS may be loosening up a bit on the requirements for look-through trusts, but it's still best to avoid using a trust for an inherited IRA.

In Chapter Nine, we went over the rules for making withdrawals from your own IRA. Uncle Sam allows only widows and widowers to roll an inherited IRA into their own accounts. Other heirs aren't allowed the same leeway, although many people mistakenly assume that the widow/widower rule applies to everyone, consequently triggering tax penalties. Take, for instance, Dorothy Galvin and Barbara Rubinstein, two sisters who inherited an IRA from their mother in 2004 that was worth $212,000. They were advised by an insurance broker to roll the money into new IRAs to avoid a big tax bite all at once. The IRA custodian cut each sister a check, which they deposited into new accounts. But at tax time the following spring, Barbara's accountant had bad news: To preserve an inherited IRA, you have to keep your hands off the money by doing what's called a trustee-to-trustee transfer into an account specifically designated for inherited funds. The sisters had to undo the new IRAs and pay taxes immediately—almost $50,000 apiece—on their whole inheritance. "I don't have any other savings down the road, and I've never married," Dorothy told us. Because of the bad advice she got, she lost the potential for decades of tax-deferred growth.

INHERITED IRA DON'TS

Handle an inherited IRA with kid gloves, double-checking with lots of experts before you touch it. Here's what you need to know:

- You cannot, under any circumstance, roll an inherited IRA into your own IRA (unless, as we said above, you got it from your husband or wife).

- You can't withdraw assets from an inherited account and then deposit them into a new IRA.

- Finally, you can't consolidate IRAs you inherit from different people into one account.

SO WHAT *SHOULD* YOU DO WITH AN INHERITED IRA?

To make the most of any IRA you inherit, stretch out the withdrawals across your life expectancy rather than taking them as a lump sum. That gives you a chance to postpone the tax bite and lengthen the time that tax-free earnings can accrue, possibly increasing your inheritance by thousands of dollars.

As long as you're clear upfront on how to take the stretched-out withdrawals, it's easy to do so. First, you need to retitle the inherited IRA so it's clear that the owner died and you are the beneficiary. Include the name of the person who died, make it clear that the account remains an IRA and say that it is "for the benefit of" yourself. For example, if the IRA owner were named Fred Jackson and the beneficiary were his daughter, the new title could read: "Fred Jackson, IRA (deceased July 15, 2006) F/B/O Sandra Jackson, beneficiary" or "Sandra Jackson, as beneficiary of Fred Jackson, IRA (deceased July 15, 2006)." Make sure, as well, that you change the Social Security number on the account to that of the beneficiary.

> **WHEN YOU INHERIT AN IRA . . .**
>
> Here are some steps to take to make sure you maximize an inherited IRA.
>
> - Retitle the account.
> - Start taking stretched-out withdrawals by December 31 of the year after the original account owner's death.
> - When you pay your own taxes, deduct any estate tax already paid on the IRA.

To calculate the minimum requirement for your annual withdrawals, you would look up your life expectancy in the IRS's life-expectancy table given on page 260. Each year, you subtract a year from your initial life expectancy, and then you divide the previous year's year-end account balance by that number to figure out how much to withdraw. Most investment firms will calculate required distributions from your own account for you, and a few are starting to do the math for inherited IRAs as well. One note: If you inherit an IRA along with other heirs, typically your siblings, you can split the account, allowing each heir to spread withdrawals across his or her own life expectancy. Otherwise, you get stuck using the life expectancy of the oldest heir.

LIFE EXPECTANCY TABLE

First, look up your life expectancy, based on your age in the year after the IRA owner's death. Then, divide that amount into the IRA's value, as of December 31 of the previous year, to figure out how much you must withdraw. The next year, subtract one from the initial divisor and then divide that number into the new account balance. Note: These numbers were current as of 2006; double-check IRS Publication 590 at www.irs.gov to make sure they are still current.

Age	Life Expectancy	Age	Life Expectancy
0	82.4	34	49.4
1	81.6	35	48.5
2	80.6	36	47.5
3	79.7	37	46.5
4	78.7	38	45.6
5	77.7	39	44.6
6	76.7	40	43.6
7	75.8	41	42.7
8	74.8	42	41.7
9	73.8	43	40.7
10	72.8	44	39.8
11	71.8	45	38.8
12	70.8	46	37.9
13	69.9	47	37.0
14	68.9	48	36.0
15	67.9	49	35.1
16	66.9	50	34.2
17	66.0	51	33.3
18	65.0	52	32.3
19	64.0	53	31.4
20	63.0	54	30.5
21	62.1	55	29.6
22	61.1	56	28.7
23	60.1	57	27.9
24	59.1	58	27.0
25	58.2	59	26.1
26	57.2	60	25.2
27	56.2	61	24.4
28	55.3	62	23.5
29	54.3	63	22.7
30	53.3	64	21.8
31	52.4	65	21.0
32	51.4	66	20.2
33	50.4	67	19.4

(continued)

Age	Life Expectancy	Age	Life Expectancy
68	18.6	90	5.5
69	17.8	91	5.2
70	17.0	92	4.9
71	16.3	93	4.6
72	15.5	94	4.3
73	14.8	95	4.1
74	14.1	96	3.8
75	13.4	97	3.6
76	12.7	98	3.4
77	12.1	99	3.1
78	11.4	100	2.9
79	10.8	101	2.7
80	10.2	102	2.5
81	9.7	103	2.3
82	9.1	104	2.1
83	8.6	105	1.9
84	8.1	106	1.7
85	7.6	107	1.5
86	7.1	108	1.4
87	6.7	109	1.2
88	6.3	110	1.1
89	5.9	111 and over	1.0

Source: IRS

Finally, make sure you don't miss this tax break: the "income in respect of a decedent," or IRD deduction, also referred to by the IRS on tax forms as the "estate-tax deduction." IRAs are subject to both income tax and estate tax. But when you inherit an IRA, you can deduct any federal estate tax already paid on the IRA from your income-tax bill. You won't want to miss it, either: The IRD deduction is usually around 45 percent of the amount withdrawn, according to Ed Slott. To take the deduction, ask the accountant who handled the estate-tax return to calculate what part of the overall bill was due to the IRA. Then, you can deduct that portion from your federal tax bill, offsetting the taxes on the IRA withdrawal you make for the same year. You can take the IRD deduction on your income-tax return every year until the entire amount is used up.

INHERITORS, WATCH OUT!

Some IRA inheritors are finding they must hold the hands of the institutions that maintain their accounts. After Carol Kenzel's father died in 2001, she split his IRA among her siblings. But during both her and her sister's annual visits to the banks that hold their inherited IRAs, they have found that the staffs are as unfamiliar with the accounts as most consumers. "After I explain all the rules to them, they call their help desk," Carol told us. "I finally get the check, and they advise me they are not responsible if I'm penalized for an early withdrawal"—even though she is actually taking a distribution required by federal law.

TAXES AND TRUSTS

Even if you set up an estate plan years ago, it's probably time to dust it off. And if you don't have one yet, it's important to realize that changes in your personal situation, tax law and the markets all mean that you need to build in as much flexibility as possible. One of the biggest changes for estate planning—a revision in the federal estate tax—is likely in coming years. The federal estate-tax exemption, which is the amount you can transfer at death before triggering a tax, already is a moving target. It's $2 million per estate in the years 2007 and 2008. In 2009, the amount rises to $3.5 million. The federal estate tax disappears entirely in 2010. A year later, in 2011, the exemption is scheduled to return, at $1 million. Some politicians are trying to get the federal estate tax eliminated permanently rather than having it return, but others want to set the exemption at an amount somewhat higher than the current level.

If you're married, the most basic estate-planning tool you should check out is a "credit-shelter" or "bypass" trust, designed so your heirs can benefit from both your and your spouse's estate-tax exemptions rather than just one. For years, the exemption sat at $1 million, so many couples with a nest egg and large home set up such trusts. Take a family with more than $4 million in assets today, with the federal exemption at $2 million. If the father dies first, without a credit-shelter trust, his assets would pass to his wife, and spouses inherit assets from each other without estate taxes. But at her death, the children would inherit her estate and get the benefit of only her $2 million estate-tax exemption. However, if the husband had put $2 million into a trust, his widow could still have access to the principal or income, depending on the way they set up the trust's instructions. And, upon her death, the couple's heirs would inherit the $2 million in the trust, along with $2 million of their mother's estate, free of federal estate tax.

Now, with the exemption in flux, you need to evaluate more closely the way those trusts would affect your financial situation. As the exemption rises, you may think that you should increase your bypass trust's size to follow. But that could leave the surviving spouse without enough money in his or her lifetime, especially if he or she needs long-term care or gets hit with big medical bills. To protect yourself, consider inserting a disclaimer in your estate plan saying the surviving spouse should receive all the assets but retain the right to disclaim any amount of the inheritance up to the amount of the estate-tax exemption.

In recent years, at least one-third of the states have taken action to keep collecting their own estate taxes, which would have dried up because of a federal law enacted in 2001. Depending on the size of your estate, this might prompt you to move to another state. You can make it more official by registering to vote, making funeral arrangements and banking in a less-taxing state. Florida, for example, has neither a state income tax nor an estate tax. Even then, figuring out whether your estate would be taxed at the state level can be tough, especially if you own homes in different states.

Another strategy, whether or not you're dealing with a potential state estate tax, is to reduce the size of the estate by giving money away in your lifetime. To avoid paying federal gift taxes, make sure you follow the federal rules for gift giving: As of 2007, you could make annual gifts of as much as $12,000 each to as many people as you want without eating away at your lifetime gift-tax exemption. Of course, there's one caveat: Don't give away any assets that you might need for your own care down the road. It's better to owe taxes after your death than lack the money you need for long-term care while you're alive. There's also a rather morbid way around state estate taxes: deathbed gifts, or large transfers made within three years of death. Such gifts are taxed by the federal government after death, as if they had remained part of your estate. But most states *don't* tax them, which means that, in the eyes of the state, you could knock down the size of your estate. Reserve this strategy for the end of life, however. Otherwise, you again risk leaving yourself without assets you might need.

You may also want to consider setting up a "dynasty" trust: With baby boomers and their parents increasingly moving assets into such vehicles, states are starting to compete for their business by passing more laws favorable to trusts. In recent years, more than twenty states have undone a centuries-old law called the "rule against perpetuities" that placed time limits on trusts, often about 100 years. Now, more states are allowing "dynasty" trusts that can last for hundreds of years, or even forever. If they are structured well, money inside such a trust theoretically could pass through many generations without incurring estate taxes, allowing it to build large gains over time.

FINALLY, THE FILING CABINET

One of our readers, Eleanor Coln, shared her system for setting up all of her financial records for her children. On a spreadsheet, she listed the name, account number, address, phone number and contact person for each of her investment accounts, including her 401(k) and IRA. She did the same for each of her insurance policies, including her auto and homeowner's insurance. She also provided her children with detailed information about her will, living will, a trust, power of attorney (both financial and health), doctors, water company and gas and electric company. She even made a list explaining how her doll collection should be distributed.

If you wish to take such an inventory yourself, there are a number of resources available. A small notebook would work for many families, as long as parents and children can remember where it's kept. You can also print out some paper alternatives from Web sites at no cost. Fannie Mae, the mortgage-finance company, offers a set of blank forms called the ElderKit at www.fanniemae.com; www.todaysseniors.com also has an array of forms.

The problem with the paper method is that after an initial burst of enthusiasm, the record-keeper rarely updates the initial entries. What's more, access to the information might be limited, especially when family members are scattered across the country. As you might expect, some online entrepreneurs are trying to create services to meet this need. For example, a service called LifeLedger, at www.elderissues.com, charges $9.95 a month for a tool that lets you keep large amounts of personal history and financial facts up-to-date. The site says that "personally identifiable information is stored in our secure data facility."

If you use the Internet for any transactions, be sure to keep a list of any access codes or passwords as well. And if you use your computer for any financial transactions, regularly print your records so you have recent information in the event that you or your family do not have Internet access.

SUCCESS STORIES:
A BALANCE OF ENGAGEMENT AND FREEDOM

The best definition of retirement we've ever heard came from a couple who, by their own admission, "flunked" their first attempt at walking away from the office.

Milt and Judy Baker found themselves at loose ends after twenty-year careers in the Navy. Looking for something to occupy a few hours of their time in retirement, the couple started a small business—a nautical bookstore and chart agency—in Fort Lauderdale, Florida. Much to their surprise, the tiny venture became a roaring success, and the Bakers' days were filled with meetings, deadlines and stress. It was a classic be-careful-what-you-wish-for story, and the couple began preparing to sell the business—and start retirement all over again.

At that point, Judy explained exactly what she and her husband were trying to do with their lives: "We're still trying to strike a balance between engagement and freedom."

A balance between engagement and freedom. Those six words come closest to describing what most people today are looking for in later life—a mix of activities that will allow them to stay involved, in mind and body, with their community, friends and family and still allow them to enjoy the fruits of years of hard work. To paraphrase Judy Baker, retirement—ideally—is spending more time doing the things you want to do and less time doing the things you have to do.

And it's not an impossible dream. We have been fortunate, in writing about retirement for *The Wall Street Journal,* to speak with numerous individuals age fifty or older who have found that mix or something close to it. In fact, their stories are among the most popular in the *Journal*'s pages. This popularity is explained by the fact that people approaching retirement have an insatiable appetite for success stories and the possibilities that await them when they leave their first, or primary, career. The possibilities, in short, are endless. We have spoken with retirees who became physician assistants and others who became ministers, rabbis or priests. We have talked with older adults who have adopted children overseas and others who have written a first novel. Still others have taken motorcycle tours of China or joined local search-and-rescue teams. Some bought ranches out West and raised emus, while others purchased vineyards in Virginia and raised grapes. They start businesses or they start teaching or they start competing in triathlons. In some cases, like the Bakers, they simply start over—again and again.

In this chapter, we'll look at some of these people and their stories. Many, when asked what they would tell others about retirement, frequently offer the same advice. Start thinking early about what you might want to do; don't wait until you're already retired. Experiment with different activities and interests and then experiment some more. Nothing about later life is written in stone.

ENTREPRENEURS ONLINE

Marcia Cooper and Harvey Levine hoped for a blissful retirement, until they both were laid off from their jobs. They hadn't planned to quit working so soon and hadn't saved enough. Feeling unprepared to compete with twenty-year-olds in the traditional job market, the sixty-something New Jersey couple turned to eBay Inc., the global Internet auction site.

Marcia and Harvey started small, standing in line to buy concert tickets for acts like Phish and Bruce Springsteen and then reselling the tickets for a profit on eBay. From there, they moved to selling wine glasses, antiques and more valuable items such as baseball memorabilia. Those endeavors turned into a business the couple named General Enterprises. The average monthly sales in their fifth year exceed $10,000.

"It's been a boon to us," Marcia told us. "We didn't expect it to grow quite as fast, because at our stage in life it's very, very difficult for somebody to enjoy what they're doing and make money at it."

Many people age fifty-five and older are turning to the online marketplace. For some retirees, eBay has become a kind of financial lifeline, supplementing pension plans or savings that may not be sufficient. Others have uncovered a latent entrepreneurial streak in themselves or simply see eBay as a creative outlet; they enjoy the sales process and the interaction an eBay business gives them with people around the world.

ADVENTURES IN HOLLYWOOD

Herb Folkman's journey to Hollywood started when he was having lunch with a friend who sat on the board of an actors' union. A former judge, Herb had retired a year earlier, just before his sixtieth birthday, and was taking a much-needed break. He was dabbling in photography and taking regular trips to the beach.

As the two discussed their pastimes, the friend suggested Herb consider doing "background" work in television and film— taking part in crowd scenes, primarily. The idea appealed to him: Many years before, he had worked as a musician, playing timbales in Latin bands and kettle drums in the Santa Monica Symphony, and he had always wanted to return to entertainment.

Herb promptly signed up with a call service recommended by his friend. His first job was as one of 5,000 people in a crowd scene for a Coca-Cola commercial. He was paid $80 a day, plus meals. He went on to do other background work for commercials, TV series and movies. Then, while working on some crowd scenes in the movie *Tin Cup,* another background actor suggested that if Herb was serious about his new pastime, he should get some training. So he signed up with schools, including the Lee Strasberg Theatre Institute, and landed an agent.

Slowly, the roles got better and he became more visible. Herb played a cab driver in the TV series *Caroline in the City* and had a recurring role as an attorney in *Common Law.* Since then, he has had speaking roles in movies, including as a Russian diplomat in *Air Force One.*

Herb found that his legal training came in handy. "This was my first go at professional acting," he told us. "But as a judge, you have to play many roles in the courtroom, so I was used to it." He was also used to working the long hours: Often, he will be on a set for fifteen hours at a time.

Herb said the toughest part of his Hollywood adventure has been getting auditions. He said the opportunities aren't as abundant for mature actors, although the situation is worse for women than men. When he does get auditions, Herb noted, he's commonly up against 100, or even 200, people. And sometimes, he'll be up against a recognizable character actor. The fact that he doesn't have to rely on acting for a living helps, however. As does his age.

"Older people are more able to tolerate disappointments," he told us. "They've been around in life and are psychologically more prepared to accept that they may go out to 200 auditions and not get a nibble. It's almost a lottery."

SEARCH AND RESCUE

"How come I have to play the dead guy?" asked Bob Boeder, plaintively. "Is it just because I'm the oldest one here?"

It's already dark, and at an elevation of 9,600 feet, the temperature is falling quickly in the Elk Mountains in Colorado. Bob is one of five "victims" of a simulated plane crash, partaking in a training exercise for the graduates of a weeklong wilderness emergency medical course. Bob's role is to lie under some willow shrubs on the steep hillside, groaning, so that his fellow classmates can locate him, diagnose his injuries (head wound and blood loss, leading, alas, to heart failure) and haul his body out to a waiting ambulance.

Like his fellow classmates, Bob is upgrading his paramedic certification, which he uses in his volunteer search-and-rescue (SAR) work. His classmates, scrambling around in the sage, are mostly in their twenties and thirties, predominantly forest firefighters and paramedics, although they also include a Secret Service agent from Park City, Utah, a handful of river guides and outfitters, a journalist and a sushi cook from Malibu, California. Unlike most of his classmates, however, Bob is sixty-one years old.

As a retiree, Bob could have gravitated to all kinds of volunteer work. But with his interest in the outdoors and his hobby of long-distance, high-altitude trail running, it isn't surprising that he ended up finding something more adventurous than supervising blood drives.

Search-and-rescue volunteers are the folks who get called out, often in the middle of the night, to look for overdue hikers, lost kids, missing fishermen and snowmobilers buried in avalanches. And increasingly, in urban and suburban areas, they also search for abducted children and wandering Alzheimer's patients and assist law enforcement with evidence searches in murder cases.

Though many volunteers are chest-thumping twentysomethings, most are in their thirties and forties, and a growing percentage are in their fifties and sixties. Many get into the work after careers in medicine, the military, firefighting and law enforcement.

Bob became the newest and oldest member of his local SAR team after he retired last year from his job of twenty years as an African specialist for the Army. After settling in Silverton, Colorado, a former mining town at an elevation of 9,300 feet in the rugged San Juan Mountains of southwest Colorado, Bob was invited to a meeting of some local search-and-rescue members.

"It seemed like a way to meet some new people," said Bob, a former college professor and Peace Corps volunteer. "Now it's like a third career."

THE RELIGIOUS LIFE

The Rev. Al Schifano knew he would have a lot to contribute when the Roman Catholic Diocese of Tucson, Arizona, asked him to help draft a policy for addressing allegations of child abuse in its parishes. But it wasn't his experience as a Roman Catholic priest they needed. Instead, they wanted to tap his knowledge in creating corporate employee-relations policies and dealing with allegations of sexual harassment. That was because the sixty-four-year-old Arizona native spent thirty-five years as a human-resources executive before becoming a priest.

Father Schifano, an associate pastor at Sts. Peter and Paul Catholic Church in Tucson, was ordained as a priest in 2001, a decade after his wife, Alice, died of lung cancer. But his experience on the church's policy-review committee helped him realize why he gave up corporate life to follow a religious calling.

"It just seemed like I was in the right place at the right time to help take care of the abused and restore trust in the church," he told us.

Father Schifano is one of a growing number of older adults who are embarking on second careers as ministers, rabbis or priests, bringing with them a wealth of life experiences and a range of perspectives. Seminary educators say a trend started to emerge in the late 1990s as baby boomers first approached retirement age and sought a way to remain active by serving their communities.

"We're thinking differently about retirement," said Father James Brackin, president-rector of Sacred Heart School of Theology in Hales Corners, Wisconsin, which specializes in training second-career priests over age thirty-five, one of whom was Father Schifano. "People are retiring now in their fifties and sixties, and they have another twenty years ahead of them, and they don't want to just kick back at the beach."

SKIING AND RAFTING

Former tax attorney Kathy Rogg, fifty-four, who was a partner at a Washington, D.C., law firm, considered herself content until a client coaxed her into leaving her cell phone at home to go on an eighteen-day rafting trip through the Grand Canyon in the late 1980s. "My life was pretty much set," she told us. "It wasn't like I sat around daydreaming about leaving my job."

But her introduction to the Southwest—coupled with her longest separation ever from the office—allowed thoughts of moving to creep into her mind. The following year, after another rafting trip, Kathy decided to move to Denver and practice law there. But after her first-ever ski trip that fall, to nearby Breckenridge, she decided to chuck it all to work for the ski resort, and she moved there that spring.

For more than a decade, Kathy spent her winters working at the ski resort. She started as an operator of snow-making machines on the night shift and eventually helped run competitive snowboarding events. In the summer, she worked as a rafting guide in Utah.

In the early years, she conceded, she occasionally supplemented her minimum-wage jobs with a bit of lawyering here and there. But other than that, she never looked back. Now, she relishes her relaxed, outdoorsy lifestyle. Her nieces and nephews have nicknamed their visits to see her as "Camp Kathy," and her siblings seek her out as a companion for other adventures.

The outdoor life in the West "was a compelling pull," she said. "I highly recommend to anyone that gets bitten by the bug to go for it. I'd done something with the first section of my adult life, and I wanted to do something different with the next part."

NAVIGATING THE "GREAT LOOP"

Several years ago, Ron and Eva Stob tagged along with Eva's sister and her husband for a weeklong trip on a rented boat through the Trent-Severn Waterway, which links Canada's Georgian Bay to Lake Ontario. "We didn't know anything about boating," recalled Ron, who had been a reluctant boater since surviving a near-drowning as a child. Instead of packing field glasses, compasses or rain gear, the two-couple crew had brought cameras, guidebooks and too many clothes to stuff onboard. "I thought that first week was enough to fill our scrapbook with memories," he told us.

In Canada, Eva saw a boat from Norfolk, Virginia, heading east and asked the owner how he had managed to get to Canada, thinking the only way there from the East Coast was via the Atlantic Ocean. She was fascinated with his answer: "By way of the Mississippi." That's when it dawned on them: Boats can cruise in a big circle, better known as the "Great Loop," around the Eastern half of the United States. "I didn't know anything about the Atlantic Intracoastal Waterway before that," said Eva. "I grew up in South Dakota and California."

The Stobs—who ended up navigating the Great Loop themselves and wrote a book about their adventure *(Honey, Let's Get a Boat)*—started America's Great Loop Cruisers' Association (www.greatloop.com), an organization of boaters who "have cruised or dreamed of cruising any or all of America's

Great Loop." The couple began writing a bimonthly newsletter, which is free with a membership; producing flags, maps, shirts and so forth; and making the rounds of boating festivals.

Do they ever want to take some time off? Not really. First, there's the necessity: "We neither one worked for large organizations and don't have cushy retirements," Eva said. Then there's the desire: "Even if we had retired from [a company like] General Motors, those people have nothing to do," Ron said. Referring to the couple's newsletter, he added, "I can't imagine not having a writing assignment in the morning."

EXECUTIVE TURNED RANCHER

Instead of pushing papers and cutting deals as he did as president of a mortgage company, Roger Morgan is pushing forty cows and cutting hay—200 tons annually—on his 108-acre Colorado ranch. "I haven't 'retired,'" he told us. "I changed my occupation. I just say I'm 'tired' now."

He has plenty of company. Lured by the Old West and the New, urban retirees and aging baby boomers are staking claims on small acreages, sometimes called "ranchettes" or hobby farms. Often, they're stocking them with cattle, camels, horses, buffalo, bees, zebras, ostriches or alligators. By all appearances, profits from such ventures are welcome, if not always essential—or feasible. Roger, age fifty-nine, and his wife Katherine, fifty-five, noted that the cash flow from their ranch covers expenses but not much more. However, they moved to this rural location for the lifestyle, the land, the physical labor and the neighborly camaraderie.

"It's something I always wanted to do," said Roger, who has also been a Navy officer, a bank president and an accountant. "There's a lot of romance."

The Morgans bought their property in 1995 after a two-year search. "We knew it belonged to us from the day we drove in the gate," Katherine said. A total of fifty-seven trips to the local dump were needed to discard a century of trash. One by one, ranching neighbors dropped by to size up the couple, suspicious of the woman on her little red tractor and a business executive turned rancher.

"They thought it was a pretense and were terrified that we'd put houses all over the last large parcel," Roger recalled. "But unlike [some new] neighbors with $2 million homes who enjoy viewing the land, we were getting dirty working it."

The couple said they earned acceptance by asking advice, pitching their own hay bales and helping nearby ranchers with their crops and cows. When a neighbor left the state because of a family death, Katherine spent two weeks overseeing nighttime calf births and pulling freezing newborns out of the mud.

Eventually, with his neighbors' support, Roger won positions on the county planning commission and the ditch board, which controls water. "They measure you by the quality of your hay, a fine stand of grass, a good calf," Roger told us. "Rural communities don't care where you come from. It's hardship and struggle, but if you work hard, you gain respect."

HELPING CHILDREN IN RUSSIA

In April 2001, nearly three years after Sam Harding retired from his thirty-year post as Russian teacher and housemaster at the private Lawrenceville School in Lawrenceville, New Jersey, he and his wife, Betsey, traveled to Yaroslavl, Russia, to volunteer at an orphanage. The program, put together by Cross-Cultural Solutions, a New Rochelle, New York, nonprofit group that organizes overseas volunteer trips, "made sense to us," Mr. Harding recalled, because it tapped his Russian fluency and the couple's experience of "having thirty kids living in our house with us all those years." The pair went to Yaroslavl as part of a group of nine volunteers, who were spread out to work among four of the eleven orphanages in the city.

The Hardings were assigned to the Pyatyorka Orphanage, where they worked with another group of thirty children, mostly ages eleven and twelve. The youngsters had little interest in learning English, "because their chances of leaving the city of Yaroslavl are so slim," Betsey told us. She enticed a small group into making sock puppets and other crafts, which they had never done before. Sam organized outdoor games. Three items that fascinated the children most were Frisbees, scented Magic Markers and Nerf footballs.

But the couple frequently had to interrupt their activities to mop up water seeping from leaky pipes down the walls of the orphanage and onto its floors. They were also shocked to see all the boys sleeping in one room and all the girls in another, with no place to bathe properly and inadequate toilets.

Shortly before they left, the Hardings learned from the orphanage's directors that they had started a project a few years earlier to renovate a condemned building next door to provide double bedrooms, a dining room and other needed facilities. The plan called for the children's current home to be turned into much-needed vocational classrooms, but the directors had run out of money before they finished the project.

At that moment, the Hardings' brief two-week stint turned into a full-time job. When they returned to their home in Jackson, New Hampshire, they began talking with friends and colleagues about starting a foundation to raise the needed funds. Eventually, the couple incorporated an organization called Friends of Russian Orphans. Three months were spent assembling a sixty-six-page application for 501(c)(3) status, so potential donors' contributions would be tax-deductible. When we met them, the Hardings had completed their second trip to Russia and were waiting for the Internal Revenue Service to approve their application before kicking their fund-raising into gear.

The couple's first goal in Yaroslavl was to build a school that would provide training through a computer lab, woodworking tools and perhaps a bakery where teenagers could learn to run a business.

"Right now as they leave the orphanage, many of them don't have marketable skills," said Sam, fifty-nine. "There's a

10 percent suicide rate [among all Russian foster children] after they turn eighteen and leave the protected environment of the orphanage. We'd like to help these kids become contributing Russian citizens. We know this is an ambitious goal."

THE WORLD'S BEST JOB

After meeting William Romey, a retired college professor turned cruise-ship lecturer, we asked him to describe what seemed to us to be the world's best job. He kindly answered:

" 'How did you get into this racket?' That's the first question people ask me when they learn what my 'racket' is—lecturing aboard cruise ships. What they really mean is, 'How can I get into this business?'

"Since retiring from St. Lawrence University in Canton, New York, I have spent at least three months each year on riverboats, exploration ships and luxury liners, teaching passengers and students about geology and geography. Simply put, it's a terrific job. My assignments have taken me to, among other destinations, the Mediterranean, Baltic, Caribbean and South China seas, as well as the Galapagos Islands and Antarctica. I get to meet and spend time with business executives, physicians, athletes, entertainers, writers, journalists, scientists and government officials. Shipboard life is great fun, too, although I have to be careful not to eat too much food.

"Yes, my background is in education. But you don't have to be a teacher to speak aboard a ship. Many lecturers come from the business world; indeed, economists and financial planners are more common than scientists. Cruise lines are learning that they have underestimated the intellectual appetites of passengers. The latter are delighted to find sessions on stock picking, estate planning, ports of call, history, foreign affairs, humor, oceanography, astronomy, archaeology, crafts and bridge.

"So, what's not to like? Well, a fair amount, actually. While my life is certainly rewarding, the job of a shipboard lecturer is far from easy—or free. I do get a cabin and meals (for my wife, too), but I'm usually expected to pay for almost everything else, including air fares to and from the ship, tips (which can be substantial) and sometimes even a placement fee to an agent. Often I get only a few days' advance notice of a job. Our accommodations have ranged from the sublime to the ridiculous (including nights spent in cabins adjacent to the bilges, with water-soaked carpets). Even in rough seas you must be on stage as scheduled—enthusiastic, bright and cheerful. And forget it if you like to gamble. Most cruise lines don't allow lecturers to play bingo or use the casino.

"Finally, even though most lecturers consider themselves independent contractors, they are expected to be part of the ship's team. As such, your responsibilities—or what you presume to be your responsibilities—could change considerably once the captain and cruise director get hold of you. I arrived on one ship with four talks ready—only to discover that the staff wanted me to deliver four additional 'informal' seminars. Could I have refused? Sure. But my booking on that vessel probably would have been my last.

"Would I trade places with a landlubber? Absolutely not. But recognize that you shouldn't be doing this kind of work if you expect simply to give three lectures a week and play the rest of the time. All shipboard life demands flexibility, because of weather, canceled landings, seasickness, etc. When I go aboard a ship, it's to participate in events as they develop, not just read old notes in front of a crowd. The unexpected may make me grumble, but it often brings out the best in me."

MOTORCYCLE TRAVELS

As vacations go, riding a motorcycle for sixty-six days from Shanghai across China and Siberia to Germany would seem more challenging than relaxing. But when Norm Smith, age seventy-seven, recently completed the trip, he found himself wanting more.

"When I met my wife and it was time to go home, all I wanted to do was turn around and run the whole thing backward," says Norm, a retired sales manager from Washington, D.C. "It would have been fantastic."

The idea of seeing the world from the seat of a motorcycle is attracting growing numbers of Americans age fifty and older. Such tours—whether brisk one-week trips in Europe or excursions across Asia that can last two months—offer riders an experience rarely found in more traditional travels. "There is so much freedom," says Elizabeth Beach, eighty years old and founder of Beach's Motorcycle Adventures Ltd. in Grand Island, New York. "You don't look at a mountain or lake through a side window of a bus or train or car. You can smell things, see 360 degrees around you and hear everything."

There is also the camaraderie. Jim Russell, age fifty-six, has been on twenty-seven group motorcycle tours since 2000 and was planning to take six more in the year we met him. "I've met a lot of people in my life, but they're all business acquaintances," says Jim, chief executive of a parts company for go-carts in Kansas City, Missouri. "Now I'm meeting people I like to spend time with."

ON YOUR MARK, GET SET . . .

Retirement, like many events in our lives, seems to come knocking at our doors sooner than we anticipate. With that in mind, we've developed a retirement "timeline" to get you started with preparations:

FIVE YEARS OUT . . .

- Set a rough date for retirement itself. Do you plan to retire at a specific age? Do you plan to take early retirement?

- Begin thinking about—and talking with your partner about—how you wish to spend your time in retirement. Develop a plan. Put your goals in writing. Start "test driving" some of your ideas.

- Take a first stab at calculating your spending and income needs in retirement.

- Consult a financial planner. Get a critique of your financial preparations.

- Get your paperwork in order. If you haven't done so already, make sure you have a will, an appointed power of attorney, health-care directives and an estate plan.

- Begin thinking about health insurance. Will there be a gap in coverage between the time you leave work and when you qualify for Medicare? If so, where will you find insurance for that period of time?

- Learn about long-term care insurance and decide whether to purchase a policy. The earlier you do so, the lower the premiums and the better the chance that you won't be denied coverage.

- Take advantage of catch-up provisions (which allow you to contribute additional funds) in your retirement plan at work.

- Determine where you want to live in retirement. If a move is a possibility, begin exploring promising destinations.

THREE YEARS OUT . . .

- Pick a firm date for retirement and begin to work toward that goal.

- Request an estimate of retirement benefits from your employer. What benefits (if any) will you receive after leaving work, and are any of these benefits subject to change?

- If you wish to "ease" into retirement, ask about the possibility of entering, or starting, a "phased retirement" program at work.

- Contact Social Security two to three months before you reach age sixty-two and evaluate the advantages and disadvantages of filing early for benefits.

- Refine your spending and income plans. Develop a firm budget for retirement.

- Consult a financial planner for a second critique of your financial preparations.

- Familiarize yourself with both Social Security and Medicare—how they work, the benefits you can expect to receive and when you should file for benefits.

- Look at your insurance needs. What coverage should you keep and what can you drop in retirement?

ONE YEAR OUT . . .

- Get a final estimate of benefits from your employer.

- If you expect to receive a pension, contact the plan administrator to verify your length of employment and benefits.

- Put a final spending and income plan in place. Spend the year before retirement living on the budget that you have prepared. Will it work in retirement?

- Set up a system (or have a financial adviser do it for you) that creates a "paycheck" in retirement. Organize your nest egg so that income flows from long-term investments into short-term investments and, eventually, into a checking account.

- Address, as best as possible, any hearing, vision or dental needs through your health insurance at work. Medicare covers almost none of that.

KEY MILESTONES:

At age . . .

50—Eligible to make catch-up contributions to 401(k) and related retirement accounts

55—If you're retired, money can be withdrawn from 401(k), 403(b) and related retirement plans without penalty

59½—Funds can be withdrawn from individual retirement accounts without penalty

60—Eligible for Social Security benefits if you have lost a spouse

62—Minimum age to collect Social Security employment benefits

65—Eligible for Medicare

66—Eligible for full Social Security benefits, if born between 1943 and 1954

70—Maximum age to begin collecting Social Security; benefits don't rise beyond this point

70½—Must begin taking minimum distributions from most retirement accounts

ACKNOWLEDGMENTS

We have incurred many debts in writing this book. Here, it's our pleasure to acknowledge them.

Ken Wells and RoseEllen D'Angelo first approached us about the possibility of sharing our thoughts about retirement with an audience beyond *The Wall Street Journal.* They also connected us with Crown Publishing Group's John Mahaney, who agreed to let us write the book as a team.

Larry Rout, our boss at the *Journal,* has been our biggest supporter since we first began writing about retirement for the paper. He encouraged us to commit to this project and spent many hours reading—and improving—our work. We thank you for your guidance and friendship.

Through the years, dozens of financial professionals and educators across the country have shared their time and expertise with us; many were kind enough to help with this book. William Bengen in El Cajon, California, Charles Farrell in Medina, Ohio, and Henry Hebeler in Seattle simplified retirement budgeting; Marc Freedman at Civic Ventures, Ron Manheimer at the North Carolina Center for Creative Retirement in Asheville and Helen Dennis in Redondo Beach, California, enlightened us about second (and third) careers; Barry Kaplan with Cambridge Southern Financial Advisors in Atlanta read and helped refine our first crack at asset allocation and withdrawal strategies; Steve Norwitz at T. Rowe Price provided and updated several key charts and tables; Ed Slott in

[285]

Rockville Centre, New York, guided us through the IRA maze, and Twila Slesnick in Loveland, Colorado, did the same for 401(k)s; finally, Deane Beebe at the Medicare Rights Center helped us decipher Medicare Part D, and James Mahaney at Prudential Financial showed us how to get the most out of Social Security. Our thanks to all.

This book would have been difficult, if not impossible, to write without the help of several current and former colleagues at the *Journal*: Doug Blackmon, Jonathan Clements, Ellen Graham, Mylene Mangalindan, Merissa Marr, Laurie McGinley, Jeff Opdyke, Tara Parker-Pope and Ellen Schultz. We benefited, as well, from the insights of Wendy Bonifazi, Ben Brown, Perri Capell, Karen Hube, Christine Larson and Shelley Lee.

Our special thanks go to Lindsay Orman, our editor at Crown, who guided us through every step of reporting and writing this book. We could not have asked for a more thoughtful and talented editor. This book is as much hers as it is ours.

Finally, to our families. Glenn wishes to thank his wife, Karen, who worked beside him through the many (many) nights and weekends of writing and rewriting. In the end, her sacrifices and her daily gifts of love and encouragement made this book—and all that he does—possible.

Kelly thanks her husband, Rick Brooks, for his unwavering love and patience, and her son, Joseph, for his understanding when she had to write. She also thanks her parents, Ed and Marian Greene, who served as her retiree focus group and biggest fans.

INDEX

ABOUT THE AUTHORS

GLENN RUFFENACH developed and now edits "Encore," *The Wall Street Journal*'s bimonthly guide to retirement planning and living, which debuted in March of 1998. Glenn joined the *Journal* in 1982 and has been a staff reporter, features editor and deputy bureau chief.

Originally from Pompton Lakes, New Jersey, Glenn is a graduate of West Point and received his master's degree from the University of Missouri School of Journalism. He and his wife live in Atlanta.

KELLY GREENE has covered retirement planning since 2001 as a staff reporter at *The Wall Street Journal,* where she works for "Encore" and writes a weekly retirement column. In 2005, she was honored with the American Society on Aging's National Media Award for her body of work. Kelly joined the *Journal* in 1996 after working for newspapers in North Carolina and Atlanta.

Kelly grew up in Winston-Salem, North Carolina, and is a graduate of Wake Forest University. She lives in Atlanta with her husband, son and three-legged cat.

The Guide in your hands is a great way
to start building wealth.

The best way to <u>keep your assets growing</u>
is to read THE WALL STREET JOURNAL!

Send in the card below and get

4 WEEKS FREE!